VISUAL & PERFORMING ARTS

It's Not All Song and Dance

VISUAL & PERFORMING ARTS

It's Not All Song and Dance

A Life Behind the Scenes
in the Performing Arts

MAXIM GERSHUNOFF AND LEON VAN DYKE

LIMELIGHT EDITIONS

Published in 2005 by
   Limelight Editions
   512 Newark Pompton Turnpike
   Pompton Plains, New Jersey 07444, USA
   www.limelighteditions.com

For sales, please contact
   Limelight Editions
   c/o Hal Leonard Corporation
   7777 West Bluemound Road
   Milwaukee, Wisconsin 53213, USA
   Tel. 800-637-2852
   Fax 414-774-3259

Website: www.limelighteditions.com

Printed in the United States of America

Library of Congress Cataloging-in-Publication Data

   Gershunoff, Maxim.
      It's not all song and dance : a life behind the scenes in the performing
   arts / Maxim Gershunoff and Leon Van Dyke.-- 1st Limelight ed.
         p. cm.
      Includes index.
      ISBN 0-87910-310-8 (hardcover)
      1. Concert agents--United States--Biography.   I. Van Dyke, Leon. II.
   Title.
   ML429.G43I8 2005
   338.7'6178'092--dc22

                                                    2004027581

This book is dedicated to the memory of my parents,
Dora Pesochinskaya Gershunoff and Aaron Gershunoff,
my trumpet teacher, Harry Glantz,
Mary Louise Curtis Bok Zimbalist,
whose generosity endowed the Curtis Institute of Music,
conductor Dimitri Mitropoulos,
choreographer Sir Frederick Ashton,
and impresario Sol Hurok.

Acknowledgments

The authors wish to thank the many who have contributed to their manuscript with facts, photos, critiques, editorial suggestions, and encouragement. We especially want to express our appreciation to James Adler, William Bast, Bridget Bogard, James Brooks-Bruzzese, John Cerullo, Javier Clavere, Joseph Conlin, Thomas Conlin, Jeffrey Coyne, Robert and Patricia Dockerty, Judy Drucker, Robert Friedman, Robert M. Gewald, Serge Goncharoff, Frieda Gronowetter, Rose Hirschel, Joseph Kluger, Floyd Landis, Maurice Peress, Joan Peyser, Maya Plisetskaya, Paul Polivnick, Daniel Saxon, Rodion Schedrin, Jose Serebrier, Harold Shaw, Andy Shreeves, Richard Talbot, Yuri Temirkhanov, Carolyn Van Dyke, Norman Van Dyke, Lee Walter, Tracy Washington, and John Waxman. We are deeply indebted to Jan Hokenson, Ph.D., and Sandra Norton, Ph.D., for their gracious assistance in shaping and editing our thoughts. Finally, our efforts also owe much to the contributions of our editor, Rosalie Wieder.

Foreword

IN MAY 2004, THE NEW YORK TIMES REPORTED THAT THE LAST BASTIONS of old-style fine French cuisine have folded up shop and been replaced by more relaxed purveyors of fine foods. These new restaurateurs cater to a clientele that no longer takes easily to the formality of jackets and ties or designer dresses when dining out. A contemporary dining customer, while spending upwards of three hundred dollars for a meal nowadays, seems to want to do so in the comfort of blue jeans if he or she so chooses. As one of the older restaurateurs phrased it so aptly: "The notion of classic has come to seem outdated."

On a previous day in the selfsame month of May 2004, the selfsame daily newspaper reported on a gifted classical cellist's efforts to "liberate" his own classical concertizing. By presenting traditional "serious" music in strikingly nontraditional environments such as rock music clubs, pizza parlors, and coffeehouses around the United States, cellist Matt Haimovitz hopes to be able to reach out to younger audiences.

This memoir reports on a golden era of classical music and dance in the United States when there was little need to "reach out" in search of audiences. Much like the entrepreneur owners of the French restaurants who held unrivaled sway in New York City during the second half of the last century, so, too, did a particular and highly individual impresario of the classical performing arts wield exceptional influence during the golden era of which we write. That man was the Russian-born American Sol Hurok.

Maxim Gershunoff's life from its very inception intertwined with that of the impresario Sol Hurok and later with those of many other stellar figures of the performing arts in the twentieth century. As an artists' manager, he has professionally represented such major artists as cellists Mstislav Rostropovich and Yo-Yo Ma, whose career he helped launch when Ma was an unknown sixteen-year-old.

Today, cellist Yo-Yo Ma can sell out large-scale auditoriums with his forays into the music of the ancient Silk Road. Young and old alike are attracted to both his celebrity and his music making. Entertainment in all of its forms sells the most tickets for those who are most celebrated. This was true when Franz Liszt and Niccolo Paganini were concertizing and remains even more so over 150 years later.

In previous decades, audiences flocked to the concerts of pianists Artur Rubinstein and Van Cliburn; violinists Isaac Stern and Nathan Milstein; cellist Jacqueline du Pré; mezzo-soprano Marian Anderson; soprano Roberta Peters; and tenor Jan Peerce. Still thousands upon thousands of others thrilled to the dancing of Margot Fonteyn and Rudolf Nureyev with the Royal Ballet of England, or the Bolshoi Ballet's Maya Plisetskaya and Vladimir Vassiliev.

During that era, concert halls throughout the U.S. and Canada witnessed an unending tide of artistry, particularly following World War II, when the country's citizenry was swollen with immigrants from war-torn Europe and there was a new sophistication regarding acceptance of matters cultural. Even eccentric million-aire aviator and filmmaker Howard Hughes dabbled in the world of ballet. Enthralled with the enchanting ballerina Zizi Jeanmaire, Hughes imported the dance company in which she starred, Roland Petit's Ballet de Paris, to Hollywood while following his dream of making Zizi a movie star.

At first radio was the best medium for enlarging live audiences for the classical performing arts. For more than half of the twentieth century, the weekly Saturday afternoon broadcasts from the Metropolitan Opera in New York City provided superb vocal artistry in living rooms from Miami, Florida, to Seattle, Washington. In those same parlors Sunday afternoons for almost three decades could be spent listening to the NBC Symphony Orchestra led by its music director, conductor Arturo Toscanini and guest conductors who were leading musical figures of their time. Alternate forms of entertainment were far fewer in those days and often called for disposable income that was even more of a rarity. Television gradually took hold, and families didn't need to venture out on Saturday nights to find entertainment when a host of comedy and variety shows could be had along with all of the comforts of home. Sunday television programming was equally gen-erous, offering the silver-tongued Leonard Bernstein holding forth on the glories of classical music with his Young People's Concerts, as well as the Columbia Broadcasting System's *Omnibus* program's presentation of classical music and dance performances. On Sunday evenings, the newspaper gossip columnist Ed Sullivan hosted a program entitled *Talk of the Town* in which vaudeville acts fea-turing gymnasts and jugglers might alternate with an operatic aria performed by a Metropolitan Opera star such as soprano Dorothy Kirsten, a musical number from a current Broadway hit, and a pas de deux as danced by stars of the American Ballet Theatre. Highly eclectic? Yes! Highly entertaining? Yes!

These were the years that emerged out of the Great Depression era. New York, Chicago, Boston, San Francisco, Los Angeles, and other great cities had large populations that had immigrated from the European continent during the first half of the century. They survived the deprivations of the Depression and the Second World War and created a strong economy. Veterans of the war attended college and became members of America's newly enlarged middle class. Racial and religious prejudices of the kind that had been a vital element in the instigation of World War II were revealed in all of their ugliness and made many reconsider their unjustified hatred. A form of prejudice that had existed since America's founding no longer could exist with any official sanction as the U.S. Supreme Court, in *Brown v. Board of Education,* decided in favor of an African-American parent who sought a good education for his child and sued in pursuit of that goal (a decision that recently reached its historic fiftieth anniversary in this year of 2004). The second half of the twentieth century witnessed the African-American mezzo-soprano Marian Anderson becoming the first black artist to sing in a production of the Metropolitan Opera. The gifted African-American ballet dancer Arthur Mitchell became a leading dancer with the New York City Ballet. Later, the celebrity Mitchell's status brought him enabled him to found the Dance Theater of Harlem. (Maxim Gershunoff also experienced prejudice on a personal level because of his Jewish heritage, although he has never adhered to any form of religious observance.) Prejudice against homosexuals plays a role in this book as well. Yet, as this is written gay men and lesbian women are marrying their life partners for the first time in this country in the city of San Francisco and the Commonwealth of Massachusetts.

As the last century hurtled towards its demise, and as the country evolved demographically and educationally, attendance at performances of the classical arts, especially in the "recital" format, began to dwindle dramatically. The student uprisings of the 1960s on university campuses across the land had college administrations relinquishing elements of authority over to student bodies. Some of that authority was vested in the presentation of artists on campus. While the heads of the music and drama departments on college campuses had previously been the principals involved in the selection of artists seen and heard in college auditoriums, students now sat on committees involved in the selection process. Where the artistry presented in prior years had been considered a necessary exposure of students to the "arts and humanities," and an informal but vital part of a university's curriculum, it now was to become student "entertainment." It has taken several decades to eliminate the classical performing arts from university presentations, and it is now almost universally the case that such presentations are comprised of rock music concerts, stand-up comics, and what are known as "bus and truck" tours of Broadway musicals featuring fourth- and fifth-run casts. The occasional former movie star will do a turn on university stages as the student selection committee's faculty adviser points the students in the direction of townsfolk who might like to see something familiar on the local campus.

Up until the 1980s, many smaller towns and cities lacking a college auditorium presented a series under the banner of "Community Concerts" at a local high school or, perhaps, a Masonic lodge auditorium. Most community concert associations were organized by Columbia Artists Management and were a major source of income for that artists management firm. Many of the management's artists found that they were able to support their growing families on the fees realized from performing hundreds of those community concerts. Being reasonably satisfied financially, such artists often did not press their management for more recognition through performances with major symphony orchestras or in important concert venues such as Carnegie Hall. But, with alternate forms of entertainment more and more available, these community concert associations began to fall apart. They were dependent upon volunteers in each town to maintain ticket sales annually, and volunteer interest waned. Columbia Artists Management, originally a subsidiary enterprise of the Columbia Broadcasting System, has sold its interest in Community Concerts, and they are now an almost totally forgotten form of artist presentation on the local level.

Another serious contributor to the decline of classical concerts has been what seems to be the complete obliteration of music instruction at the elementary and secondary school levels in the U.S. Marching bands are still a mainstay of participation in holiday parades and at school sports events. Instruction for school bands does not require the elevated level of musical knowledge that training for participation in an orchestra with a full complement of string sections does. Funding for such music instruction if it is still available is often made only through the continuing efforts of students' parents organizing cake and rummage sales, as well as games of chance to raise needed monies. America's body politic has largely abandoned any form of encouragement of the arts in education. Those politicians who might wish to support the arts through legislation have ceded their influence in this area as they fight what they see as bigger battles with their opposition.

The purpose of this memoir is to set forth for the curious reader a significant part of the history of a golden era in the classical performing arts and, especially, that of a participant in their presentation from the 1940s through to the end of the twentieth century. Having been professionally involved in the performing arts for most of my own almost seventy years, and having been a friend and business partner of Maxim Gershunoff's for most of my years, I can testify as to the verity of his recollections. As a matter of fact, I have been able not only to record his stories via computer, I was actually able to help him recall some of his own lifetime experiences.

A highly successful local presenter in California perhaps summed up Maxim Gershunoff's life experiences in the performing arts best when he told him, "Max, you may not have become a very rich man in your work, but you certainly have led a far more interesting life than I have. I can truly say, I am jealous of you and your life's experiences."

Maxim Gershunoff and I believe that these recollections contribute a unique and personal perspective on a vanished era in the cultural history of this country and, as such, have their own intrinsic value.

LEON VAN DYKE
Fort Lauderdale, Florida
June 2004

Preface

TRAINED AS A MUSICIAN FROM AN EARLY AGE, I ENTERED THE FIELD OF ARTS and artists management while still in my twenties, and since then have handled many aspects of getting artists onto a stage. Although the lives of performing artists are increasingly a matter of public record, particularly in this age of celebrity, the people who work as hard as, and sometimes harder than, the artists themselves at creating the opportunities and circumstances in which artists flourish are rarely acknowledged. We are often dismissed as mere flesh peddlers, and our contributions to making an artist a "known quantity," and sometimes even a household name, are seldom appreciated, especially by the artists themselves. I am stating this as fact and not by way of complaining about my lot. But I do believe it is important that readers have the opportunity to learn for themselves what transpires behind the scenes.

The work involved in preparing public performances can be complex, even hair-raising at times. It can involve risking large sums of money that can be lost at the whim of an artist or a fickle public, let alone the occurrence of an event sparking an international conflict. The story I want to tell is not simply a matter of name-dropping. The reader will find humor in these pages, as well as some surprises.

To those readers who may be disturbed at startlingly negative descriptions of some of their heroes in action, I extend my apologies. However, I do not deserve recriminations for the misdeeds of others; it is they who should be blamed. I offer readers the chance to gain some insight into how it all happens, both onstage and backstage, as well as offstage, and in the process to perhaps gain a broader familiarity with these heroes.

I have enjoyed a rich life in my quest for a livelihood in the arts, and I continue to be active in that pursuit as I write this at the age of eighty. The tale I wish to tell is the story of my life and my work, starting from my days as an active musician in major symphony orchestras and continuing on to my transition into the business aspects of the live performing arts, work that involves not only the arts, but everything life has to offer, including international politics. I will attempt to keep my recounting of experiences with many artists as close to the truth as possible, without embellishment, overglamorization, or distortion, and to tell it as it really was.

It is my desire that this book serve not only as a bridge between generations by communicating in realistic terms with younger readers, but also as a means to spark in those who have lived through the decades of which I write a desire to learn more about some of the great icons of the performing arts, both past and present, of whom they may have known very little heretofore.

Perhaps by recounting my experiences I can help both types of reader to better know artists as the human beings they actually are when not in the public eye, or at least as I have found them to be in my work and in my travels with them.

Prologue

I OWE MY VERY EXISTENCE, AND MY MEANS OF EXISTENCE, TO TWO EXCEEDINGLY different leaders. The first, nameless leader led a band of hooligans in the free-wheeling early revolutionary era of the Soviet Union. The second leader was the symphony and opera conductor Dimitri Mitropoulos, a former monk turned musician who has been described as a "priest of music."

Perhaps I would never have been born had my mother not been gifted with the ability to think quickly and lie effectively. She utilized those gifts to great advantage by saving her own life and that of some fellow travelers in the beginning days of the USSR.

As a young woman, my mother, a professional cellist, was returning home to Odessa one night by train after a concert when the train was halted by a group of drunken, renegade hooligans on horseback looking for an evening of "fun." Their leader got off his steed, climbed aboard the train, stomped through each railroad car, read the identity papers of each of the passengers, and demanded that all identified as Jews get off the train and stand along one side of the tracks. His followers remained astride their horses with sabers at the ready.

The leader, apparently, happened to have heard my mother perform, and approached her. She was standing in line with two of her seatmates, along with all of the other Jewish passengers. He addressed her, saying, "You are the cellist. Get out of this line." My mother was reluctant, explaining that she was with her two sisters and pleaded that they be allowed to come with her. He handed her a kerosene lantern and told her to start walking down the tracks to the next town and not to look back. By doing so, she and the two other women, actually total strangers to her, were saved from being beheaded by the saber blades of the horse-riding hooligans.

FOLLOWING A HEART ATTACK IN 1951, DIMITRI MITROPOULOS, THEN PRINCIPAL conductor of the New York Philharmonic, was recuperating for three months at my home in California. A doctor who was treating the maestro in New York City had telephoned me in Los Angeles. Apparently, this doctor had recommended that Mitropoulos not conduct for at least three months after he left New York Hospital, where he had been treated. A warm climate was also prescribed for recuperation. A flight to a Mediterranean country would have been too stressful. California could be the solution, since he already had an invitation from Spyros Skouras, chairman of Twentieth Century-Fox, a fellow Greek countryman, and still another invitation had been proffered by famed violinist Joseph Szygeti and his wife.

The doctor who called me regarding Dimitri said, "The maestro keeps saying, 'The thought smiles me most is to stay with Max if I am to go to California.'" This man who had grown up in a monastery very seriously believed that his talent was a God-given gift. He felt that it would be sinful if any of the monies that he earned with his gift were used to indulge himself. On the contrary, and without fanfare, he used whatever excess funds he had by helping many individuals, including Leonard Bernstein, further their education. During Lenny's studies at the Curtis Institute of Music, Mitropoulos provided him with a stipend to help cover his living expenses, which were not provided for by Lenny's scholarship.

As a philosophical form of counterbalance, Mitropoulos's preference was to recuperate and be helped in the home of someone not possessed of substantial means, namely myself. Besides which, he would be comfortable with both me and my parents, as all of us were musicians. Since the length of time needed for his recovery was to extend to three months, he would feel more at home in these surroundings. Without hesitation, I agreed to have Dimitri come and stay at my place. Dimitri loved mountain climbing, and being able to live in my small, recently leased penthouse on Hillside Avenue, overlooking Los Angeles from an elevation of 1,000 feet, gave him a visual sense of freedom. My new apartment was only a couple of blocks away from my parents' home on Kings Road, where I had been living. This was often convenient for the dinner hour, when my mother would provide Dimitri and me with sensible nourishment. Paul Strauss, a young conductor whom Dimitri had been mentoring, came to stay for a while as well, and he helped me care for Dimitri. Eleanor Peters would help, also. When Dimitri arrived on the airplane and we met him in the terminal, he could barely walk. Little by little, with lengthening neighborhood walks, he regained his strength.

Dimitri recounted to me a visit he had with conductor Fritz Reiner while he was in New York Hospital. They were "talking shop" and exchanging thoughts on Reiner's imminent departure from the Metropolitan Opera, where he had con-ducted for some time. Dimitri asked Reiner who would be replacing him. Shocked, Reiner said, "Replacing? I am irreplaceable." Dimitri, recalling that he had heard this while lying on his back in the hospital, couldn't digest Reiner's concept of being irreplaceable. Laughing, he said to me, "We are all replaceable."

But there was no way Dimitri was going to let his brain rest, and in the three months of his recuperation he memorized five new symphonic scores. I was interested by his reaction to letters he received from composers who wished him to review their new scores and offered a recording of their work for his approval. His response was that of someone who had been slightly offended. On occasion he would reply to them explaining that he would gladly look at the score but didn't need to hear a recording, since he could "read" a score and didn't even own a Victrola (the name of the early wind-up record player). As the time went by, spending three months in the company of this almost saintly genius turned out to be more than a privilege and affected my life very deeply.

We engaged in long, long conversations over the months, and Dimitri, being the nurturing man that he was, insisted that I look at the way my life was unfolding personally and professionally. While I enjoyed the lifestyle of a moderately successful freelance musician in California, Dimitri could offer me the opportunity of a seat in the New York Philharmonic, and he held that out to me as an option for my life's path. But, as he grew to know me even better over the months of his recuperation, Mitropoulos said that I would likely grow bored over time as a tenured musician in New York City. He advised me to consider pursuing a line of endeavor that had always interested me: management of the performing arts. I had dabbled here and there prior to this time. For instance, I had been the road manager for a tour with orchestra by a famous Viennese composer/conductor in the late forties, billed as "An Evening with Oscar Strauss." With this perceptive suggestion, Mitropoulos refocused and redirected my love of the performing arts.

Chapter One

I WAS BORN ON NEW YORK CITY'S EAST 99th STREET OFF PARK AVENUE IN what was then and is now known as Spanish Harlem. My parents had only recently settled in New York City, having been sequestered in a displaced persons' camp in England for a number of months before they were able to emigrate to the United States. Their entry was made possible through the husband of an aunt of my father's in New York City. The aunt was Bertha Koot and her husband was Charlie, a jeweler in New York City's Bowery district. Charlie was a very close friend of the newly emerging impresario Sol Hurok. Charlie elicited a favor from Hurok, who provided my parents with a contract inviting them to tour the U.S. as musicians on his roster of artists. His letter to them, dated December 10, 1923, on letterhead reading "S. Hurok, Inc." with an address at the old Aeolian Hall on West 43rd Street in Manhattan, was a ruse. For bureaucratic purposes only, it nevertheless smoothed the path with United States immigration authorities. As a result, then, my mother, Dora, father, Aaron, and brother, Alex, were permitted to enter the Port of New York in early 1924, and I was born in June of that year. The letter had served to get around the quota restrictions on Jews imposed by the U.S. Immigration and Naturalization Service.

My parents and brother would otherwise have had to immigrate to Argentina, their alternative plan in case they could not enter the U.S. In the camp in Southampton, England, along with my family was a cousin of my father, Alberto Gershunoff, who did become an Argentine citizen. There he was to become a highly respected author and was known as the "Jewish Gaucho." He was a firm believer in integration rather than the "ghettoizing" of ethnic groups. Today there is a boulevard in Buenos Aires that bears his name. So, whenever I have had business dealings with anyone in Argentina, they have no problems, either with pronouncing or recognizing my surname, and all ask if I am related to their famous writer.

My parents later moved to the far reaches of Brooklyn, to 1406 Avenue Y, in a neighborhood called Sheepshead Bay. During that era, Italian immigrants who were primarily local fishermen mostly inhabited Sheepshead Bay. In character it was like an Italian village. The men played bocce ball, maintained grapevines in their backyards, and filled barrels with grapes to make wine in their basements. My mother and father wanted my brother and me to grow up in a less urban atmosphere than Manhattan. My brother and I attended elementary schools in our neighborhood. My parents were also insistent that the entire family speak the English language at home. They felt that they had to learn the language of their newly adopted country, and that this would certainly make things much easier for their children once they began their schooling.

In 1934, Franklin Delano Roosevelt's new administration had the United States of America formally recognizing the Union of Soviet Socialist Republics. With diplomatic relations established between our countries, tourism was encouraged. It now became possible for émigrés, such as my family, to visit relatives in the USSR. As former Soviet citizens, my parents felt that it would be highly risky to travel to the USSR unless I, their American-born child, traveled with one or both of them should they return to visit. With an American citizen in tow, there would be little likelihood of the Soviet authorities detaining any former Soviet citizens and never releasing them. Although my father had no desire to return to his homeland, my mother very much missed her family in Odessa.

It was decided that my mother, my brother, and I would visit her family in Odessa now that such travel was permissible. On June 16, 1934, we set sail on the luxurious French liner the *Ile de France* in first-class accommodations. Fellow passengers on board included the movie stars Janet Gaynor and Charles Farrell. At ten years of age, I found Miss Gaynor to be most attractive. I would go to the ship's gym every morning to watch her work out. My brother, Alex, and I had brought model airplane kits with us for amusement on the trip. After the framework was assembled, a paper skin was required to finish off the models. Though unable to complete the models while aboard the *Ile de France,* we discovered that the toilet tissue provided on board our ship would make an excellent alternative to the covering provided by the toymaker and decided to augment the paper provided in the model kits. However, we didn't take enough of the toilet tissue with us, as we were to discover later to our sorrow.

We disembarked at Plymouth, England, and went via train to London, where we boarded a Soviet vessel, the SS *Smolny.* From there we set sail via the North Sea to the Baltic Sea, by way of the Kiel Canal, and through the Gulf of Finland, arriving in Leningrad, now once again called St. Petersburg. The time spent on the SS *Smolny* was pleasant. One of our diversions was winding up a Victrola record player and listening to Russian folk songs, as well as disks of classical music. Occasionally members of the crew would play on accordions and balalaikas and sing together as a chorus. As on the *Ile de France*, safety drills were de rigueur, except they happened more often. As before, we were directed to our assigned lifeboats. The only difference aboard the Soviet ship was that there were gas attack drills, for the crew only. I had never seen people with gas masks on their faces before. To a ten-year-old and a twelve-year-old the sight was frightening. We were alarmed as to what would happen to us should there be an attack involving gas because we had none of those masks.

Our late-night arrival in June in Leningrad coincided with the "midnight sun." My brother and I were certainly unaccustomed to this northern phenomenon. We were met at the dock by one of my mother's sisters, Ethel, who had traveled by train all the way from the Black Sea port of Odessa to greet us and accompany us on the train ride to my grandmother's home there.

In Leningrad we stayed at the elegant Astoria Hotel. In later years, Hitler would plan on hosting his victory dinner there, and he went so far as to have invitations printed for the occasion. Thanks to the heroic efforts of Leningrad's citizenry during the Second World War, such an event never took place. Ironically, in that same hotel, Soviet dictates prevented my Aunt Ethel from being allowed to dine with us in the hotel's dining room, which was for tourists only; no Soviet citizens were allowed, even as guests.

The best that could be done under the circumstances was to sneak Aunt Ethel into our suite, where we could enjoy room service together after the bellman had left the room. In reality, she wasn't even allowed into the hotel. A "security" concierge who kept an eye on all hotel occupants and their visitors oversaw each floor. I do not know how my mother managed to get my aunt through the lobby, up in an elevator, down a hallway, and into our suite. Based on what I later learned about Soviet citizens masquerading as foreigners by donning foreign-made clothing, perhaps my mother had my aunt wear some of her American-made dresses, shoes (very important), and some lipstick. She would have told Aunt Ethel not to speak, and they would enter the hotel together.

The train trip from Leningrad to Odessa took several days. We made a stop in Moscow, where we stayed overnight at the Metropole Hotel, which to this day still accommodates travelers. We then traveled through endless miles of wheat fields while heading south through Ukraine. Along the way, treats for us children were the "cherries on a stick" for sale at the railroad stops en route. Tightly bound together by having their stems woven onto a tree twig of around twelve inches in length, the sweet cherries were a substitute for candy treats and very refreshing in those un-air-conditioned times.

When we arrived at the railroad station in Odessa we were met by my grandmother, Naomi Pesochinskaya. This grandmother had been the mother of five daughters, who all played piano, as well as other musical instruments, and one son, who became a cellist. My grandfather had died long before in one of the mysterious epidemics of the earlier twentieth century. The prospect of spending three months with a grandmother I didn't know had made me somewhat apprehensive, as I had no idea of what she would be like. I didn't know whether I would love her or hate her. My fears immediately dissipated as it turned out that I took an intense liking to my grandmother. Though I could not speak Russian yet, the tone of her voice, her very beautiful blue eyes, and a friendly, earthy yet elegant warmth all captivated me. From our first meeting until her death many years later in America we were good and close friends.

Much as in New York's Central Park of today, we were driven in a horse and carriage to the Hotel London. The horse and carriage were not for effect; this was the lone mode of transportation available. The hotel was situated on a boulevard overlooking the Black Sea and just to the right of the famous Potemkin Steps. It was a beautiful, classic hotel of an earlier era with an inner open-air courtyard and fountain. My grandmother lived on the same boulevard several blocks to the left of the Potemkin Steps. Although our accommodations had had to be paid for in advance in New York City, my mother preferred that we all stay with my grandmother. We would, however, retire to the hotel for certain creature comforts on occasion, such as taking a bath in privacy and using actual toilet paper, which was provided there. We discovered that the newspapers on hand at my grandmother's apartment were not up to date but may not have been read anyway. They were torn into strips and used for other purposes, and that is why my brother and I were sorry we had not robbed the *Ile de France* of more of its nice toilet tissue.

My grandmother's living quarters were a far cry from our rooms at the Hotel London. In a building that had formerly housed a foreign consulate, she lived on the ground floor in one very large, high-ceilinged room. There was a community kitchen shared by the other tenants on the floor. The cooking stoves used were one-burner Primuses, much as are used on camping trips. In the building's courtyard was a fountain that was a source of drinking water. One filled a pail and brought it into the kitchen. There was other water available for washing dishes, but the fountain provided potable water. Tenants filled their samovars for tea with water from that fountain as well. Charcoal was the fuel used in the samovar, and it was lit while you were still in the courtyard, immediately after having been filled with water. Toilet facilities were also shared, and there were two of those, where one always found lots of old newspapers. To bathe, everyone went to public bathhouses.

Alex and I spent our daytime hours on the boulevard dressed as American children would dress during the summer months, and we found that the Russian youngsters would mutter comments that we later learned translated as "shitty Americans." Later, when we had gained our street smarts, we would go out dressed as we saw our Russian counterparts were. This meant we went shoeless and wore shorts.

There were many homeless children in our midst. Buying a packet of sunflower seeds in the streets, we soon discovered, involved some defensive reactions. If we were not cautious, hands would appear from nowhere and slap the pack of seeds from our hands. The scattered seeds would be scavenged from the ground and the thieving culprit would race off.

While spending three months in Russia, as children we were able to quite easily pick up on the language we were not learning at home in Brooklyn. We made some friends who asked us if it was true that Americans sleep in a "special suit" when they go to bed. We said, "You mean pajamas?" As if we were doing them the greatest favor, they asked if they could come with us and see what pajamas looked like. We accommodated their curiosity and they reacted with delight on their discovery of pajamas. Evenings, several times during the week, could be spent in the huge square above the Potemkin Steps at the outdoor free showings of a "kino" (movie). There were no seats available; the audience, comprised of hundreds of people, simply stood and watched the somewhat distorted film projection.

Alex and I were shown the place where he had been born. We visited the beautiful Odessa Opera House, an almost exact replica of the Paris Opera. It was at the Odessa Opera House that my mother's father had been employed and my father had received much of his musical education. We also frequented the "lemon beach," a public beach that was famous for its therapeutic black mud baths. One simply applied the wet soil along the shore to one's body. Most bathers were nude. They lay in the sun and let the mud dry on their naked forms. When they had had enough, they uncaked the baked-on mud and went into the water to remove its last vestiges.

My grandmother maintained a chicken coop in the apartment house's rear courtyard. She had a total of fourteen birds when we arrived, and I thought of them as pets. One by one, they were disappearing. Little was made of their disappearance and I was told that the chickens were off wandering. By the time our visit was nearing its end in August, the last two chickens I had seen one morning were gone by the evening. We were having chicken soup for dinner, and only then did the truth of the chickens' disappearing act actually dawn on me. I refused to eat and, packing my bags, announced that I was leaving immediately to meet my father in Paris, where he was expected. I was allowed to talk myself silly, complete with mournful tears. Having little choice, I reluctantly obeyed my mother's admonitions and stayed until we were all ready to leave Odessa. But, from that point forward I always chose dogs to be my pets.

At one point during our stay in Odessa, we were all witnesses to a variation on

Victor Hugo's *Les Misérables*. At a courthouse on the same square above the Potemkin Steps, a trial was in progress. As it was open to the public, my mother, brother, and I were able to be present at two days of hearings for an accused criminal. It was one of the Stalin-designed public "show trials." If attendees were crowded out of the actual courtroom, the proceedings were broadcast over speakers to those standing in the square. The defendant ran a government-owned bakery where bread was sold by the kilo. He was accused of having cheated customers on bread weight so as to privately speculate on the difference at the end of the day by selling the bread he had accumulated. He was considered not only to have deceived the Soviet government but also to have stolen from the Soviet people. Such a defendant was labeled an "enemy of the people."

The trial was held in two sessions. In the first session the case was reviewed, while the second was for the sentencing. The culprit was found to be guilty. He was sentenced to death. I have never forgotten the sounds of that baker screaming as he was hauled out of the room.

Odessa is an international seaport, and, hearing of an incoming Italian luxury liner, the Roma, we eagerly anticipated that ship's arrival in the port. To accommodate the expected arriving tourists from the liner, massive marquees were erected for banquet festivities along the boulevard on either side of the Potemkin Steps. Human chains of policemen blocked all of the streets emptying off into the boulevard. The apartment buildings overlooking the boulevard had their front entrances locked, and tenants could enter and exit their buildings only through the courtyards in the rear. My brother, dressed as a young Russian and ever the contrarian, took his bicycle out of the courtyard and rode along the blockaded boulevard despite having been told not to do so. As he attempted to go through a blockade, the police grabbed him from his bike and threw him to the ground. Some of the neighbors witnessing the action quickly told the police, "He's okay! He's an American. He can do that." Upon his return to my grandmother's flat after that incident, Alex and I decided we had had enough of our masquerade dressing as Russian children did. Our appetite to mix and mingle with the tourists from the ship became desperate. We told our three female cousins to put on American dresses and shoes that my mother had brought as gifts for them. Alex and I also put on our American clothing, and once the girls were in their unaccustomed garments, we all proceeded to the Hotel London, telling the girls not to speak a word. We did not want them to be recognized for the Russians they were.

After having been subjected to Russian culture for several weeks, we had had our fill of it! It was a joy to arrive in the lobby of the Hotel London and to hear the English language being spoken once again by some of the tourists.

During the summer of that year, there was great political unrest in Europe, which alarmed my father at home in New York City. Realizing that in the USSR we were actually in a "closed" society, he thought he would be very clever and, hoping that my mother would understand, he cabled: VERY HOT. COME HOME AT ONCE. With little or no news of an international nature available to ordinary Russians, my mother innocently answered my father's cable by replying: IT'S VERY HOT HERE, TOO. IT'S AUGUST. The next telegram to my mother reflected my father's complete exasperation. He wrote: AM ABOARD THE ILE DE FRANCE. MEET ME IN PARIS AT THE HOTEL LAFAYETTE, specifying a date in late August. Reacting to my father's sense of urgency, my mother booked space for us on a deluxe international train heading north through Poland, into Germany, Belgium, and, finally, France.

We had a suite of compartments aboard the train. There were tufted velvet couches that converted into our beds at night. Classical music was piped into the compartments, and we could listen to it on earphones that were as big as earmuffs. The cars were wagons-lits and were quite luxurious, appointed much as one envisions the old Orient Express to have been. Our arrival in Berlin involved a seven-hour layover. As we approached that city, looking out of the train window, we saw Nazi flags lining both sides of all the streets. Our arrival in the German capital coincided with the day of Hindenburg's funeral. Being isolated from the rest of the world, as we had been, we had no idea that he had died.

When the train came to a halt, uniformed Nazi officials, replete with swastika armbands, boarded it. They had come aboard to check all passenger documents. When they came to our compartments, they insisted that a steamer trunk be removed and put in the baggage car, which was five cars behind. As we had traveled with the trunk in our compartments through all of Russia and Poland, and in Germany as far as Berlin with no problem to that point, we inquired why it could not remain where it was. The Nazis were adamant and declared it to be unsafe. If it must be moved, my mother asked, how could porters be found to move the trunk? Their reply was "A German doesn't carry baggage for Jews." Fortunately, two of our fellow passengers were physicians from Persia. They had been quite friendly with us during our trip from Russia and they volunteered their assistance in carting the trunk to the baggage car. My mother felt obliged to at least accompany them on their walk down the station platform to the fifth car back. Afraid that we might wander off, she expressed her concern that Alex and I should not wander but stay put in the compartment until her return. As history has recorded, that day in August of 1934 was the seminal turning point in Hitler's rise to political power.

Without further incident, we arrived in Paris and were met by my father. We spent a few days there awaiting the arrival of the *Ile de France* at the port of Le Havre. I recall my parents purchasing two handsome navy-blue overcoats at

Paris's Galeries Lafayette department store for my brother and me. We were able to see many of Paris's famous landmarks, including the Paris Opera, and enjoyed much more sophisticated dining than we had had at our disposal in Odessa. I was not going to be eating chicken for some time to come.

As we again boarded the *Ile de France* for our return to New York, my perspective was now somewhat different. I was now a "seasoned traveler." I knew the ship quite well, and that unto itself was like a homecoming for me. Probably the most stellar fellow passenger on the return trip was an "old lady" in my youthful estimation. From the moment she would enter the dining room at mealtimes and be escorted to her table by a solicitous maitre d', much fuss was constantly made over her. She was rather a stately figure. Her name was Sara Roosevelt, mother of our American president at the time, Franklin Delano Roosevelt.

In those times and aboard such an ocean liner, both adults and children were required to dress for dinner. As we sat at one such proper dinner in our formal attire, the ocean was acting up because of some bad weather we were experiencing on the return voyage. My brother, Alex, possessing no "sea legs," became nauseated at the sight of the food and immediately threw up into his empty soup plate as the waiter ladled soup into my plate. The waiter, with total aplomb, saying nothing at all, grabbed a table napkin and, in one smooth gesture, placed it over Alex's offending plate and removed it from the sight of our table's occupants.

Chapter Two

IN 1938, WHEN MY FAMILY MOVED FROM SHEEPSHEAD BAY IN BROOKLYN to an apartment on Riverside Drive in Manhattan, I was in for a bit of a cultural shock. I was transferred to Stuyvesant High School in midtown Manhattan. It was supposed to be a school excelling in teaching mathematics to its all-male student body. I played trumpet as a member of the All City High School Orchestra, which had its rehearsals at Stuyvesant. Because of this, the school administration was delighted to have me transferred to its school.

I found that the surroundings were rather unpleasant compared to Abraham Lincoln High School, which I had attended in Brooklyn. A "moment of truth" occurred for me during a class when a knife went flying at someone and flopped onto the surface of my desk. Not knowing at whom the weapon had been targeted, I simply got up from my desk, walked out of the room, went down to the principal's office, and announced, "I am checking out. I can be reached at home. Good-bye." Naturally, my parents were telephoned and were told that I must be placed in another school within a period of two weeks. I then tried to apply to George Washington High School, a coed school that was said to be much more disciplined, and found that I lived several blocks out of its zone. I also applied to the High School of Music and Art, but they would not take me because I was no longer in the first term of the school year. I ended up attending DeWitt Clinton High School in the Bronx. This involved a one-hour subway commute each way from our apartment on Riverside Drive at 90th Street.

I was becoming more and more disturbed at being pulled in different directions by my academic and musical studies, and at what I felt to be wasted time on the subway each school day. A friend, Allen Golden, was encouraging me to enroll at the private school he was attending. However, though I was only fourteen years old, it was my belief that my parents' tax money should have provided me with public schooling sufficient for my needs. During this period I even entertained the thought of running away from home, with no particular place to run to in mind. I simply wanted to escape from my educational dilemma.

A mutual friend with whom I grew up, Jeanette Stone, had moved to California. When she visited New York City that year, a friend of hers from California, Mitchell Lurie, came up from Philadelphia to visit Jeannette. I was introduced to Mitchell at that time and learned that he was attending the Curtis Institute of Music in Philadelphia, where he was pursuing a major in clarinet. As I got to know Mitchell during his stay and expounded on my own problems as a young musician, he suggested a possible solution. It was an avenue I had not even thought of exploring. If there was to be an opening for a trumpet student, the Curtis Institute would be holding auditions the following April. So, why didn't I apply for a scholarship, much as he had during the previous year? Curtis would offer me a musical education both on trumpet and piano and would also provide a private academic tutor at no cost whatsoever to my parents. My parents, however, would be responsible for my living expenses. It was a challenge, as the entire student body was comprised of only 135 youngsters. They came from all over the world and their instructors were world-famous musicians. So, obtaining a scholarship was a highly competitive process. As there were only four trumpets in the school's symphony orchestra, there were only four openings for trumpet students. One could only be accepted if one of those four students graduated or left for another reason. Unlike the Juilliard School, the Manhattan School of Music, and the majority of such conservatories of music, the Curtis Institute of Music maintains a policy of an all-scholarship student body that does not pay for tuition.

In order to better concentrate on my musical studies and have more time in which to do so, I had to transfer schools once again. The only school in my area was Haaren High School on Tenth Avenue at 59th Street. Although this school and its raucous students hardly were conducive to anyone's peace of mind, I would only have to be enrolled there for the second term of my sophomore year in high school as long as I obtained a scholarship to the Curtis Institute. At that juncture, I thought the only other solution might be suicide, whatever that meant to me in my youthful ignorance.

As luck would have it, an opening for a trumpet student was available at the Curtis Institute of Music, and on a rainy day in that April of 1939, I entered its front doors for the first time. The building was a converted mansion that had been the former town house of Philadelphia's noted Drexel family, on Rittenhouse Square at 18th and Locust Streets. In no way did the atmosphere of the building connote "institution." Rather, it was like entering the large and beautiful urban residence of an enormously wealthy household. Two white-jacketed porters greeted students as they entered and would even assist you in removing your coat at a convenient cloakroom. A receptionist awaited your inquiry and accommodated your needs by directing you appropriately. I played my audition for instructor Saul Caston in one of two enormous parlors on the second floor of the mansion. Several other students were waiting for their auditions on trumpet. The competition was real indeed.

To some, my description of the surroundings at Curtis makes it seem to have been a somewhat "stuffy" environment in which to nurture young students. To me, though, it was a breath of fresh air. I was quite overwhelmed by the contrast between this welcoming environment in Philadelphia and my experiences with the public school system in New York City. More than ever I now hoped that I had played well enough to be accepted and could escape my educational problems at home. Not long after, I received a letter telling me of my acceptance as a scholarship student at the Curtis Institute of Music. It was both a joy and a relief, and now suicide was definitely out of the question. Although both of my parents were pleased, I had not thought that my father would put forth conditions on my new good fortune.

Dad's main concern was that I should not turn out to be like some of the Curtis graduates of his acquaintance. He told me that for the most part they were snobs who felt that they were superior to those around them. If I was to turn out like those he knew, he would rather that I not go to Curtis at all. The Curtis alumni my father knew were now professional musicians in New York City. He, like many of his colleagues, did not hold them in high regard due to the attitudes they possessed. Impressing upon me that I must never use such people as role models, he finally agreed to allow me to accept the scholarship I had been offered.

An example of how serious my father was about such attitudes can be seen in an event that occurred after I had been at Curtis for a year or so and had some of my fellow students over to my family's apartment in New York City one weekend afternoon. One of those fellow students was horsing around at our piano. He was exaggeratedly satirizing the famous pianists of that era, including his teacher Rudolf Serkin. My father, hearing the performance, took umbrage at the inappropriate arrogance of the student pianist and demanded that the pianist, Eugene Istomin, get up and immediately leave the apartment.

NOW THAT I HAD JUST TURNED FIFTEEN AND WAS TO BE A SCHOLARSHIP student at one of the world's finest conservatories, another opportunity presented itself for both my brother and me in lieu of our usual summer sojourn at a children's camp in Westchester County. So it was that my first trip to California was made in that summer of 1939, traveling with my brother Alex aboard a sleeper bus of the All-American Bus Company. The bus accommodated a total of sixteen passengers. As on a railroad Pullman car, it had upper- and lower-berth beds by night, with a porter converting them all back to eight seating compartments by day. There was also a toilet aboard the bus, which was unusual for the times. The cost from New York to Los Angeles and back was a total of $72! The price of the ticket included a cash allotment for three meals a day at designated stopovers. The allotment, in Depression-era currency, was twenty-five cents for breakfast, thirty-five cents for lunch, and half a dollar for dinner. An extra piece of pie cost another ten cents, which came out of your own pocket. It took several days to get to Los Angeles. We were to meet at the home of Gregory Stone, a wonderful musician and composer who had written the musical arrangement of Benny Goodman's theme song, called "Let's Dance." My brother Alex, Gregory Stone's daughter Jeanette, Benny Goodman's youngest brother Jerry, and I usually spent our summers at children's camps in Upper New York State.

Jerry Goodman played the trumpet, and it was through him that I had first become very interested in that instrument while we were at children's camp. Although my first musical instruments, starting at age five, were violin and then piano, I truly did not excel at either one. Because the trumpet was the first musical instrument about which I showed no rebellion, my father took my new interest seriously. He happened to be a close friend of Harry Glantz, principal trumpet player of the New York Philharmonic at that time. He prevailed upon Harry to give me lessons. Harry found that with my basic knowledge of music already deeply instilled, I had a natural talent for the trumpet. It turned out I became the only student Harry Glantz had ever started as a complete neophyte. I could not have been more fortunate in my father's choice of an instructor and role model for me. Harry, whom I always called "Mr. Glantz," is still remembered as one of the finest exponents of symphonic trumpet playing and was Arturo Toscanini's favorite. Toscanini spirited him away from his position with the New York Philharmonic to have Harry play principal trumpet with Toscanini and the NBC Symphony Orchestra.

Again, with my father's help, I had had some additional coaching from another instructor prior to my audition at Curtis. His name at the time, as a trumpeter, was Sam Shapiro. He felt that I needed to exhibit more versatility in my approach to playing my instrument. In more colorful language, he made every effort to assuage my trepidations concerning my upcoming audition by advising me that my auditors would be just people like me, and like me they also had to utilize toilet facilities. Sam Shapiro achieved success later under another name and in another guise. He became known as "Sandy Spears" and was music director and conductor for all of comedian Jackie Gleason's television shows.

After arriving in California in the summer of 1939, Jeanette, Jerry, Alex, and I were to continue on for our stay on Santa Catalina Island along with the Benny Goodman band. Benny's band was the main attraction at the round casino building on the shore of the island, a very visible landmark. We were there to provide company for Benny's youngest brother, Jerry. As kids in our early teens, we were to be cared for by Benny's sister Ethel. It all was a complete joy for us youngsters to go to sleep at 2 a.m., as our nightly activity was to hear Benny's great band. The band's makeup included Gene Krupa on drums, Lionel Hampton on vibraphone, Ziggy Elman on trumpet, and Toots Mondello on sax, and featured Helen Forrest as vocalist. Following our excursions to the casino each night, as we walked back to our house we could smell a heady mixture of aromas: night-blooming jasmine, orange blossoms, and the scent of donuts being freshly made. We would all adjourn to the bakery and buy donuts to munch on as we headed back to go to sleep, as only kids with cast-iron stomachs can do.

That summer left a deep impression on both Alex and me, and upon returning to New York City our desire was to return to California one day. California eventually was to become a major element in my life in the performing arts, and Santa Catalina Island would become a part of it again in 1960.

ONE OF THE FIRST RESPONSIBILITIES I HAD AS A NEW STUDENT IN Philadelphia was to find housing, as the Curtis Institute did not have any such facilities for its students. They did have a list of approved nearby rental offerings for the music students. Mitchell Lurie and Morrie Boltuch already were living in a rooming house where I could also be accommodated. Owing to my youth, my mother was also very much involved in this process. She wanted to be certain that wherever it was that I would be housed was up to her standards. So, she made the trip down to Philadelphia with me to have a look. We walked along South 22nd Street, lined with red brick row houses graced with white marble steps, and just across the street from the address where Mitchell and Morrie roomed was a beautiful row house that had flower boxes in its windows and polished brass on its front door. It did make for a definite contrast to the surrounding houses. My mother, thinking that the entire block might consist of rooming houses, thought that the beautiful townhouse was the place to start looking for my living arrangements. When she rang the doorbell, the door was opened by a uniformed housemaid. Now, it seemed silly to ask, but, nevertheless, my mother inquired, "Do you rent rooms?" The maid, nonplused, simply said, "No, this is the residence of Meyer Davis, but they rent rooms across the street to the young musicians." (During that period and for many decades following, Meyer Davis was America's leading bandleader for the social affairs of the well-to-do and for political occasions where there was dancing. Davis was the parent of two sons and a daughter. His eldest son, Gary, became rather notorious by renouncing his U.S. citizenship and becoming a "citizen of the world." His other son, Emory, a clarinetist, later was involved in his father's enterprises. I know nothing about the Davis daughter other than that she was younger than us Curtis students and we thrilled at observing her undress from our windows across South 22nd Street.)

My mother and I went across the street to Mitchell's and Morrie's rooming place, and she finally approved of that establishment, where meals were included. Coincidentally, fellow Curtis student Leonard Bernstein lived just down the street, as did many other students. The following school year, however, Mitchell, Morrie, and I did not return to that rooming house. We located an apartment nearby on Locust Street and South 23rd Street that suited us better. We preferred to take turns preparing our own meals, though we had to wash our dishes in the bathtub. The meals at the rooming house on South 22nd Street had never really been satisfactory. As both Morrie and Mitchell were older than I, they served as a stabilizing influence on me and we remain friends to this day. I served as best man at Morris Boltuch's wedding to his wife Betty. He later became a member of the New York Philharmonic.

To earn some spending money for myself during the school year I would moonlight by teaching a student younger than myself who lived in the suburbs, receiving three dollars per lesson. I would also play a dance job of a Saturday night back home in New York in order to afford the luxury of occasional weekend visits with my parents, my brother Alex, and my smooth-haired fox terrier named Sargeant (after the flea soap). The band with which I played was called The Midnight Echoes. A group of us had started it up while we were all high school students in Brooklyn. Actually our band was quite good, and a dance job would pay $3.50, which required that we play until 1 a.m. A job on New Year's Eve would pay anywhere from five to ten dollars. My usual weekend financial formula in New York worked out to be almost a complete wash, as some jobs only paid a flat three dollars. The money was spent as follows:

> $2.10–Round-trip bus fare (Philadelphia/New York City/
> Philadelphia via Quaker City Bus Line)
> 0.10–Subway fares
> 0.85–Meal at a Chinese restaurant following the dance job

SUCH AN EXCURSION BY CURTIS STUDENTS INTO THE REALM OF EMPLOYMENT in a jazz band was seriously frowned upon. The frown included the possibility of losing one's scholarship. Jazz was certainly contrary to the knowledge of classical music performance that Curtis made every effort to impart. Today's musicians require greater versatility, and learning to play in various styles is the only method of achieving such versatility.

On one of my weekend visits to New York City, Jerry Goodman called me at my parents' apartment on Riverside Drive from the Goodman family's apartment on Central Park West, inviting me to come over. Since I was already a student at the Curtis Institute of Music, I was considered to be a "longhair." Jerry assumed

I would be very interested in Benny's latest accomplishment, a classical recording of Mozart.

Benny was not there when I arrived, and we went into Benny's bedroom to listen to the new recording. The reason for choosing the bedroom, which had its own sound system, was that it was the only room in their magnificent apartment with an air conditioner installed in one of the windows. This was a great luxury in those days and afforded the exceptionally busy Benny Goodman the comfort of a good night's rest during New York City's sultry summers.

I was very uninhibited and basically quite honest in my reaction to the new disk. I commented that although Benny played well, his vibrato, as far as I was concerned, was still that of a jazz musician and was not legitimate enough for my classically trained taste. Not incidentally, I had become very accustomed to an unusually high standard of classically legitimate clarinet playing from listening to my roommate Mitchell Lurie, who was already a superb young clarinetist. If I wasn't practicing on the trumpet, Mitchell was practicing on his clarinet. As it turned out, Mitchell became first clarinetist in the Pittsburgh Symphony Orchestra under Fritz Reiner, and when Reiner left Pittsburgh for the Chicago Symphony Orchestra, he took Mitchell along with him to become the first clarinetist of that orchestra. Although I admired Benny and his unique talents as a jazz musician, word of my youthfully sassy reaction may have gotten back to him. In any case, he later took to being coached by the first clarinetist of the NBC Symphony Orchestra, Gus Duques.

Benny Goodman was intent on improving not only his own image but that of jazz and swing as well. These forms of musical expression were not entirely acceptable yet for the concert hall. They were considered dance music for dance halls. If dance hall patrons stopped dancing and stood listening to bands such as Benny's or Stan Kenton's, the dance hall proprietors would become highly agitated. So, as it became more and more evident that his listeners were craving the experience of hearing him and his music "in concert," Benny wanted to elevate the public's perception of him via this new recording. He wanted the prestige of being recognized as a valid "concert artist." Only such classical artists' talents were regularly exposed on the stage of Carnegie Hall. Although every kind of entertainment is heard and seen in concert today, in that era to be able to perform on the concert stage had an entirely different connotation. A couple of decades previously, Paul Whiteman had much the same intention when he organized a concert at New York City's Aeolian Hall. There he commissioned a number of contemporary composers to write in the jazz idiom for a program to be directed at audiences in concert halls, rather than from the dance floor. Ordinarily, his orchestra could be heard a few blocks away at the Palais Royal dance hall.

Whiteman's concert presented the premiere of George Gershwin's *Rhapsody in Blue*. The concert might be remembered to this day for that if for nothing else. However, it became known as the concert that "made a lady out of jazz," as it was christened by a famed classical musician of the time, Walter Damrosch. Six decades later, jazz in America is accepted as a thoroughly legitimate musical art form. Not only has the Lincoln Center for the Performing Arts in New York City sponsored a series entitled "Jazz at Lincoln Center," led by trumpet player Wynton Marsalis, but a concert hall dedicated to jazz performance has now become a part of the Lincoln Center complex. For perhaps the same reasons as Benny Goodman, Wynton Marsalis has gone the route of "crossing over" and performing classical music, recording an excellent rendition of the Haydn Trumpet Concerto. Marsalis's recording includes a cadenza that is unusually difficult and very impressive in its execution. Such artistry and technical virtuosity does not really need the approval of "longhairs" today to establish its legitimacy. Jazz has finally arrived, as Whiteman and later Goodman hoped that one day it would.

Sadly, like thousands upon thousands of other American families during the Second World War, the Goodman family suffered a loss when Jerry, having enlisted in the U.S. Army Air Force, was among those killed in action.

As I have mentioned, world-renowned musicians instructed the Curtis students on a regular basis. Famous artists visiting Philadelphia were also invited to this unique school and often participated directly in our curriculum. Many gave private recitals for us while they were in town to appear as soloists elsewhere. We regularly attended the concerts of the Philadelphia Orchestra and delighted in doing so. There was limited seating in the two boxes maintained by the Curtis Institute at the Academy of Music for its students, and a staggered rotation of students was necessary in order that we all could attend. If there was a highly desirable program being performed, those who had tickets and had already entered the theater would drop our ticket stubs from a fire escape down to fellow students waiting below. Once these other students passed the ticket takers with our stubs, they would scan the hall for an empty seat. If none could be found, they would run up to the Curtis boxes, and they would seat themselves — two to a chair. Our musical appetites were voracious.

The Christmas seasons were always highly festive and enjoyable times at Curtis. There was an elaborately decorated tree in the wood-paneled common room, where a huge fireplace always had large logs ablaze during the season. Of course, there was a Christmas party and seasonal concerts given at Curtis as well.

We received special training in how to conduct ourselves at social events. It was felt that should any of us achieve a high level of success as musicians, we should be able to at least "balance a teacup." Each Wednesday afternoon, there-fore, the Curtis student body was invited to tea. Often, Mrs. Mary Louise Curtis Bok, founder of the Curtis Institute in 1924, would preside at these social affairs along with her cocker spaniel named "Scandal." Most of the Curtis students, although exceptionally talented as musicians, came from families whose normal circumstances did not equip them for the different social milieus into which their talents would take them. Even the mature Leonard Bernstein was capable of a social gaffe and would later be harshly criticized for publicly kissing former First Lady Jacqueline Kennedy on the cheek at the premiere of his Mass, which opened the Kennedy Center for the Performing Arts.

Rarely would Arturo Toscanini appear as a conductor with any orchestra other than his own. However, on one occasion Toscanini was to conduct the Philadelphia Orchestra and was invited to a tour of Curtis on the Wednesday afternoon preceding his Thursday morning rehearsal with the orchestra. He was highly impressed with the special atmosphere of our school and, while at tea, became very expansive. He reciprocated the hospitality to which he had been treated by inviting the students of Curtis to attend his rehearsal the following morning. We all got reasonably brushed up and attired and arrived before the rehearsal began. Debussy's La Mer was the work chosen to begin the rehearsal. All went well and, of course, we were thrilled to be able to observe the great maestro at work. However, there are several measures in the work that are rhythmically very tricky for the cello section of any orchestra. Toscanini zeroed in on that par-ticular problematic musical phrase. Perhaps because Toscanini himself was once a cellist, or perhaps because he was simply in a cranky mood, he exploded with one of his famous outbursts of profanity, in several languages. When intermission was called, a group of the orchestra's principal musicians who were also teachers at Curtis went to the maestro to remind him that although he certainly could rehearse as he wished, he had invited guests in the auditorium that morning. Those guests were their pupils, and his use of foul language had been both embar-rassing and demeaning to these faculty members. If he wished to work with the orchestra's musicians in that manner, it would be okay, but then he should not have guests. At Toscanini's request, then, and without hesitation, we Curtis stu-dents were instructed to leave the Academy of Music before the rehearsal con-tinued. We later heard that he had really laid into the orchestra in the second half of the rehearsal that day.

No conductor desirous of being reinvited to appear as a guest with a sym-phony orchestra today would dare to behave in this manner. While one might get away with it in a first rehearsal during an initial engagement, a representative of the orchestra's musicians would alert the orchestra's management. The conductor would be visited by management during or immediately following the rehearsal and informed that the conductor's behavior was not to be tolerated. On the contrary, conductors today who might be known for obnoxious behavior elsewhere will often treat the musicians of orchestras they are guest conducting to a "sweeter" version of their behavior to dispel talk of their manners in order to be reengaged.

When we were students at the Curtis Institute, Leonard Bernstein was the student of Mme. Renée Longy Miquelle in score reading and solfège, Fritz Reiner for conducting, and Isabelle Vengerova for piano. When we woodwind and brass students had our separate orchestral rehearsals to learn the repertoire, Lenny would have to play the string parts on the piano, filling in for the missing strings. This class was also a means for him to practice reading from the entire score of a symphonic work. Marcel Tabateau or Alexander Hilsberg would conduct these classes. Tabateau was the first oboist of the Philadelphia Orchestra, and Hilsberg its concertmaster. Fritz Reiner conducted full orchestra rehearsals.

There was a wonderful family living outside Philadelphia on the Main Line. Walter (called "Billy") and Irene Wolfe were very much into classical music. Walter's hobby was playing classical flute, and Irene's mother was the famous violinist Leah Lubeshutz, who was on the faculty at Curtis along with Efrem Zimbalist. The Wolfes were famous for their annual Christmas greeting cards, so much so that their cards were once displayed in *Life* magazine. It started with the family group posing in a canoe one year, then, as the family grew, on a four-poster bed. Continuing to grow almost annually, in time the family posed on a railroad freight car.

As is true of so many homes on the Main Line, the Wolfes' large house was situated on many acres of wooded land and can only be described as an estate. Every so often, particularly during the winter months, the Wolfes would invite the Curtis "kids" to their home on a Sunday. We would all receive railroad tickets, and looked forward to being able to play and run around in the woods all day, ride bikes or sleds, and play ping-pong in the game room. Young cigarette smokers were enabled to maintain their habit by stocking up from the Wolfes' cigarette boxes, which were generously displayed and well stocked throughout the house. The kids would naturally help themselves to more than just the occasional smoke, taking an ample supply for the week ahead. After a full day of fun, we would be treated to a late-afternoon buffet featuring filling foodstuffs for growing youngsters.

The purpose of these Sunday outings for Curtis students at the Wolfes' residence was not for our pleasure alone, but also for that of our host, Walter Wolfe, who would enjoy sitting in and playing second or third flute as we concluded our

Sunday outing by getting together to play orchestral repertoire. Although we usually had the privilege of having Fritz Reiner conduct us on these occasions, as he was also an invited guest, there was a Sunday when he was unavailable. Maestro Reiner was stuck in Pittsburgh, where he held the position of music director of the Pittsburgh Symphony Orchestra. There had been a snowstorm and his return trip to Philadelphia had been canceled. Irene Wolfe called and spoke with me and my roommates, Mitchell Lurie and Morris Boltuch, telling us about the problem and explaining that even Eugene Ormandy and Leopold Stokowski were not in town that weekend. The only solution would be to have Lenny Bernstein come out to conduct. What would the kids think? Would they come? Consulting with certain key players in the Curtis Symphony on that day, we discovered that most would prefer to put off the pleasure of our usual outing to the Wolfes' home for another time when we could have a genuine conductor. We returned Irene's call and informed her of the students' preference of a movie as an alternate to performing under the baton of Leonard Bernstein. Needless to say, many who refused to perform on that occasion found themselves performing professionally under Lenny's direction years later and loving it.

While visiting Philadelphia many years later I joined Billy and Irene Wolfe in attending a Philadelphia Orchestra concert conducted by Leonard Bernstein and given in his honor, as well. A standing ovation ensued, and Irene turned to me and smilingly, even proudly, asked, "Remember when?"

My partner, Leon Van Dyke, is fond of saying that if all of the graduates of America's music conservatories attended classical music concerts, there would be no problems with the size of audiences today for those in our profession who perform classical music. There are literally thousands of students graduating annually from such schools as the Shepherd School of Music at Southern Methodist University, the University of Michigan's school of music, the music schools at the University of Southern California, Pennsylvania State University, Indiana University at Bloomington, San Francisco State, Ohio State, Oberlin College, Louisiana State, and Yale University, and, yet to be mentioned, the highly visible Juilliard School of Music, Peabody Conservatory, Manhattan School of Music, Mannes School of Music, New England Conservatory, and Eastman School of Music, as well as my own alma mater, the Curtis Institute of Music. Many such graduates drift into other professions, still others teach at the secondary and higher levels of education, fewer still take seats in American and foreign symphony orchestras. Only a miniscule fraction are able to achieve a degree of distinction as soloists or guest artists with symphony orchestras in their own country and around the world.

I was fifteen when I entered Curtis. All students attended on a full-tuition scholarship. Admission was based on your demonstrated potential as a musician on the instrument of your choice. While attending the Curtis Institute, I, like every other student, was tutored in basic academics for my age level as part of the curriculum. Those whose parents could not afford housing were also allotted funds to cover that aspect of their schooling. It was the height of the Depression, starting with the 1939/40 school year, and many of the scholarship students were joined in their housing by their parents, who were ailing financially. Fellow students of varying ages included then unknowns such as Giancarlo Menotti, Leonard Bernstein, Samuel Barber, and many others who would go on to international acclaim through their performances and compositions. The Curtis Institute of Music continues to this day as one of the few such educational facilities having an entire student body comprised of talented youngsters on full scholarships. Today, a significant proportion of the student body at the Curtis Institute is made up of fledgling musicians from Asia.

Chapter Three

IN 1942, HAVING JUST TURNED EIGHTEEN YEARS OLD IN JUNE AND NOT yet having completed my studies at the Curtis Institute, I was living in New York City and was eminently draftable. Through the grapevine that seems to have existed forever among musicians, I learned that the U.S. Army was seeking fine musicians. There was a man affiliated with the American Federation of Musicians who was compiling a list of such draftable, first-rate musicians for a relative of his, an officer at West Point. The United States Military Academy was in the process of expanding its instruction of cadets to include flying. The students would receive their flight training at the newly constructed Stewart Air Force Base, which was officially being annexed to West Point.

The base was situated in Newburgh, New York, near West Point on the western bank of the Hudson River. The officers in charge of the base wanted to have an orchestra of the highest caliber as a source of both pride and entertainment. In actuality, they wished it to outshine the existing West Point band. So a scheme had been devised to form such an ensemble from the pool of excellent musicians available in nearby New York City.

Pressure was on to get this group formed, and quickly. Stewart Air Force Base wasn't entirely completed, and its officers' club was one of the elements still under construction. The target was to have the orchestra members enlisted, inoculated, issued uniforms, trained as soldiers, rehearsed as an orchestra, and ready with a stellar program for the official opening of the Stewart Air Force Base Officers' Club. The incoming officers of Stewart Field were of a competitive mindset and wished to top anything that emanated from nearby West Point, particularly in wartime when top talent was draftable.

I found myself fortunate enough to be included on the list of those who were being inducted into the U.S. Army to form the new orchestra at Stewart Air Force Base. It turned out that at eighteen, I was the youngest member of the entire group. Among the many men involved were: Joseph Kahn, pianist with the NBC Symphony Orchestra; Harry Schulman, oboist of the NBC Symphony; Martin Grupp, also of the NBC Symphony (and a member of the Midnight Echoes, our teenage dance band); Joseph Leavitt, a percussionist (later a crackerjack adminis-trator of symphony orchestras); Mischa Borodkin, a violinist in the New York Philharmonic; Arkady Berkenholtz, another violinist with the Philharmonic; Warren Parmentier, a fine saxophonist; Fred Klein, principal horn with the CBS Symphony Orchestra; Martin Fried, pianist accompanist to Al Jolson; Sam Musiker, a terrific jazz sax and clarinet player; and vocalist Don Cornell of Sammy Kaye's band. Still later, composer Samuel Barber joined us. These are but a few of the names that comprised the membership of the new orchestra for Stewart Air Force Base, and they certainly exemplify the caliber of musicians at these army officers' disposal.

It was arranged that we all meet at 52nd Street and Madison Avenue in New York City, outside the CBS Radio studios at 11:30 p.m. one night. We were driven in U.S. Army staff cars to the Thayer Hotel at West Point, where we were billeted for two days until our induction. This process was turning into some-thing of a charade. For example, we were required to jump fifty counts on the right foot and another fifty counts on the left foot. When the officer conducting the physical exam started to count, he proceeded thusly: "One, two, three, forty-nine, fifty. Next foot. Forty-five, forty-six, fifty." If none of us died after this exhaustive examination, we were qualified as acceptable specimens for the U.S. Army. In actuality, the majority of the men in the orchestra were already in their late thirties. The swearing-in to the army was done en masse. We were then driven to our new and sparser accommodations at Stewart Field, where we were issued our wardrobe, which in other circumstances would be called uniforms. Some of the gear provided came in handy as we found there were no paved streets, sidewalks, or other such amenities. There was lots and lots of mud. Boots were more than appropriate for such a venue. We received our medical shots, and many came down with temporary illnesses from the inoculations. We were trained to march in formation, to prepare us for exhibition band playing. We were issued M-2 rifles and taught how to present arms. We were never taught how to use the rifles, or such niceties as disassembling and cleaning the guns and reassembling them, which other new soldiers are expected to learn. The only other compulsory feature of our training was attendance at the showing of films on how to avoid venereal disease. The primary objective for our unit as soldiers was to get to the officers' club and start putting together a show for its grand opening. Music had to be assembled: orchestrations for band playing, arrange-ments for dance music, and concert material all had to be either obtained from publishers or newly created. On a number of occasions we rehearsed well into the night. The extent of our physical training for our combat readiness at the officers' club was to stand "reveille" at 5:30 a.m. Although it was beautiful country, we stood at attention, often with the thermometer registering well below zero degrees Fahrenheit, and were accounted for before running off to breakfast in the mess hall. We were not even subjected to any form of calisthenics.

Al Jolson sat in on a number of our rehearsals, and to motivate us in our efforts under the leadership of a band conductor by the name of Murray Kellner, Jolson would say, "Keep at it. I'll get you weekend passes." This was a definite perk for all of us New Yorkers who wanted to get down to the city, which was less than fifty miles distant. We kept at it and he delivered on his promises. The officers' club opened with great success, with Al Jolson emceeing the affair.

Heading the new hospital at Stewart Field was a Colonel Henry Ross, of the U.S. Army, a medical doctor who was married to the then famous blonde film actress Glenda Farrell (who had attended the officers' club opening). Colonel Ross had been present at our medical examinations at West Point. At the time of those exams, he had been a major and then was promoted when he became head of the new medical facility. Tommy Farrell, a comedian and entertainer and Glenda's son, had been assigned to our unit, so Colonel Ross was most familiar with our unit from its inception.

Three or four months elapsed, during which we fulfilled the entertainment needs at Stewart Field. Then a new regulation was announced, mandating that all soldiers over the age of thirty-eight could be immediately and honorably discharged should they wish. The texture of our unit changed almost overnight as at least half of the unit chose to leave the army.

An element that we had not been aware of surfaced at that time. We had been under the impression when we were enlisted that we were an "official" band. Now, we discovered we had been enlisted as anything other than musicians, from cooks to engineers. Putting aside the relative cushiness of our positions in the U.S. Army Air Force, we now realized that not only had we had been duped, but that without notice we could be transferred individually into combat units. We, of course, were totally unprepared for such an eventuality. Not only would we be in mortal danger, but we would place the lives of those around us in more danger than usual with our ignorance of combat skills.

We asked to meet as a group with the officer in charge and reviewed our situation from its beginnings. We were told that every effort would be made to apply to Washington, D.C., for official recognition of us as the U.S. Army Air Force Band. Technically, we had been fraudulently enlisted and could have walked off the base without any formal complaint. Most of us, however, would have been the immediate targets of our local draft boards. We agreed among ourselves that it would be best to sweat it out and await Washington's official pronouncement of our legitimacy. Our compliance would also avoid a potential major source of embarrassment for the West Point command during wartime.

After a wait of a couple of months, we were officially named the 369th Army

Air Force Band and continued wearing the West Point insignia we had initially been assigned. Along with that, we were placed under the command of a young, new warrant officer by the name of William Carney. New musicians were arriving to replace those who had chosen to leave due to their age. The caliber of musicianship declined and the mood of the unit was not the same. I began to feel that Warrant Officer Carney was singling me out for less than favorable treatment, and when the unit was given weekend leave for Mother's Day, I was restricted to the field.

Nothing in my behavior merited this kind of action on Carney's part. I approached him and asked, "What's the problem?" His answer was that he did not like my attitude and that I should remain on the field and use the time to think about it. I told him that if I had done anything, I certainly wanted to know what I was being punished for. Because, otherwise, the only one he would be punishing would be my mother on Mother's Day. Harry Schulman, suspecting something was not right, called his fiancée, telling her that he was not coming into New York City for the weekend. He remained at Stewart Field over that weekend to keep me company. I have never forgotten his act of kindness. My friend Marty Grupp also suspected strange happenings and put in for a cleaning detail so that he could clean Carney's office. While so occupied he could rifle through correspondence and try to decipher what was happening with our unit and its new warrant officer.

I learned, too, from Warren Parmentier, that he had been asked by Carney "How much Jewish blood do you have in you?" Taken aback, Warren could only answer Carney by saying, "Why do you ask?" Carney replied, "I don't know why you hang around with the wrong people." Although Warren was not Jewish, this remark of Carney's did not sit well with him.

While cleaning Carney's office, Marty uncovered correspondence with a trumpeter friend of Carney's at Cornell University who was about to be drafted. The substance of the "plan" the letter described was to create an opening on trumpet in the 369th Army Air Force Band by removing me from the band. Once I was out of the picture, or at least on my way out, Carney would request that his friend from Cornell be my replacement.

Now that I had put all the pieces together and had a clear picture of what was happening, I found it necessary, at the age of eighteen, to try to find a way to protect myself from what I perceived as an injustice. I wanted to do so quickly before the situation came to a head and got completely out of hand. I could have made a public sensation out of my predicament by going to the New York press. I did deliberate about the possibility of making such an exposé surrounding the farce of our unit's induction at West Point. However, I decided that it would be far too much of a public embarrassment to the military during the height of war, especially at West Point. The only one whom I knew I could safely approach was Colonel Ross at the base hospital. He knew the entire story of our unit from its strikingly unusual beginnings.

Colonel Ross was kind enough to let me meet privately with him, and he was most understanding. He assured me that my sudden transfer to any other unit, including a combat outfit, would require my having to be cleared through the base hospital first. He suggested that we wait for such an occurrence and then deal with it when it happened.

One day, not long afterward, Carney did tell me that I was soon to be transferred. Carney was completely aware of our unit's limited training and of the fact that we had been falsely credited "on paper" with full training for combat. I was astounded at how Carney could literally be sending me to my death. I had to face the reality of a very serious second war, a private war unfolding between Carney and myself. He was arranging to quite literally sacrifice me to get his trumpeter friend into our unit in my place. At that juncture, I was no longer willing to be the victim of a superior's intolerance. Although I had very few options at my disposal in dealing with this warrant officer's bigoted behavior, I was not going to be a lamb led to my inevitable slaughter.

I met again with Colonel Ross and told him, "This is it." I told Ross what had been happening, including Warren's encounter with Carney. Ross, it turned out, was also Jewish. He told me that there was no one, including the commandant of the field, whom I could speak to about the prejudice that existed.

Ross used the tactic of describing a scenario for me, thus providing a way out of my dilemma. Everything was outlined for me in the third person, with the suggestion that a soldier with some knowledge of Russian had the vague possibility of being transferred to some division of the Intelligence Service. Alternatively, an eighteen-year-old had enlisted and found that the idea of the carnage of war was deeply affecting him. The young soldier could no longer eat meat. He also envied a fly on a toilet that had the freedom to fly away from a military base at will. Such a young soldier could easily crack up. In his mental condition he could become a financial liability medically to the U.S. government, possibly for his entire lifetime. Colonel Ross also pointed out that since that soldier was not drafted but had enlisted, he should have no feelings of guilt. He said, "If you want to think about it, it is for you to choose." By that time, I was completely and utterly wrung out emotionally. I told Colonel Ross that I really wanted to get on with my own life somehow if at all possible. He said, "Fine. I will send you to the Halloran General Hospital on Staten Island, where you will probably be required to stay under observation for six or seven weeks. They sometimes offer patients there passes to go into New York City. It would be recommended not to accept such inducements. Just remain in the hospital and 'do your time' there. I will check it from this end." Colonel Ross then arranged for me to be transferred by a private staff car, accompanied by an air force captain from the hospital at Stewart Field, and I was registered as a patient at Halloran General Hospital. When it was determined that I was to be hospitalized, I telephoned my parents in New York City from Stewart Field and told them what was happening. I said that I would not be seeing them for around two months and they would not be hearing from me by telephone during that time, either. With their background and experiences in the USSR, they were petrified with fear for my well-being.

As Ross had also suggested to me, whenever I was asked, "How are you?" while at the hospital, I replied, "The same." If threatened with being placed in a work camp if I did not shape up, I was to simply shrug my shoulders. All took place as outlined by Colonel Ross, and finally one day I was told that I would be leaving the same day with an honorable medical discharge. I had made friends with many of my fellow patients during my stay at Halloran. Many of them were victims of combat wounds, and I had the opportunity to witness first hand what my future might have had in store for me, if I survived at all. When I left the hospital, a very large, very warm-hearted and outgoing black man lifted me onto his shoulders in a triumphant gesture and marched me through the ward and out the doors, saying, "Well, you made it!"

Later that year, I learned that there had been a major transfer of personnel from Stewart Air Force Base to a combat unit that was involved in the invasion of France in 1944.

Now a veteran, having served in the U.S. Army Air Force for an odd and eventually terrifying ten months, I was back in civvies in New York City once again. Fortunately, there was an opening in the Pittsburgh Symphony Orchestra, for which I auditioned and was accepted.

My connection with Colonel Ross did not end. As we corresponded, he expressed pride at my having been accepted for a position with the Pittsburgh Symphony. We maintained a connection for a number of years until his death. It might truthfully be said that I owe that good man my life.

For the entire music season of 1943/44, I was a member of the Pittsburgh Symphony Orchestra under the musical direction of Fritz Reiner, my former teacher at the Curtis Institute of Music. In January of 1944, Leonard Bernstein was invited to guest conduct the premiere of his *Jeremiah* Symphony, with soprano Jennie Tourel as soloist. At Curtis, we students had played the "Lamentation" movement, which was written before the other two movements, under Lenny's direction. However, this occasion in Pittsburgh was to be the actual first performance of the work in its entirety. At rehearsal Lenny, as conductor, was having a great deal of difficulty in keeping the orchestra together. The attacks were all uneven. Reiner, who sat out in the hall of the Syria Mosque listening to the rehearsal, found it necessary to get out of his seat, move to the stage, and literally give Lenny a lesson in front of the entire orchestra. Reiner demonstrated what Lenny needed to do in order to keep the orchestra together, and it worked. Although a great fuss was already being made about Leonard Bernstein in the press and elsewhere, at the age of twenty-four he was still young enough to accept such direction without undue embarrassment. Reiner found it necessary to assert his professorial stature over his student, as there was a turf battle going on over possession and credit for this prize pupil. Knowing that Bernstein was cozying up to Serge Koussevitzky as a potentially more influential mentor, Reiner clearly demonstrated his authority over Lenny in front of the entire orchestra. Lenny, while unusually multitalented, was still highly inexperienced at rehearsing a symphony orchestra playing a work new to the orchestral repertoire. Rehearsals can tell the trained orchestral musician more about the abilities of a conductor and the limitations of his "stick technique" than actual performances can reveal to an audience and the critics. When Lenny had made his debut conducting the New York Philharmonic during the previous fall season, highlighted by the drama of his being a "last minute" replacement for the orchestra's ailing musical adviser, Bruno Walter, he had elicited a slightly exaggerated acceptance, replete with hyperbole, by the New York press. But the Philharmonic's musicians were very familiar with the contents of the program performed that Sunday afternoon, and Lenny still had much to learn, as pointedly made evident by Fritz Reiner that following January in Pittsburgh.

Seated next to me in Pittsburgh during this process was a fellow trumpet player of German descent who had started out with the Cincinnati Symphony Orchestra. He got fed up and crushed the sheets of his trumpet part to the score of *Jeremiah* on his music stand. Then, recovering himself slightly and straightening out his part, he placed it back on the stand and muttered, "God damn fucking Jews." We were still at war with Germany and I hardly needed this reminder of the fact sitting next to me. After the rehearsal I proceeded directly to Maestro Fritz Reiner's dressing room. Once there, I told the maestro of the foul anti-Semitic language to which I been subjected. Reiner asked me to repeat the language in question. I was somewhat shy and, out of respect for him, said that it was a four-letter word. He wanted to know whether it began with an *S* or an *F*. I told him it was the latter. He asked, "Did he say 'fucking Jews'?" I answered, "Yes." At full volume, Reiner began screaming for Edward Specter, the orchestra manager. "Specter, Specter," he yelled. Shouting out the guilty party's name, he said, "Get rid of him. He said 'fucking Jews.'" I hadn't realized that Lenny's music of Hebraic inspiration could so aggravate people.

Fritz Reiner himself, was not always the kindest of humans in his remarks to musicians. When rehearsing he would sometimes look at the string section and, if he was displeased, he would continue conducting while shouting at them "Schweiner! [Pigs!]." One day at rehearsal, he stopped the orchestra and, singling out the assistant concertmaster, Louis Krasner, in front of the entire orchestra, said, "You're a catastrophe, the major disappointment of the orchestra." Everyone remained still, and the mood of the orchestra members became very heavy indeed. Actually, Louis Krasner was a renowned violinist and a dedicated musician who had commissioned Alban Berg to write his violin concerto and subsequently recorded the work. When that rehearsal was over, I found that the incident had been upsetting to me personally, although it had nothing to do with me. I went to Maestro Reiner's dressing room immediately following the rehearsal. I confronted him, without addressing him as "Doctor Reiner," which was his expected form of address. I said, "Mr. Reiner, if anyone is a major disappointment in this orchestra, you are to me." He was seated, and looking up at me through half-moon reading glasses, he appeared genuinely surprised to hear this from me, a nineteen-year-old. I said, "I can't understand how you expect to get results from people when you behave like that." He seemed to back off from his lofty posture and replied, "Well, I have Mr. Hitler to blame. If not for the war, I would have the musicians that I deserve to have in this orchestra. Sometimes when I lose myself, as I did today, it makes me sick." I continued, "I heard that you were a very intelligent man when we were at Curtis, but out in the profession this is not the way an intelligent man achieves the results he wants."

Following a lunch break after that morning's rehearsal that was to begin again at 2:30 that afternoon, the orchestra had reassembled and was ready for Reiner to make his usual grumpy entrance. Instead, the assistant conductor, Vladimir Bakalainikov, announced, "Gentlemen, I will conduct this rehearsal. Reiner called and said that he would not come in this afternoon. He is sick." Reiner's reaction to our chat turned into a private delight for me and a constructive rehearsal for the orchestra that day.

The Pittsburgh Symphony Orchestra was the orchestra in residence at the Chautauqua Festival in the New York State Finger Lakes region during the summer season. Franco Autori was the conductor of the "Chautauqua Symphony Orchestra," as the group from Pittsburgh was known for the summer's duration. A Protestant religious institution, the Chautauquas once were available throughout the U.S. To this day, as it did during the war years, the Chautauqua Festival in New York State offers a broad array of cultural events, including appearances by pop stars. Yet one still is able to hear lectures by authorities on a wide spectrum of topics, from current affairs to travelogues. The community, situated on beautiful Lake Chautauqua, boasts quaint Victorian summer homes ranging from mansions to cottages, as well as hotels for the convenience of short-term guests. One restriction was that no alcohol was allowed into the community.

One of the orchestra musicians, however, had a telephone call from the gate informing him that a box of books had arrived but that it was leaking. Much to the musician's embarrassment, he could not accept the package.

I was flattered when a young couple, regular guests at Chautauqua, who had a sailboat invited me to spend the afternoon sailing with them. They wanted the opportunity of getting to know young artists better. While sailing, they introduced me to the sport of jumping from the boat while holding a line, in order to be towed by the moving boat. I didn't know that one was to lie on one's back while pursuing the sport. Instead, as I surfed with my chest as my surfboard, water was forced into my nose and mouth and the surrounding water succeeded in completely removing my bathing trunks. All in good humor, and somewhat embarrassed, we became better friends.

Our orchestra played for opera productions as well as symphonic programs over the course of the summer. Percy Grainger, the Australian pianist and composer, was one of the soloists that summer. He was something of an eccentric and was reported to be off sleeping in the woods during his stay in Chautauqua. I clearly recall his having arrived at rehearsal with a knapsack on his back, so there must have been some credence to the rumor of his "camping out." We musicians did not have to camp out, as our rents cost us individually around five dollars per week. The sole inconvenience we experienced was having to share a bath.

Before leaving Pittsburgh that summer, I had not yet signed a contract for the upcoming 1944/45 season with the orchestra. During that period, musicians did not have tenure with an orchestra; one was either given a contract for the following season or received notice of termination. I had received neither. Regardless, I went to fulfill my duties at Chautauqua and returned to New York City. Once back on my home grounds, I started freelancing.

Much to my surprise, I received a telephone call from Edward Specter, the Pittsburgh Symphony's manager, telling me that Reiner wanted to see me the following day at 9:30 in the morning at Steinway Hall. I asked Specter, "Why so early in the morning?" All he said was "Just be there at 9:30 and you show him." I asked, "Show him what?" "Oh," Specter said, "bring your trumpet, he wants to hear you play something." I was shocked. I told Specter, "After I've played for him for a couple of years at Curtis and a season in Pittsburgh, if Reiner doesn't know how I play by now, he never will know." What Reiner was doing, I knew, was being his sadistic self. He was devising a scheme to musically intimidate me. He was seeking his revenge for my having confronted him after his outburst belittling Louis Krasner in rehearsal. I had also heard that Reiner had auditioned two oboists a few weeks earlier in New York. He had them both play Ravel's *Le Tombeau de Couperin* in front of one another. Then, Reiner told one he had a better technique, while he told the other that he had the better sound. Reiner had thereby intimidated both of them and was able to select the oboist he actually wanted at the salary of his choosing. I was not going to submit myself to Reiner's subjugation, and I told Specter to give Reiner a message for me, that I was not a horse and didn't wish to have my teeth inspected. I always admired Reiner's conducting and musicianship, but his dictatorial attitudes and diplomatic short-comings were the least admirable of his traits.

Reiner's more admirable and sensitive side, which rarely prevailed, must, how-ever, be mentioned. The Pittsburgh Symphony Orchestra had just rehearsed an orchestral work of Bela Bartok. As musicians, we were privileged to have Fritz Reiner conducting this work because he so thoroughly understood the composi-tion's folk music sources, which emanated from his own Hungarian background. The interpretation simply thrilled the Pittsburgh orchestra's musicians as it was revealed to us through our rehearsals of the work. Following the rehearsal ses-sions, we asked Reiner if we could privately record the concert performance of this new concerto. During that time, according to the strictures of the American Federation of Musicians under James Caesar Petrillo, such a recording would never have been allowed. Taping devices had yet to be invented, and the only resource at our command would be a relatively primitive home recording device utilizing a 78 rpm record. However, if Reiner did not object, we could get away with such a recording for our private use only. Reiner was surprised at our request. He asked why we wanted to record Bartok's opus. We said that it was such an adventure, expressed a real joy in music making, and was relatively new and interesting for its time. He was pleased with our reactions and agreed to the recording. He said, "I'm glad you all feel that way. I will tell you why. After the concert, I will be returning from Pittsburgh to New York to see my friend Bela Bartok, and I am sure that this reaction from you musicians will make him very, very happy. You see, his work thus far has not been very well appreciated or accepted. My friend is expected to die in the very near future." Bela Bartok died the following year. His works are now considered standard repertoire with today's major symphony orchestras.

I was able to freelance and play with the NBC Symphony Orchestra in New York City during the course of the next several years. In 1946, I was playing in the orchestra for a broadcast concert led by guest conductor Dimitri Mitropoulos, at the time the music director of the Minneapolis Symphony Orchestra. I was needed to play during only the first half of the broadcast. The final half of the program was a premiere of a work by composer Elie Siegmeister. Since there was no need for me to remain, I left Studio 8-H and, intending to go home, was approaching the bank of elevators in the RCA Building at Rockefeller Center when Leonard Bernstein walked out of an arriving elevator. Mitropoulos had arranged for him to serve as guest conductor of the Minneapolis Symphony to cover his current absence. Lenny agitatedly said that his plane had been late, but Dimitri had wanted him to hear the Siegmeister work. In no way would they now let him into Studio 8-H because the broadcast was already in progress. He said that some pompous head of guest relations was being totally inflexible. Lenny had already been invited to conduct the NBC Symphony Orchestra during the coming summer, but he was not yet a familiar enough public figure to conduct during the more formal winter season. So, he certainly held no sway over the pompous official. Thinking the situation a bit ridiculous, I took Lenny back with me around the corridors of the studio, with which I was highly familiar. Although the broadcast was in progress, as professionals we went quietly into the control room for Studio 8-H. The producer, Don Gillis, who was also a composer, was delighted to see us. Perhaps for more reasons than one. Apparently Don had just finished composing a work of his called *Symphony Five and a Half*. While we were listening to the Siegmeister work, we also were being importuned by Don Gillis concerning his new composition. He wanted Lenny to see the score, and Lenny suggested that Don send it to him. Don said, "It's a wise composer who personally shows a score to a conductor." At the conclusion of the broadcast Lenny and I were on our way out of that control room when we saw Al Walker, the head of guest relations, approaching with two policemen. We were going to be placed under arrest according to provisions of a wartime law that made it a federal offense to break into any broadcasting facility. As we were escorted along the corridors surrounding the studio, our group passed Dimitri Mitropoulos's open dressing room. Dimitri, calling out happily to Lenny, said, "Oh, you made it!" Lenny said, "Made it? We're being arrested."

Expressing shock and dismay at the absurdity of the situation, Dimitri announced that he would not leave the building until the matter was cleared up. "After all," he declared, "this man is going to be guest conducting the NBC Symphony this coming summer and he is not street trash." In spite of that fact, we were all marched down to the second floor, to the NBC "officer of the day." Al Walker, in reviewing his complaint, related that Bernstein was told that he could not hear the broadcast while it was in progress and that, disregarding his orders, Bernstein and Gershunoff had entered the control room. Further, there had been so much conversation in the control room that it might have impeded the engineers' ability to work the dials. Walker compounded his accusations by adding that we had both been drinking. At that point, Dimitri interjected, saying, "Gershunoff played the first half of the program and his instrument is a trumpet. Had he gotten that out of hand on alcohol, the broadcast would have been a catastrophe. This whole thing has been complete nonsense. Just forget that any of it happened." At that juncture, Lenny chimed in and said, "Who knows? Someday this incident may become history." Now it has.

Not only had Mitropoulos invited Lenny to guest conduct the Minneapolis Symphony Orchestra while Dimitri conducted the NBC Symphony, he had also suggested that one day Lenny might join him as assistant conductor in Minneapolis. Although Mitropoulos was always encouraging toward him, Lenny's ambitions were at odds with Mitropoulos's estimation of his readiness. Mitropoulos had the same attitude regarding the young conductor Thomas Schippers at a later date. He resisted encouraging the premature overexposure of such youthful gifts and their potential exploitation. He believed that the brain of a conductor needed to age fifty years in order to absorb the symphonic repertoire, as well as to "season" both the human being and conductor.

Chapter Four

With my fond recollections of the state, I had finally moved to California in 1947. After a long, uneventful drive cross country, upon arriving in Los Angeles I was stopped on Sunset Boulevard by a motorcycle cop who announced that he had to give me a citation. Still used to the idioms of World War II, the idea of a "citation" represented a compliment. When I thanked him for the compliment, he asked if I was being sarcastic. Much to my amazement, the policeman was actually giving me a ticket for a traffic violation. I seemed to have gone through a yellow caution signal without what he considered to be the appropriate manner of stopping. That first day in the state I had been instantly introduced to the realities of driving in California.

Unfortunately, following the war too many musicians living on the East Coast shared an attraction to the glamour of Hollywood and California's movie studios and made their move to the Golden State. As a result, restrictions had been imposed by Hollywood's Local 47 of the American Federation of Musicians, intending to serve as a deterrent to this mass migration westward of musicians that threatened the livelihood of its members already residing there. The new rules for transfer members would not allow for steady employment as a musician in the Los Angeles area until one had been a resident of the state of California for a full year. Musicians transferring from other locals were only allowed to take single engagements during that first year.

Conductor Werner Jansen, whose family owned the famed Jansen's Hofbrau restaurant in New York City's Commodore Hotel and who was married to movie star Ann Harding, had just been appointed music director and conductor of the Portland Symphony Orchestra. In order to raise the level of his new orchestra, he imported certain principal players. He negotiated permission from Local 47 of the A.F. of M. in Los Angeles to credit me with my full year's residence, although I would actually be playing a full season as first trumpet in Portland, Oregon. I became a reluctant celebrity in Portland as a result of being the highest-paid member of that orchestra, the newspapers commenting that my salary exceeded that of the concertmaster. While the recognition was flattering, and the position financially gratifying, the attention did make me somewhat uncomfortable.

While I was in Portland playing with the Portland Symphony Orchestra, the Ballet Russe de Monte Carlo was on tour and appeared there. I was acquainted with the conductor of the Ballet Russe, Paul Strauss, who introduced me to Eleanor Hirsch Peters. Her family was connected with the Northwest's local Meyer and Frank department stores. We got on exceptionally well and we remain dear friends to this day. Eleanor, a divorced woman and mother of two, Pat and John, was a devoted patron of the arts who played hostess to many of the artists who performed in Portland and Seattle, her home. She maintained friendships with a diverse legion of artists including mezzo-soprano Marian Anderson, conductor Dimitri Mitropoulos, ballerina Alexandra Danilova and her frequent dancing partner, Frederic Franklin, soprano Jarmila Novotna, choreographer George Balanchine, ballerinas Maria Tallchief and Alicia Markova, Markova's partner, Anton Dolin, and actress Judith Anderson. It was through Eleanor that I first met the great pianist Vladimir Horowitz and a Seattle-based, teenaged dancer by the name of Robert Joffrey. Eleanor would drive her daughter Pat, Bobby Joffrey, and Gerald (Gerry) Arpino to school in Seattle. My year in Portland awaiting certification as an employable member of Local 47 flew by as a result of Eleanor's friendship and frequent hospitality and the opportunity to earn a living in the meantime. The restriction imposed by Local 47 was found to be illegal some ten years later.

Eleanor Peters enjoyed spending time in Los Angeles. Each summer she would come to Los Angeles and rent a house large enough to accommodate her family and house guests, who generally were artists. One year she asked me to find a house she could rent where she and her children would be comfortable for a summer's stay. I found a large mansion in the fashionable area known as Hancock Park. The house had a swimming pool, and the back lawn opened onto a golf course. It was suitable for large-scale entertaining. However, after the family had settled in we found the house to be haunted. It seemed that a ghost, or what we began to call the "friendly ghost," could be heard at night walking up or down the huge grand staircase in the entryway. Occasionally, water faucets would be flowing where no one had turned them on. While speaking on the guest telephone beneath the grand staircase one day, I observed the huge front door open, then shut and, moments later, the back door leading to the pool area do the same. No visible entity was responsible for this coming and going and it was not a windy day. Chills went up and down my back.

As more and more guests arrived for short stays in the house, the ghost disappeared. We surmised that the ghost was happy with the current occupants. Although not a believer in paranormal things such as ghosts, I still do not to this day understand why I experienced chills running down my back when the ghost seems to have made its presence known to me. Some years later, while I was in

New York City, a very excited Eleanor called me from Los Angeles where she had just returned from a cocktail party, telling me she had made some new friends. Coincidentally, she found that they had rented that same house in Hancock Park. They related that they had recently moved into the rented house with their two children and a maid. They went out for the very first evening and upon returning found that their maid was immediately leaving their employ and did not intend to remain for the night. She told them that when she went into the huge living room she was shocked to see the figure of half a man, viewed lengthwise, seated near the fireplace. She simply flew the coop. Breaking their lease, that family left the house in Hancock Park the following day. Coincidence or otherwise, as Eleanor related this new story of the Hancock House friendly ghost, chills once again ran up and down my spinal column.

Following that summer's rented house, Eleanor Peters purchased the Warner Brothers movie star Jack Carson's home. The house was situated on two acres on Longridge Avenue in Sherman Oaks, in the San Fernando Valley just over the mountains from Hollywood and Beverly Hills. Her neighbors down the street were actress Alexis Smith, composer David Rose, comedian Lou Costello, and red-headed movie star Susan Hayward. It had an Olympic-sized swimming pool; a huge pool house containing a walk-in fireplace; both men's and women's dressing rooms; saunas and a barbecue area; and a separate garage with servants' living quarters above. The only drawbacks at that house were the occasional rattlesnake that might wander down the hillside to the pool area and the parades of tourist buses during the Christmas holiday season to view the display of lights on Longridge Avenue. The house later was leveled and became the site of a home for television star Tony Danza of *Taxi*.

When I finally began to work as a trumpeter in Los Angeles, having been cleared for full local union membership, I began to support myself by playing such radio shows as the *Lux Radio Theatre,* with which I remained for seven years. With the advent of television in the early fifties that show dovetailed with *Lux Video Theatre,* for which I played for five years. Many freelance calls in Los Angeles involved recording for films, such as *September Affair* with Joan Fontaine and Joseph Cotten; *Stalag 17* with William Holden; *The World's Greatest Show* with Betty Hutton and Cornell Wilde; and a number of musicals at MGM. I also played in the pit orchestras for the live musicals performed by the Civic Light Opera of Los Angeles and for a season of musicals at the Greek Theatre in Griffith Park. That latter season of musicals, in 1950, was fairly distinguished, as it included *Annie Get Your Gun* with Martha Raye; *Finian's Rainbow,* featuring two of its original Broadway stars, Ella Logan and David Wayne; and *Gentlemen Prefer Blondes* with Gertrude Niesen as Lorelei Lee. Despite such an exciting theatrical season, the then producer of the Greek Theatre, Gene Mann, was unable to pay Los Angeles County taxes, thereby rendering his lease on the outdoor 4,800-seat amphitheater null and void.

During this period the impresario Sol Hurok imported Roland Petit's company, the Ballets de Paris, which had appeared in New York City with great success. After the Second World War, Americans took a renewed interest in France, and particularly in Paris. New designers, such as Dior, Givenchy, and others, were doing everything within their power to get their creations exposed in the U.S. American filmmakers were making films that appealed to the American fascination with France, such as *An American in Paris*. The success of the sensational French import, the Ballets de Paris, in the Big Apple led to a national tour that wound up on the West Coast in 1951. The company's starring ballerina was Renée (Zizi) Jeanmaire, who was spectacularly featured as Carmen in Petit's ballet of the same name. It has since been incorporated as a staple of the repertoire of many ballet companies throughout the world.

When the Ballets de Paris appeared in Los Angeles, I played trumpet in the orchestra for its performances there. Unlike many of my colleagues in that orchestra and the others with which I had played, I was interested in what was happening onstage and who was performing. I enjoyed comparing artists' performances in various roles. Being first trumpet in such pit orchestras, I was seated near the pit railing separating the musicians from the audience. In order to see what was happening onstage, I would attach a mirror to the railing at an angle so that I could occasionally glance at it and watch the action on the stage.

Final theatrical performances traditionally allow for cast members to take some liberties. It is a form of "breaking the mold," and of easing the stress often built up under trying performance conditions. While observing Roland Petit and Zizi Jeanmaire perform the last Los Angeles matinee of Petit's *Carmen*, I witnessed the following: At the most dramatic point in the entire ballet, Carmen (Zizi) is menaced by Don Jose (Roland), and in fear for her life she darts away from him, dodging his threatened physical contact. In this climactic scene in which Don Jose stabs and kills Carmen, the actual slaying is preceded by sixteen measures with no music other than repeated tympani beats in groups of four that escalate in a crescendo building to the moment in which Don Jose reaches beneath his cape for his knife to finally stab the ill-fated cigarette girl. During this "special" performance, Carmen found herself being stabbed by Don Jose not with the usual prop knife but with a weapon in the form of a limp, melting bar of Hershey's chocolate. Although Roland thought he might break Zizi's concentration and get her to laugh or even be rattled, fortunately for the audience, no such lapse in her performance occurred. There was a big laugh by the cast and crew backstage, however, which carried on into the curtain calls.

It is my belief that composers, instrumentalists, choreographers, and other creative types have the tendency, at one point or another in their lives, to spoof themselves, although with tongue in cheek, once they have achieved a certain level of success. For example, instrumentalists may interject a false note for a laugh; composers may utilize one of their colleagues' musical themes in their new compositions as a form of joke; choreographers other than Petit depart from their own choreography, as I mention elsewhere in the case of Frederick Ashton taking liberties in his *Cinderella* when performing as an Ugly Stepsister; conductor Erich Leinsdorf once played a pair of cymbals while conducting a march with the Boston Symphony Orchestra.

It was my good fortune that I played well enough to get away with my "mirror trick" with the conductors under whom I was playing. Some didn't even realize I had a mirror placed on the railing. It really bothered me that I couldn't share a mutual interest in the total musical production with any of my fellow musicians. For the majority, their only interest was in playing their part in the orchestra and then going home. I think this was yet another factor that contributed to my restlessness as "just a musician." I could not see devoting my future entirely to what was to me, rightly or wrongly, a one-dimensional life.

I found myself easily making friends with the artists appearing onstage. I became very friendly with "Zizi" (Renée Jeanmaire) and Roland Petit when they appeared in Los Angeles. They nicknamed me Trompète, and to them I remain Trompète to this day.

I wasn't the only person in Los Angeles interested in the Ballets de Paris. Howard Hughes, then owner of RKO Studios in Hollywood (among his many holdings) was fascinated both with the company's performances and with Jeanmaire as well. Hughes wanted to make a movie star out of her. She was flattered but had no interest in abandoning Roland Petit or the company. She had literally grown up with Roland, adored him and was frightened of him, respected his talents, and ignored his shortcomings. Despite Hughes's enticements and the glamour of Hollywood, her loyalties remained steadfastly with Petit and their dance company.

Hughes, however, could not accept a rejection. So, he purchased himself a solution. He kept the entire Ballets de Paris company in Hollywood for a year. The dancers were housed in groups of threes and fours in houses he rented for them, while Roland was provided with a house in Beverly Hills a few doors away from Elizabeth Taylor's residence at the time. Zizi was ensconced in a lovely house with the requisite swimming pool overlooking Sunset Boulevard in West Hollywood. Coincidentally, Zizi's house was very conveniently located near mine on Kings Road, also above Sunset Boulevard, about five blocks away. The company took their daily ballet classes at the RKO studio. To improve Zizi's English, Hughes insisted that she have tutoring in the language, reflecting his interest in her becoming a movie star. She was shy in her attempts to communicate in English, yet somehow was very comfortable when speaking with me. I found her very knowledgeable about classical music, and she was blessed with excellent musical taste. As our friendship grew, we found that we shared many interests.

We often took long drives to the ocean at Malibu. In the early fifties the Pacific Ocean at Malibu was very clean. We would walk the beach and be able to enjoy an impromptu lunch by picking up clams from the sand and eating them right there on the beach. To feed our more sophisticated appetites, we would attend symphony concerts together. On our excursions, Zizi would try to converse with me in English, and if we had any problems communicating, I would fall back on my limited knowledge of French. Somehow, we understood each other. But I insisted that she always attempt to speak English first when addressing me.

Once when we planned to attend a symphony concert in downtown Los Angeles, Zizi telephoned and asked me not to pick her up. She would meet me in front of the theater. I was puzzled, since we lived near each other and I usually drove the two of us to concerts. Zizi said she would explain the change in plans when we met at the theater.

Zizi, who had arrived in a chauffeur-driven limousine, seemed agitated when we met. I asked her what had happened. She said, "I just told the driver to go and not to wait as I will go back on my own." As it turned out, Zizi was very disturbed about Howard Hughes.

She said that he had wanted to know where she was going that evening, and she told him, "I'm going to a concert." Hughes then asked, "Are you going with the same guy that you've been going with for the last three weeks?" She replied, "Yes, it is Trompète. We are very good friends." She then found out that Hughes had had us followed for the previous three weeks. Justifying his behavior, he said, "I have too much money invested in you to have anyone drive you other than my driver."

She told me that she would straighten out the situation with Hughes, which, apparently, she later did because we were not followed anymore.

As we walked into the theater and were seated, everyone looked at the now highly recognizable Zizi with her famous *gamin* haircut that was unique at the time. The concert, which was to be conducted by Maestro Alfred Wallenstein, included Beethoven's *Pastorale* Symphony. To my mind, and those of many others, as a conductor, Wallenstein was not a very exciting interpreter. Zizi was still irritated about Howard Hughes's personal CIA following us for three weeks, so her mood was anything but "pastoral." As the performance droned on, Zizi leaned over to me and, remembering I wanted her to talk to me in English, she said in a much too loud whisper, "Ach, he is sheeit." The same opinion in French, "Il est merde," sounds so much nicer to the American ear, and I wished she had spoken French in the first place. All of those in the surrounding seats overheard her accurate but embarrassing criticism.

Zizi took me with her when she visited with Gene Kelly at his home in Beverly Hills. Kelly was still very much in his *American in Paris* creative phase and may even have been putting the finishing touches on that film during this period. He was a very cordial host, and we enjoyed a highly informal visit together. I found it somewhat bothersome that Kelly dwelled so frequently on his heterosexual identity. During the course of the evening, he insisted on separating himself from other male dancers. Although even in Hollywood American society at the time may not have been as liberated as it is today, one would have thought someone with Kelly's Hollywood achievements and New York theater background might have recognized that his creativity and talent, not his sexuality, were interesting to fellow artists.

On another evening Roland and I went to Zizi's house, where the three of us opened a bottle of wine and spent the time chatting. Zizi had received a trunk-load of clothes from one of Paris's leading haute couture designers. He wanted her to wear them around Hollywood to give his designs exposure. Roland asked her to model some of the clothing for us. The radio was playing, the mood was mellow, and Zizi happily agreed. She turned her modeling into an improvised dance as she changed from one garment to the next. Roland couldn't tolerate just remaining seated and watching, so he joined in to partner her. As the game went on, when Zizi would remove a blouse, Roland would remove his shirt, and what had been a modeling session became a striptease that literally ended with both dancers sharing one handkerchief in a final gesture to modesty. Just then, however, the telephone rang. It was around 2:30 or 3 in the morning. Who was it? Howard Hughes. Zizi, now in the buff, shrugged her shoulders and answered the phone, dutifully reporting in to the boss.

During the year the Ballets de Paris stayed in Hollywood, the company enjoyed the hospitality of many local residents. Leslie Caron was among the circle of French dancers then living in Hollywood. At one gathering Leslie met George Hormel. "Geordie," as the younger George was known, was the eldest of three sons of the head of the major American meat-packing family. Their mother, a Frenchwoman, had also been a dancer. Young theater people were always welcome in her home, as well as their latest jokes and scandals. Geordie Hormel eventually became Leslie Caron's first husband. The Hormel family home is in Minnesota, but they also maintained a magnificent Spanish-style villa in Bel Air.

With its six-car garage, capacious grounds, and elegant furnishings, it looked almost like a resort hotel. The Hormels hosted some memorable parties, inviting many of the Ballets de Paris company members to mingle with the usual movie star guests. I recall one day shortly before a Christmas holiday we were asked to appear at the Hormels' Bel Air home promptly at 5 p.m. It was to be a surprise for Leslie. The surprise, a gift to her from the Hormel family, turned out to be the arrival of Leslie's entire family from France to spend the holidays in Bel Air.

I was very impressed with both Geordie and his brother Tommy. I had only one occasion to meet their youngest brother, Jimmy. Much later, and by then a noted philanthropist, he was President Bill Clinton's ambassador to Luxembourg. Both Geordie and Tommy had an innate natural musicianship. They could play improvisational jazz and have great fun doing it. Geordie did pursue a career as a professional jazz musician for some time, while Tommy's interests lay more in the areas of photography and recording. In the tradition of the Hormel family, Tommy wound up marrying yet another French dancer, Simone Mostavoy, Roland Petit's cousin and also a member of his Ballets de Paris. Leslie Caron had once unsuccessfully auditioned for Roland Petit in the hope of becoming a member of his company. Ironically, Leslie eventually became a movie star rather than a Ballets de Paris premier dancer. Another member of the Ballets de Paris, Liliane Montevecchi, was also making a name for herself in Hollywood and getting occasional featured roles in films.

I recall that year Howard Hughes subsidized the Ballets de Paris as one of youthful joy enhanced by the sparkling personalities of the French dancers. They added liveliness to any occasion and made parties or just plain old gatherings fun. On Sunday afternoons, either Roland Petit in Beverly Hills or Eleanor Peters in Sherman Oaks would play host to the corps of dancers and many of their new Hollywood acquaintances. A young Shelley Winters, Farley Granger, and others such as Claire Trevor would usually drop by.

When Tommy and Simone married they had a new home built in Bel Air, where they entertained lavishly. I remember one July 14 (Bastille Day) they gave a party that lasted until dawn. It was a truly gala and memorable occasion, with red, white, and blue French flags, the swimming pool flaunting a mountain of floating red, white, and blue balloons illuminated from below, dancers from Hollywood films and movie stars galore in attendance, and dancing that included dancing star Fred Astaire. As the party wore on into the early hours of the morning and after the "elders" had taken their leave, the warm night air seemed to beckon the remaining younger partygoers to use the pool's dressing rooms to disrobe. With the seeming freedom of birds all of us dove naked into the inviting mountain of balloons. The erotic combination of the warm evening, the balloons popping, champagne corks popping, and the beautiful bodies of trained dancers could not have been more symbolic of liberty, fraternity, and equality for any country.

Years later, no longer living in Los Angeles, I was visiting my old hometown of Hollywood and decided to renew my friendship with Tommy Hormel. I telephoned him, and he invited me to visit, saying he no longer lived in Bel Air but had a place on Pico Boulevard. He and his wife, Simone, had divorced after about twenty years of marriage, and he was living alone. Simone was living in Malibu. I must have registered some surprise at the idea of a Hormel living on Pico Boulevard, which traverses an industrial area of Los Angeles. In order to be certain of the address, I asked Tommy to repeat it, and he said, "Don't be confused. It's a block of storefronts, just go to the right number and ring." Once I found the right address, Tommy opened the door and I was amazed. He had taken four storefronts, using the first storefront as a living room cum crash pad and wet bar; the second storefront was fashioned into a completely and professionally equipped recording and photography studio; the third area was an open-air atrium containing a huge exotic tropical garden; and the fourth was Tommy's bedroom. From the street, no one could possibly have imagined Tommy's fantastic re-creation on the other side of the industrial facades. I have seen many industrial lofts transformed sumptuously in New York City and elsewhere, but few have rivaled the marvel that Tommy Hormel created on the very drab and grayish Pico Boulevard.

DURING 1951, MY INVOLVEMENT WITH THE GREEK THEATRE, AN OUTDOOR amphitheater in Los Angeles's Griffith Park, was to go far beyond merely playing in the pit orchestras for summer musicals being presented there. An acquaintance of mine by the name of James A. Doolittle telephoned me asking for my opinion on, as well as cooperation and participation in, his upcoming plans for the future. While he had a desire to be involved in the presentation of the performing arts, Jimmy Doolittle acknowledged that, without expert input, he was incapable of going forward with any such plans. Being a native-born Los Angelean and having connections with the Los Angeles County Parks Department, Jimmy felt that he could get the lease on the Greek Theatre, which had remained uncommitted for the forthcoming summer season, just four months away that year of '51.

There were a few elements that had to be dealt with immediately. In order to apply for the lease, the lessee had to submit a complete program for the season and show that a substantial amount of cash was immediately available. Another item to be dealt with was the opposition of Mrs. Norman Chandler, wife of the owner of the *Los Angeles Times*. This woman did not take competition lightly. As a matter of fact, she would rather eliminate it entirely than have any rivalry for the activities she and her fellow board members undertook as sponsors of the

Hollywood Bowl. I convinced Jimmy not to lose the opportunity, and he set up a corporate entity called the Greek Theatre Association, its charter describing it as a "nonprofit cultural institution." Jimmy's expertise in the arts was restricted to an opera production of *Il Trovatore,* since his Beverly Hills fiancée, Nonnie Friedman, was an opera singer. I called upon my friend Eleanor Peters with her connections and still another friend, William Westcott, for his talents in public relations to help me put together an emergency menu for a season to begin within four months. Bill Westcott's family, lending us some necessary funds to begin the enterprise, made the terms of the loan easy ones for us all. This funding was made available at no interest and was to be returned in three years, if we did not fall on our collective faces. In the end we were able to propose an offering that included Japan's Fujiwara Opera Company, appearing in the U.S. for the first time performing *La Bohème* and *Madama Butterfly,* as well as ballet highlights featuring the famed balletic duo Alicia Markova and Anton Dolin with an orchestra conducted by Robert Zeller, an unusually exciting ballet conductor. The coup de grace, and key to obtaining the lease, was Eleanor Peters's ability to finally convince George Balanchine not to accept the prior offer by the Hollywood Bowl for the New York City Ballet to make its first appearance on the West Coast in its outdoor amphitheater, which seats about twenty thousand. The New York City Ballet's roster of principal dancers at the time included now legendary figures such as Maria Tallchief, Nicholas Magallanes, Francisco Moncion, Andre Eglevsky, and Melissa Hayden. Eleanor knew that Balanchine's aesthetic sensibilities would favor accepting the more intimate surroundings of the smaller Greek Theatre with better sight lines and much better natural acoustics than the Hollywood Bowl. Balanchine agreed, and now, for the Los Angeles County parks department, everything had to be proven in favor of the newly formed "cultural institution" of the Greek Theatre Association. Surviving on meals of homemade sandwiches and coffee, and utilizing the offices beneath the Greek Theatre, Eleanor, Bill, Jimmy, and I set to work with no salaries, working countless hours every day and night of that season. Not only was it my responsibility to find and engage the finest orchestral instrumentalists for the newly created "Greek Theatre Orchestra," I also had to double as a player, and Balanchine and his conductor, Leon Barzan, were demanding a high musical standard.

That first season of the Greek Theatre Association turned out to be a tremendous success and was greeted with great reviews that were appropriately laudatory given the high artistic standards achieved. Soon after, we began planning the next season. The mood in the office, by way of activity, was in sharp contrast to the silence of the preceding season. People called us instead of our having to reach out as we had had to do in the previous year. I began making tentative plans for Dimitri Mitropoulos to have a Sunday chamber music series, as I had shown him to the site I'd chosen and he loved it. His imagination started to spin. This all seemed wonderful until Jimmy said to me, " Max, what are we going to do with Eleanor this coming year?" Puzzled, I asked him what he meant. He said, "Oh, well. Do we really need her? She has lots of money." Dumbfounded by his seemingly easy dismissal of someone who was instrumental to his new success, I said, "Jimmy, what kind of a person are you? Who the hell would want to work with you?" Jimmy's reply was "Well, if you feel you don't want to, you don't have to." I said, "I most certainly would not." In hindsight, I realized that this man had led me into a trap. Having used us to create an immediate impact, he then was able to walk away with the whole project and take all of the credit. We had been so immersed in creating the successful first season's format and seeing it through that we had no idea we were being bamboozled, and used by Jimmy to authenticate his questionable credentials with the Los Angeles County Board of Supervisors and Department of Parks. I had been given the nondescript title of "Director of Music." Eleanor was tagged as a "Coordinator," and Bill was "Director of Public Relations." Only after Eleanor and I departed did it occur to any of us that Jimmy had deliberately neglected to include any of our names in the charter documentation of the Greek Theatre Association. Though disenchanted, Bill Westcott had to remain through a third season to see that the matter of the monies advanced by his family was resolved. Jimmy hired other public relations firms to bolster his image as the genius behind the resurrection of a Los Angeles County "white elephant."

The Greek Theatre Association after our departure, under the continued leadership of James A. Doolittle, became the local outlet, for the most part, for mixed programming consisting largely of a spillover of Las Vegas acts. He continued on that somewhat successful path for forty years.

Many years later it was necessary for me to telephone Jimmy from my office in Florida. I had visited with the Bolshoi Ballet's administration in Moscow to discuss a potential American tour of the company. They had asked me to resolve something surrounding a previous correspondence with Doolittle. The subject in question, if resolved, would have to go through my office. Therefore, I felt that I needed to telephone Jimmy in Los Angeles. I placed the call and gave my name to his secretary. A few moments later Jimmy came on the line and said, "Jesus Christ! Forty years later." We had a few laughs and arranged to meet two weeks later in Los Angeles. On the designated morning I phoned Jimmy once again to set the exact time of our meeting for that day. He sounded delighted and said, "Come on over to my apartment at eleven this morning, or as soon as you can." When I arrived, Jimmy greeted me and practically smothered me in a big bear hug. He explained to his secretary, "We go a long way back." Jimmy apologized for the condition of an outside hallway. The walls were being broken through for a new office space for him so he would not have to travel to his office at the Dorothy Chandler Pavilion in downtown Los Angeles.

We then sat around while he showed me some photographs, and we actually enjoyed one another's company as we chatted about our various accomplishments over the intervening years. Although there were many contingencies to discuss surrounding the Russian dancers of the Bolshoi, Jimmy and I experienced no differences that day. Jimmy commented that over the years he thought I had had a much more interesting life than the parochial life he'd led. When I departed, again I got a big hug, and he said he thought that it should be sooner than another forty years before we met again. I hope this wish is not granted—as it happened, that same day, James A. Doolittle had a fatal, massive heart attack in his apartment. I have often wondered if this old Russian adage applied that day: "Under the hat of a thief, the head sweats." Perhaps Jimmy was actually deeply discomfited by recollecting his past misbehavior toward my helpful friends and me.

STILL ANOTHER HOLLYWOOD DENIZEN CALLED UPON ME TO ASSIST WITH yet another musical endeavor during the 1950s. The Academy Award–winning film and classical composer Franz Waxman asked me to work with the manager of his Los Angeles Music Festival, Dorothy Huttenbach. Waxman, who was a German-Jewish refugee from Hitler, arrived in Los Angeles in the early 1930s from Paris, where he had composed the score for the film *Lilliom* starring Joseph Schildkraut. Waxman went on to become the composer of many distinguished film scores, including those for *Humoresque, Sunset Boulevard, A Place in the Sun, A Nun's Story, The Spirit of St. Louis,* and many, many others. His classical output includes the incredibly difficult work for violin and orchestra entitled *Carmen Variations* that Waxman wrote for Jascha Heifetz. Each year Franz Waxman used his income from one of the films he scored to help fund the Los Angeles Music Festival. The venue for the festival was Royce Hall, a 1,980-seat concert hall at the University of California's Los Angeles campus. UCLA's concert box office handled ticket sales, but all other management aspects of the festival were dispensed either to Mrs. Huttenbach's home in Beverly Hills, Waxman's residence on Mulholland Drive, or my house in West Hollywood. Managing the festival required a great deal of work, and it would keep me busy for a number of years. Unlike many of today's festivals with huge budgets and large staffs, including administrative interns, we were limited to very few workers. We considered it normal to fulfill many functions and "wear many hats." Interestingly, today many symphony orchestras have administrative staffs almost exceeding the number of musicians in their orchestras. Back then, however, Dorothy Huttenbach, I, and a few volunteers churned out budgets, payrolls, contracts with musicians and guest artists, publicity releases, radio and television spot announcements, mail-outs, and program copy and took care of the attendant logistics surrounding any large-scale operation such as transporting artists to and from airports, hotels, rehearsals, and performances.

A consistent problem each June was ferreting out stellar guest artists to appear at the L.A. Music Festival. Most artists at that time committed to European appearances during the summer months. There were only a few summer music festivals in the entire U.S., including Red Rocks outside of Denver, Lewisohn Stadium in New York City, the Tanglewood Music Festival in Massachusetts's Berkshire Mountains, the Carter Baron Festival in Washington, D.C., the Ravinia Festival outside of Chicago, the Chautauqua Festival in New York State, and Robin Hood Dell in Philadelphia. By contrast, it seemed that every small town in Germany, France, England, Italy, Switzerland, and the Netherlands boasted a festival, many of them having major importance to the music profession in terms of prestige. Consequently, Waxman, for instance, needed to call in a favor in order to engage a famous guest violinist who would be a box-office draw at the L.A. Music Festival.

I have mentioned that Franz Waxman composed the score for the film *Humoresque,* which starred Joan Crawford and John Garfield. Garfield played the role of a violinist who, through necessity, had given up the violin to pursue boxing. His role called for a high standard of virtuosity when it came to playing the violin in the movie. Naturally, this element would have to be dubbed, and several violinists were called on to fulfill the requirement. The first priority was to obtain the services of a great violinist of the day, such as Yehudi Menuhin. Despite the exceptionally large sum of money offered, Menuhin had to decline because of other contractual concert commitments. Jack Warner, the head of Warner Brothers Studio, which was backing the film, grew impatient on learning of Menuhin's refusal and that of yet another giant violinistic talent, Jascha Heifetz. He told Hal Wallis, the film's producer, "Get a kid." Since a decision had to be made, Waxman thought of a relatively unknown young violinist from San Francisco who was just beginning to make a name for himself. Waxman flew to San Francisco and auditioned the young artist. Waxman found the young man's standard of playing would more than certainly meet the movie's requirements. Not only would it help this young musician toward building his career, but it would provide him with a great deal of money ($25,000). The young musician happily accepted the assignment, and it was a job well done.

So now, more than a decade later, Waxman, in his annual search for stellar guest artists, called upon this violinist whom he had helped establish as a household name to return the favor. Waxman called him again, and again, and again, and again. Each time Waxman spoke with the violinist's wife, who said that

Waxman's call would be returned. It never was! Franz Waxman never received the courtesy of having a favor returned by a seemingly ungrateful Isaac Stern.

The repertoire performed on the Los Angeles Music Festival's programs each year was varied and represented both contemporary and classical works. The music of Igor Stravinsky, also a resident of West Hollywood, was prominently programmed and would feature the composer himself conducting. The Stravinsky repertoire performed at the Los Angeles Music Festival was impressive, including *Les Noces* and excerpts from *Le Rossignol.* Repertoire from other contemporaries included Honegger's *King David* and *Joan of Arc,* narrated by Vera Zorina.

Stravinsky was not a clear conductor. Robert Craft would conduct rehearsals. When the orchestra was totally prepared, Stravinsky would do the final run-through, or dress rehearsal. Interestingly, during the course of such a final rehearsal, if a musician had a question about a specific musical note, Stravinsky would start shouting to Bob Craft for the answer. For reasons of royalties, many works were updated and notes were changed here and there to accomplish renewed copyright benefits. I drove Stravinsky to morning rehearsals. He sat in the auditorium with a towel around his neck and a thermos bottle filled with cold milk at his side while Craft conducted the rehearsal. Every once in a while the elderly gentleman drank from his thermos. I later learned that it contained iced milk laced with Scotch whiskey. On one occasion, after driving Stravinsky home from a rehearsal, I joined him and Bob Craft there for lunch. In true Russian style, we drank long drafts of vodka served at the table in tea glasses before starting our lunch. Even though he was a member of Stravinsky's extended household, Bob was having some sort of a tiff with Stravinsky, and they were not speaking. Bob refused the lunch offered. Instead, leaving us to a more ordinary repast, and to further illustrate his antagonism toward his mentor, he went to the refrigerator and returned with a leftover cold lobster. The dynamic of that lunch was somewhat odd, with a varied menu but no conversation between Craft and Stravinsky. I did not wish to interfere in what was a family squabble of sorts, and there was very little conversation at that table at all.

After lunch, Stravinsky would excuse himself and retire for an afternoon nap. He liked to break up his day into two parts, and the second part, upon awakening from his nap, would be devoted to composing well into the night.

Earlier, at the renowned composer's request, I had assembled the orchestra for the premiere recording sessions of his score for the George Balanchine ballet *Agon.* I was driving a delighted Stravinsky back to his house in West Los Angeles following the final session at the recording studio when out of the blue, in his deep Russian basso voice, he remarked to me, "Max, don't always believe everything you read!"

Puzzled by his sudden remark, I asked him what he meant.

He replied, "Ach, young writers and young critics do not want to hear the truth. If you tell them truth in an interview, is not interesting. They want to over-intellectualize everything." He continued by recalling the premiere in France of the ballet *Sacre du Printemps*.

"Max," he said, "vas scandale. Now, today's critics ask me, 'Maestro, when the lights on the stage backdrop reveal the symbol of infinity, how was it possible for you to create music so descriptive of infinity?' You ever heard anything so stupid? You are younger, Max, but did you ever see silent movie?"

I said, "Yes."

He further expounded by saying, "Nu [so], if pianist in the pit played by accident what is happening on the screen, he is genius!"

A YOUNG MUSIC ARRANGER AND CONDUCTOR AT MGM WOULD OFTEN ATTEND rehearsals. He later became one of the music directors of the Los Angeles Philharmonic. He was an extremely versatile musician, and I often made a point of driving to the Encore Restaurant on La Cienega Boulevard in Hollywood to hear him playing piano in a jazz combo. He was fabulous. The musician's name was André Previn.

Another interesting participant in the L.A. Music Festival was the pianist, raconteur, and neurotic wit Oscar Levant. It was decided that I would personally pick him up and drive him for the rehearsals and performance to ensure that he would be on time. So it was that on one memorable morning I drove to Oscar Levant's very beautiful Beverly Hills home to drive him to an orchestral rehearsal of the Gershwin Concerto in F for the festival. When I arrived, his daughter took me directly to the doors leading into his library. In response to his daughter's tapping on the doors, Oscar shouted, "Who the fuck is there?" I was somewhat shocked, although he did not know that I had arrived to fetch him. I later learned that he had had a terrible fight with his wife, June, that morning and had broken a few of her ribs. I then realized that all the stories about the legendary difficulties created by this man were absolutely true. The following afternoon he was expected for a second rehearsal. Once again, I went to his home. Once there, I was told to go to Eddie Fisher's Beverly Hills house. It was growing closer to the rehearsal hour, and I realized I was getting pressed for time. I quickly drove over to Fisher's home and was received by some rather crude flunky who could well have been cast as an old-time Brooklyn gangster. I asked for Mr. Levant and the reply was, "He's upstairs wit Eddie and dey can't be distoibed." Under pressure from the situation, I simply stood at the staircase in the entry hall and shouted up at Oscar, "Come on down or you're going to be late for your rehearsal." He came down but offered no apologies for the inconvenience he'd caused me. He went directly to my very beautiful Mark IV Jaguar. On the rear seat, luxuriously covered in pigskin, were two baseball caps. Oscar suddenly bolted, screaming, "I'm not going to wear any of those hats." After dealing with so many other artists, I realized at that point that this person was a "patient."

When I got him to the rehearsal I noticed a complete change in his personality. Two of his old friends, Adolph Green and Betty Comden, had shown up for the rehearsal. His behavior from that point on was less childish. When the rehearsal was over, I returned him to his home and we made our arrangements for the following night's concert. I thought: "Here we go again!" Since Oscar was scheduled to play after the intermission, which according to my careful guesswork would be at approximately 9:15 p.m., he did not want to sit around but wished to arrive at the hall in time to just get out of the car, proceed to the stage immediately, and start playing. Timing traffic in Los Angeles on any given day is a roll of the dice. At Oscar's house I waited for him to start toward the car to go to the concert. As the time we needed to be there drew nearer, I prompted him with "Let's go," but he kept procrastinating. After he had done so several times, he announced that he was not going to go and he was not going to play. Weary of his hopeless and inexcusable conduct, I said, "Oscar. Cut it out and get in the car because I'm leaving anyway." I got up and walked out of the house. I guess I communicated. He came out and got in the car. Not a word was exchanged on the way. We drove in total silence. With an audience waiting we couldn't be late. As it happened, Lady Luck was with us. We arrived, and with conductor Franz Waxman propelling him forward, Oscar walked out onto the stage, treating the world once again to his self-proclaimed genius.

I found it really irritating once again to see that horrific personality change as backstage after the performance Oscar Levant graciously received and accepted the compliments of his intimate friends: Betty (Lauren) Bacall, Comden and Green, and any number of others from the Hollywood movie colony. But I was really relieved to know that I wouldn't have to go through any more of Levant's antics during that festival season.

DURING 1960, THE LOS ANGELES MUSIC FESTIVAL INVITED THE UNION of Soviet Composers, which was then headed by Tikhon Krienikov, to send a delegation of its leading members to a composers' symposium to be held in 1963 at UCLA. The delegation that finally arrived in Los Angeles included Dmitri Shostakovich, Aram Khachaturian, and Tikhon Krennikov. Since a dialogue had now been established with the festival, Franz Waxman was invited to conduct Soviet orchestras in Moscow, Kiev, and Leningrad during February of 1961. Both his second wife, Lella, and I would accompany Waxman on the trip to the USSR. At that time the Soviet Union was still a very closed society. Once we arrived we found that the mood, although very hospitable, was clearly defined by the Soviets' expectation that their guests would observe certain "do's and don'ts." We were treated to wonderful ceremonial luncheons at which all of the then famous composers were in attendance. There were many, many of the requisite toasts, so dear to the Russian heart, with Georgian champagne and Russian vodka. Waxman was very pleased to find that the Soviet orchestral musicians were extremely cooperative and took their work very seriously. That certainly contrasted sharply with the attitudes of the American musicians with whom Waxman was accustomed to work, particularly at the Hollywood movie studios.

Although we were official guests of the Soviet government, questionnaires accompanying our visa applications had to be answered in detail. One "Yes" or "No" question posed a problem for me: "Do you have relatives in the USSR?" If the answer was "Yes," the visa applicant had to submit the names and addresses of his or her relatives. At that particular moment in time, many Soviet citizens were uncomfortable, if not petrified, over contact with American relatives. However, the only answer I could mark on the visa application was "Yes." But I added, "The names and addresses are unknown to me at this time." The truth was that I did know the names and addresses of my relatives, including my mother's sisters and their children. I decided that if they would allow me into the Soviet Union despite my dissembling, it would be fine, but if they did not grant me a visa, that would be fine too. The Waxmans claimed no relatives in the USSR, so the question posed no problem for them.

Leaving from Los Angeles, we had an overnight stopover in Copenhagen and arrived the following evening in a snowy Moscow. A car and driver met us at the airport. On the long drive through the thick birch forest that lined the road into Moscow in those days, we finally reached the first traffic signal on the outskirts of the city. It was a very long red light. We were all engaged in a conversation in the rear of the cab, so we didn't notice that the driver had disengaged the engine. During a conversational lull, Waxman, in an attempt to be friendly, remarked to the driver that our car certainly had an incredibly smooth, quiet motor. The driver remained stone-faced and did not respond. When the light turned green at last, the driver reached for the ignition, turned the key, and revved up a very noisy engine. Seated in the rear of the auto, we poked one another and tried to remain stone-faced ourselves. The humor far exceeded any possible embarrassment. After we had been in that country for a while, we discovered that Soviet drivers hardly, if ever, would talk with us. We also learned that the drivers were compelled to turn their motors off at lengthy stop signals in order to conserve fuel. To the Soviet people conservation was of paramount concern. Whenever we returned to our hotel rooms all lights would have been extinguished by the maids and all plugs pulled from their outlets in the walls.

Franz Waxman immediately set about rehearsing with the Moscow Philharmonic. He led that orchestra in a highly successful concert at the Moscow Conservatory's concert hall. Following that event, we had an evening when we were free to find our own amusements. We chose to remain at the hotel and simply enjoy a leisurely dinner in its main dining room, where huge windows faced the street at ground level. This hotel hosted guests from various countries, and each table in the dining room had a flag representing the country of the persons dining there. After finishing our rather lavish meal, which included champagne and other wines, we decided to venture outside into the cold and snowy Russian weather for a breath of fresh air. Since my coat was in the checkroom but the Waxmans had to go up to their suite to collect theirs, we decided to meet outside on the hotel's entrance steps. I went out, took a deep breath, and remained standing waiting for the Waxmans. Some pedestrians passed by, and one of them, an older woman, her head covered in the traditional Russian babushka, stopped and turned to me. She asked me in Russian, "What is your name?" Under normal circumstances this would have puzzled me; I hesitated but decided to answer: "Max." She continued to stare at me while nodding her head up and down. Something about the woman's face, almost hidden by her babushka, reminded me of my maternal grandmother, who had already passed away in the United States. Somehow, it occurred to me that this might be my mother's youngest sister, Ethel, whom I had met in Russia when I was ten years old.

I asked her, "Are you Ethel?"

She replied, "Yes."

"What are you doing here? How did you know I was here?" I asked.

"I was watching you eat through the window," she replied.

Despite the circumstances, it nevertheless was a shock to me that my aunt, a Russian, was not permitted to enter into a hotel lobby in her own country and greet her American nephew. Instead, unknown to us, she stood in the snow, content to look through a window while we indulged ourselves in what was comparative luxury in terms of the Soviet lifestyle of the time. Nothing had changed since I had visited as a ten-year-old boy, when Ethel had experienced the same sorts of restrictions while visiting my mother, brother, and me at our hotel in Leningrad in 1934.

Ethel knew of my arrival because all of my relatives were musicians, and my mother had let it be known through some discreet network that a conductor from California would be coming to Moscow. Using a code name she assigned to me, she also let it be known that I would be accompanying him. When the Waxmans came down to the hotel entrance to join me in a breath of fresh air, I introduced my aunt to them. My mother, by then a longtime resident of California, had seen us all off at the airport in Los Angeles, and the contrast that could be seen when they met my mother's youngest sister in Moscow was a shock to the Waxmans. They saw for themselves the toll that the hardships of life in the Soviet Union had taken on this woman, who was years younger than my mother but seemed almost decades older. I decided to accompany my aunt for a walk of a few blocks. Serious conversations could best take place outdoors on sidewalks, for fear of being overheard even in your own household. The Waxmans, taking in the situation, thought it would be advisable to let my Aunt Ethel and I go our separate way that evening. During our walk, I arranged with Ethel to visit with my other relatives on my next free night in Moscow.

Adjusting to this new and alien environment, as well as meeting my responsibilities to the Waxmans, I felt obliged to obtain the permission of some authority to visit with my relatives.

I approached the interpreter assigned to us and told her of my plans. She told me it was wonderful that I had found my relatives and went so far as to suggest that I could even visit ten of them, if I so wished. She said, "If you want to go on your next free night, I will go with you. What time would you like to go?" As cautiously and diplomatically as possible I explained that my relatives were older people and that it might be uncomfortable for them to be confronted with a nonrelative, as they might be very emotional under the circumstances. The interpreter, stating she understood, said she would order a taxi for me at around 7:30 in the evening. When the taxi appeared at the appointed hour, I chose not to give the driver the actual address of my relatives, but instead gave the names of nearby intersecting cross streets. I knew that my cousins were posting themselves on the sidewalks at a distance of three blocks in either direction from their building's entryway.

The evening was certainly gratifying and emotional. However, I heard family stories that were hair-raising to me. There were incidents of incarcerations recounted along with beatings and other horrors attendant on such imprisonments. I learned that along with an aunt and uncle of mine who had been imprisoned by the government, others in the group of Jewish musicians from Moscow who had been jailed included pianist Vladimir Horowitz's sister and relatives of violinist Nathan Milstein, as well as cellist Gregor Piatigorsky. As was Soviet custom, my aunt, as the wife of an "enemy of the people," had also been imprisoned with my uncle two years after his arrest. Their crime had been receiving U.S. dollars. My mother had occasionally sent cash to my aunt so that she would be able to purchase medications for one of their sisters, Sarah, who had died from her illness during the war years. After my uncle had been in prison for five years of his seven-year-long sentence, and my aunt imprisoned in the same place along with him for three years of her five-year sentence, one day the guards announced to both of them and to all of the prisoners, "This is a good day. You can go home." Having been abused and constantly frightened by such guards, the prisoners did not know how to react to such news. They were afraid that if they left the prison compound, they might very well be shot as they left. However, they were assured, "No! Khrushchev gave a new order. You can all leave. It was Stalin's mistake." My uncle, a cellist with the Bolshoi, had been subjected to a beating with the heel of a boot. As a result of that and other beatings, he lost his hearing in one ear. Although released from prison, the partial deafness affected his ability to earn a living afterwards.

It has been impossible ever since for me to erase from my mind my uncle's descriptions of that Soviet prison. One practice of the Soviet guards was to choose a prisoner at random for a show of discipline and to force him into a coffinlike box standing on its end. My uncle was subjected to that particular torture and felt only joy and relief when he knew that his swollen legs had crumbled and he had begun to faint. Those stories of life in the Soviet gulag later came back to me vividly as I read of the tortures endured in Iraq at the hands of the U.S. Army and U.S. intelligence operatives there in 2004.

The contrast between being officially wined and dined during the day by the elite of the Soviet musical world and the nightly accounts I heard of the horrors endured by my relatives in their actual day-to-day life in a controlled society was very difficult for me to absorb. I was being torn apart and emotionally drained. During all of this, of course, I was unable to express any anger and resentment toward Soviet officialdom. I had to maintain an appropriate facade of cordiality for the remainder of the trip to the USSR with the Waxmans. Following Franz Waxman's final concert in Moscow, as we were leaving to board the famed "Red Arrow" night train for Leningrad, the Moscow interpreter came to see us off and introduce us to our newly assigned Leningrad interpreter. Before she left the train, the Moscow interpreter asked if she could speak with me. She suggested that we go to the end of the railroad car in order to talk. Once there, she said, "Max, do you remember the night you went to visit your relatives?" I said, "Yes," and in anticipation of being questioned regarding that night, I froze and my mouth turned to cotton, as I could not forget the horrible stories I had heard that evening. The interpreter continued, "I had occasion to use the same taxi you had the next day. I asked the driver if you had arrived at your destination comfortably. The driver told me that he didn't think you went where you said you would be going, as he had to let you out on the street." Just happening to use the same taxi as someone else in Moscow is as likely as experiencing a similar coincidence in New York City. No way, Jose! Again controlling my anger, I replied, "Please remember, I am your guest. If I said I was going to go somewhere that is exactly what I did. I would suggest that you first check on the honesty and the motivation of your taxi driver before you check on the honesty of your guests." She then kissed me and said, "Please forget that I ever asked."

Later, while in Kiev, our third stop, I was backstage during the beginning of a rehearsal. Seated on a chair in the wings was a young Ukrainian who asked me if it would be okay for him to remain there to hear the rehearsal. He loved classical music. Such encounters were hardly unusual in the USSR. Young people were accustomed to hearing classical music from childhood and took great interest in its performance, going so far as to attend any rehearsals at which their presence would be tolerated. I told the young man that it would be okay, but he could go into the concert hall if he liked. I asked him if he was a musician. He replied, "No, I am an actor." He was dressed somewhat shabbily, and unshaven, so it was difficult for me to accept him as a member of the acting profession. However, taking a second look at his face I saw that he most certainly could be an actor. When he saw me focusing, he looked at me, then smiling and nodding his head said, "Yes, like Tyrone Power." I told him to stay where he was, I would be right back. I went out into the hall and got Lella Waxman, asking her to come with me right away. Lella's background was as the assistant to Arthur Freed, producer of the legendary MGM musicals. At the studio she had been known as Lella Simone and worked closely with Roger Edens of the MGM music department. Trained originally as a musician, Lella was Belgian born and had immigrated to America during the thirties. She certainly was well connected with all of Hollywood from her days at MGM. I thought she would be as astonished as I was. I brought her to the young actor and said, "Who does he look like?" "Oh, my God! It's a double for Tyrone Power," was her reaction. We couldn't let him go, and we arranged with officialdom to have him dine with us at the hotel. It was interesting to hear about his acting career. He told us that he was usually cast as an unappealing, smooth bad-guy character, such as an American, because he didn't have the image of a Soviet romantic lead. His looks were far too refined for the Soviet ideal of a rugged working-class male lover. As far as his future was concerned, he felt there was little hope for him in Soviet films because he was so readily typecast as a foreigner from the Western world. Somewhat akin to a struggling American actor, he lived with his wife and mother-in-law in one room. He commented that by living that way, "Love can soon go out the window." While she knew her suggestion to be a futile one, Lella commented to Franz and me that if we could bring him with us back to California, he would have a sensational professional welcome there. The best that we could do was to give him a gift of some underwear. He would not accept any outer garments, even socks, as gifts because they could be seen. He might be questioned as to the source of such foreign goods. It was an interesting experience for the Waxmans. They saw for themselves the world of suspicion and paranoia in which the citizens of the USSR existed.

Chapter Five

In 1953, while playing trumpet in the touring orchestra for England's Royal Ballet in Los Angeles and then again in New York City, when the National Broadcasting Company televised choreographer Sir Frederick Ashton's production of *Sleeping Beauty*, I got to know many in the ballet company quite well. In that time, private trains were used as transport for such major touring by big ballet, opera, and theater troupes. Thus I came to know conductors Robert Irving and John Hollingsworth, dancers Alexander Grant, Margot Fonteyn, and Bryan Shaw, and Sir Frederick. Contrasted with tours by airplanes, the old-fashioned train travel was so much more fun and allowed for conversations regarding not only the arts but also everyone's professional ambitions, not to mention their sex lives.

At that time I shared my feeling that I did not wish to devote my professional life to playing the trumpet despite my musical background and experience. I had already completed a course in California real estate law, merely as a way to learn more about business practices. My experience at the Curtis Institute of Music was in many ways so "nineteenth century" that one didn't feel comfortable speaking to strangers unless one was properly introduced. After moving to California and becoming more comfortable in business dealings, I had already begun exploring managerial projects, which turned out to be quite successful.

Speaking of the nineteenth century, Frederick Ashton was not one who had advanced that far into the twentieth century himself. The contrarian view, of course, is that the dance world benefited enormously by such a perspective through his re-creation of such nineteenth-century ballets as *Sleeping Beauty, Swan Lake, La Fille Mal Gardée*, and others. "Freddy" was not one to suffer fools lightly. I recall being at an opening-night party one year honoring the Royal Ballet that was hosted at the Ambassador Hotel by the presenter of the Los Angeles engagement, John Moss. I was seated at one of the many tables with Freddy and his friends in the company. The waiter approached and asked that we present him with our "meal tickets." Freddy questioned the wording "meal tickets" and asked, "What are we? Beggars?" He shouted, "Barbarians. They're all barbarians!" He arose from his seat at the table and said, "Come on. Let's get out of here." Whereupon our host, seeing the exodus of a large complement of the Royal Ballet's principals, who were leaving along with Freddy, was practically tearing his hair out. He pleaded with all of us to "please sit down. I can't explain but I will take care of everything."

On a subsequent tour of the Royal Ballet in which I had no involvement, Freddy telephoned me when the company arrived (once again by train) in Los Angeles. On hearing his voice, I said "Freddy, welcome. How was the trip?" His reply was "Barbarians. They're all barbarians. Our first time in Texas, and how crude that, by law, one has to carry alcohol in a paper bag." Actually, the reason for his telephone call was to tell me that some managerial problems had developed during the course of that particular tour. Apparently Sol Hurok had commented that some of the problems were due to his office's mishandling of certain details. Hurok had noted that it was very hard to find individuals who were knowledgeable in ballet, music, and business. Freddy continued by saying, "Max, I've arranged for you to meet old Sol. Come to the Ambassador Hotel tomorrow at five o'clock. I have told him about your background and your projects, and I think you two should meet."

To me, it was like being asked to meet practically the most important person in the American performing arts. I considered the opportunity a great privilege and was prompt. After being introduced, it turned out that Sol Hurok and I were able to talk for a few hours, and the evening was absolutely delightful. Toward the end of that evening, Mr. Hurok said he had heard much about me from Ashton and would like me to consider joining his organization.

I was elated at Mr. Hurok's invitation (with my upbringing, I never could bring myself to call him anything other than "Mr. Hurok" simply out of respect for the man). Later that evening I went to my parents' home and told them what had just occurred. My father asked me if I would be coming there the following day, as he thought he had something for me. The next day my father presented me with a document, saying, "I think from now on this should be yours." Much to my surprise, it was a contract written on December 10, 1923, on Hurok's stationery and was the actual document that enabled my parents to bypass the quota for Russian immigrants and enter the U.S. legally, as otherwise they would have had to immigrate to Argentina. By the way, it is interesting to note that some of the names included on his stationery (1923/24 season), which established his office as being located in Aeolian Hall at that time, were only considered successful contemporary artists rather than the legends we now know them to be, including Mme. Ernestine Schumann-Heink, Feodor Chaliapin, Efrem Zimbalist, Anna Pavlova, and Artur Schnabel. I had not known of this contract until that moment.

My parents, Dora and Aaron Gershunoff, and my older brother, Alex, together with me at age three in 1927. (Collection of Maxim Gershunoff.)

On Catalina Island in 1938, with the Wrigley mansion seen in the background. *Standing, left to right*: Teenagers Alex Gershunoff and Jerry Goodman (Benny's youngest brother), my best friend at the time. *Seated*: Jeanette Stone and me. (Collection of Maxim Gershunoff.)

My mother, Dora Gershunoff née Pesochinskaya, as a cello student in Odessa, Ukraine, in 1912. (Collection of Maxim Gershunoff.)

S. HUROK, Inc.

MANAGER DISTINGUISHED ARTISTS

AND CONCERT TOURS

Suite 714-717, Aeolian Hall

NEW YORK

December 10, 1923.

SEASON 1923—1924

Ernestine SCHUMANN-HEINK
Contralto

FEODOR CHALIAPIN
Basso-Cantante

EFREM ZIMBALIST
Violinist

ALMA GLUCK
Soprano

JOSEPH SCHWARZ
Baritone

ANNA PAVLOWA
and her Ballet Russe

INA BOURSKAYA
Mezzo-Soprano

RUDOLPH POLK
Violinist

ALFRED MIROVITCH
Pianist

CHERNIAVSKY TRIO

ARTUR SCHNABEL
Pianist
(Season 1924—1925)

and Other Stars.

Mr. & Mrs. Gerchonoff,
Easthigh,
Southampton, Eng.

Dear Mr. & Mrs. Gerchonoff,

As per personal conversation had with Mrs. Koot at my office to-day, this will certify that both you and Mrs. Gerchonoff are to be under my exclusive management for the season of 1924-1925.

It is understood that I am to arrange your concerts on a percentage basis and receive Twenty (20%) percent of the gross receipts as my compensation. You are to pay all expenses such as advertising, printing, railroad fares, etc.

Very truly yours,

The 1923 contract letter from Sol Hurok that helped gain entry into the U.S. for my parents and brother. This was sent before my birth in the U.S. in June 1924. Notice Hurok's 1923 roster of artists, including names that are now legendary: basso Feodor Chaliapin, soprano Alma Gluck, ballerina Anna Pavlova, pianist Artur Schnabel, contralto Ernestine Schumann-Heink, and violinist Efrem Zimbalist.

My father, Aaron Gershunoff, as flutist with the NBC Symphony under Arturo Toscanini in a candid shot taken sometime in the forties. (Collection of Maxim Gershunoff.)

Igor Stravinsky and me at the 1958 recording session of his score for George Balanchine's ballet *Agon*, staged later that year by the New York City Ballet Company. (Courtesy of Sergei Goncharoff.)

Sergei Goncharoff

Dimitri Mitropoulos made a thank-you note out of a publicity portrait. (Collection of Maxim Gershunoff.)

Susan Hoeller

Left to right: Conductor Paul Strauss, Harry Weiss (orchestra manager of the Lux Radio Theater), New York Philharmonic conductor Dimitri Mitropoulos, Eleanor Peters, and me in a snapshot taken at Eleanor's home in 1951 during Dimitri's convalescence. (Collection of Maxim Gershunoff.)

A Sanford Roth photographic portrait of Dimitri Mitropoulos emphasizing his strength of character. (Collection of Maxim Gershunoff.)

A snapshot of me at home in California circa 1956. (Collection of Maxim Gershunoff.)

Another "Sandy" Roth portrait of Maestro Mitropoulos, taken at the Hollywood Bowl and later published as a postcard. (Collection of Maxim Gershunoff.)

Oscar Levant, who made several appearances at the Los Angeles Music Festival. He is seen here during a rehearsal for a performance of a Shostakovich piano concerto. (Collection of John W. Waxman. Used by permission.)

Igor Stravinsky autographed a rather artistic photo portrait for me when we worked together in 1958 at the Los Angeles Music Festival. (Collection of Maxim Gershunoff.)

Autographed photo of Franz Waxman, composer, conductor, wartime Hollywood refugee, Academy Award winner, and founder and artistic director of the Los Angeles Music Festival. (Collection of Maxim Gershunoff.)

A film studio publicity photo taken during the recording sessions for *Humoresque* starring John Garfield, *right*, as a youthful Isaac Stern, *left*, demonstrates violin technique to the movie star. Franz Waxman, who composed the film's famous score, hovers above. (Collection of John W. Waxman. Used by permission.)

With Bolshoi Ballet principal choreographer and artistic director Yuri Grigorovich backstage at an unidentified theater. (Collection of Maxim Gershunoff.)

Left to right: Robert Craft, Igor Stravinsky, and Franz Waxman in a publicity photo taken for the Los Angeles Music Festival. Craft always "pre-rehearsed" orchestras for appearances by Stravinsky and later was responsible for many important publications about Stravinsky, his life, and his music. (Collection of John W. Waxman. Used by permission.)

© John W. Waxman

The great impresario Sol Hurok happily conversing with the Royal Ballet of England's principal choreographer, Sir Frederick Ashton. (Collection of Maxim Gershunoff.)

With Lella Simone Waxman and Franz Waxman. We are being seen off on our way to the Soviet Union in 1962. I looked much happier on departure than I did when I returned from that eye-opening and emotionally upsetting trip. (Collection of John W. Waxman. Used by permission.)

Bob Hoffman

Dmitri Shostakovich

From left: Head of the Union of Soviet Composers Tikhon Khrenikov, Lella Waxman, Franz Waxman, Armenian composer Aram Khachaturian, and me at a party in Waxman's honor in Moscow. (Collection of Maxim Gershunoff.)

With, *left to right*, Russian composer Rodion Schedrin, famed cellist and conductor Mstislav Rostropovich, Maya Plisetskaya, and an unidentified friend of theirs in Daytona Beach for a festival there in 1997. (Collection of Maxim Gershunoff.)

Maya Plisetskaya and Alexander Godunov appeared to great acclaim in Roland Petit's staging of his *Rose Malade* to the music of Gustav Mahler for the Bolshoi Ballet. (Collection of Maxim Gershunoff.)

The Bolshoi Ballet's prima ballerina Maya Plisetskaya autographed this portrait for me early in our acquaintance. (Collection of Maxim Gershunoff.)

Maya Plisetskaya in perhaps her most famous performance, that of the "Dying Swan." (Collection of Maxim Gershunoff.)

When next I saw Sol Hurok, I said, "You know, Mr. Hurok, I am deeply indebted to you."

He responded, "For what?"

I replied, "Were it not for you, I would not have been born an American. Do you know the name Charlie Koot?"

Hurok was surprised. "How do you know Charlie Koot's name? He was my best friend."

I responded, "Well, before I was born he asked you to do him a favor: to write a contract for two musicians so that they would be able to enter the United States. Charlie Koot was my uncle, and the two musicians were my parents."

With so much time having passed, Sol Hurok himself had no immediate recollection of having dictated the letter and signed it on my parents' behalf. He was shocked and very moved. He embraced me and, as it turned out, I would say that over time he actually became a second father to me.

So in 1962, I started working for Hurok, at first in his West Coast office in Los Angeles. I was booking artists in the Western states when, suddenly, I was told to pack my bags and go to San Francisco the very next day. I was to be prepared to be away for six to eight weeks. Further, I was told not to ask any questions; all would be explained to me on arrival in San Francisco. Apparently, the American male interpreter for the Bolshoi Ballet tour that season had to be dismissed immediately. What with Soviet-American tensions at an all-time high over developments in Cuba, the Soviets had uncovered information that the interpreter was an active member of an anti-Soviet organization. Hurok had to oblige the Bolshoi Ballet administrators traveling with the company and let the man go. I was to be the interpreter's replacement.

Interpreting was not and is not my profession, however conversant in the Russian language I might be. I was assigned to interpret the Russian technicians' backstage stage and lighting cues for their American counterparts. While I may have been able to hold my own speaking Russian socially, I really could have screwed up performances. The people I was supposed to be helping seemed to fare better without my foul-ups. During the first few days, I found my reception by the Russians to be very strange and sensed a wall between the company and myself. At first, they thought that I had been sent by the CIA to replace the previous interpreter. Then, little by little, in communicating with the Russian conductor Kopilev and some others, I asked them if they knew any of my relatives in Moscow. All of my relatives there were musicians. For instance, the first oboist of the Moscow Philharmonic, under Kiril Kondrashin, was Simon Trubachnik, my first cousin. At long last, the Russians leveled with me after they knew who my relatives were and they became more comfortable having me in their midst. From that point forward the assignment began to blossom. I learned how to recognize and deal with some of the Russian personnel traveling with the company as "arts administrators" who actually were something other than their titles made them out to be. If the arts were the subject of a discussion, they were very limited in their knowledge and conversational abilities. Often I would see these individuals taking turns doing all-night "guard duty" in the lobbies of the hotels in which the company stayed while on tour. I was becoming "streetwise" to my new environment. I uncovered the fact that Soviet dance companies touring in the West were divided into groups of ten, out of which one individual dancer would be responsible for the whereabouts of the nine others in the group, who always traveled at least in pairs and never individually. Every dancer had to be accounted for by someone at all times. It was also very interesting to find that the touring symphony orchestras from the USSR tightened the formula and reduced the monitoring group number to four, with one of the four musicians responsible for three others. I couldn't quite understand why the ratio was that different. Apparently, there were more Jewish musicians than Jewish dancers, so the risk of defection on the part of musicians was greater. My cousin Simon had toured with Kondrashin and the Moscow Philharmonic. In order to be able to participate in tours of the West, Simon, as a Jewish "risk" who was nevertheless an essential member of the orchestra, had to join the Communist Party. When the Philharmonic was in New York City, his group of four would collect in my apartment. Each would venture forth on his own, and then later the quartet would regroup at a mutually agreed time before returning to their hotel seemingly as innocent as choirboys. When Simon, or "Senya," the diminutive by which he is known in our family, was finally able to leave the USSR, he was refused permission to immigrate by the United States because of his former membership in the Communist Party. His life's path has routed him first to Israel, then to Belgium, and finally, and happily, to Canada, where he is a much respected member of the faculty of the Royal Conservatory of Music in Toronto.

During this period of touring with Soviet artists, I was in a "no-win" situation when it came to outsiders' perception of my identity. In those tense times full of political paranoia, many of my fellow Americans would whisper their suspicions of my being a Soviet operative posing as an American traveling with the various artists or groups from the USSR. And, unless they knew me better, the Soviets suspected me of being assigned to travel with them by the U.S. government. As an example, movie star Natalie Wood had invited Maya Plisetskaya and two others to spend the day on a yacht she had chartered for the day in San Francisco. The writer Mart Crowley (*Boys in the Band*), then her secretary, was among the other guests invited, along with one of Natalie's sisters. Natalie had asked Maya if she would be comfortable on her day off if Max, the Soviet watchman, came along. Maya assured her there was no government connection, and that she and I were indeed friends.

During a later tour of the Bolshoi Ballet under the aegis of Columbia Artists Management, I personally experienced yet another "cloak-and-dagger" twist involving an English-speaking principal soloist in the Bolshoi Ballet who became a very friendly traveling companion during that tour with the company. Somehow, we always managed to be seated together on any airplane in which the company flew. Our hotel rooms were always next to one another. After performances, we would go out with two of the ballerinas, and occasionally Alexander Gudonov (who defected one year later) would join us as well. My newfound friend insisted that I come and visit him and his wife and stay in their Moscow apartment. I reminded him that Americans were required to obtain special permission to make such a visit under the political circumstances of the time. He said, "It is not necessary because in my country, if you know how to steer around the obstacles, we have complete freedom." He went on to describe his marvelous apartment, which he, so deserving an artist, was able to get from the former first oboist of the Moscow Philharmonic, who had left Mother Russia. Much to my amusement and shock, I said, "You mean Senya? I have been in that apartment many times, Senya is my first cousin." In a strange and pleasant way, somehow this made us personally closer. On a day off, when we were in Los Angeles, I invited him to spend the day with me and he willingly accepted. So, off we went to my brother's home on Malibu Beach. We had a great time swimming, eating, and playing with my nieces and nephews. The one other day that we had free during that stay in Los Angeles, the company was scheduled to go to Disneyland. My Russian "buddy" assumed that I was going also and was somewhat disturbed when I informed him of my own plans for the day. I had been to Disneyland on countless other occasions and told him I was going back to visit with my brother and his family in Malibu and that he was welcome to accompany me there once again. He became very sullen. I asked him about his change in mood. He then very seriously replied, "Max, I have come to know you quite well, and I know that your interests are purely in the arts and you are not at all a political sort of person. How can I explain to you that if you don't go to Disneyland, I cannot go? Therefore, I may never get to see Disneyland in my lifetime."

I said, "I don't understand, please explain what you mean."

Reluctantly, but honestly, he replied, "I am supposed to be with you, if at all possible. So, if you are not with the company on our trip to Disneyland, I cannot account for where you have been or whom you might have seen, or to whom you might have reported."

Although, I am certain the Soviets already had an extensive dossier on my personal life and professional activities, I had incurred added suspicion by becoming involved in the "rescue" of the Panovs. After much fuss in the media, these dancers from Leningrad's Kirov Ballet Company, who had recently immigrated to Israel, were preparing to come to the U.S. to perform here under my aegis. As a result, to the Soviets I had now become suspect as a "traitor." Therefore, I had been assigned my very own "keeper." Regardless, our mutual respect for one another prompted me to acquiesce, even as a free American, and that day I dutifully traveled to Disneyland with the Bolshoi Ballet to visit with Mickey and Minnie Mouse once again.

An example of the Soviets' attention to the minutiae surrounding famous artists who had defected is the way they dealt with Sol Hurok when he was presenting the English Royal Ballet in the U.S. with the world-famous dancer (and Soviet defector) Rudolf Nureyev as a guest star. The Soviet government, through its ministry of culture, lodged an official complaint with Hurok about his hiring of Nureyev to tour with the Royal Ballet. The complaint was certainly made with the hope of impeding Nureyev's burgeoning career. They went so far as to suggest that it would be unlikely for them to continue their almost exclusive arrangements with Hurok on future tours of their great artists. Their efforts failed when Hurok presented his trump card. He asserted that Nureyev was not on his payroll. Nureyev had been hired by the Royal Ballet and was being paid directly by them. Having made their best effort to impede the dancer's appearances, with that technicality the Soviets let the matter rest.

Adding to my suspicion that the Soviets might no longer have considered me someone who could be trusted with their artists and, therefore, a dangerous security risk if I assisted those who defected, I have always harbored the thought that my father's death in Israel was of a suspicious nature.

My father had traveled with me to Israel during one of my business trips there on behalf of the Panovs. On that particular trip, I received much local publicity in Israel associated with my arrival there to assist the former Russian dancers, and I have always felt that my own notoriety there may have worked against my father and me. During our stay, my father suffered an appendicitis attack and required emergency surgery. His postoperative recuperation in the hospital was going very well. Though I had to leave him in the hospital and travel back to New York City, I had been assured that he was well on his way to recovery. My cousin Senya Trubachnik, oboist with the Israel Philharmonic at the time, visited my father daily in the hospital, and they were very close. So, I felt the situation was well in hand and was comfortable returning to New York, and planning to return to Tel Aviv within a matter of ten days.

Within four days, however, I was shocked to be telephoned with the news that my father had died of blood poisoning while still in the hospital. Could it have been that some Soviet operative had had a hand in my father's demise, as a means of getting even with me for my dealings with the Panovs? I will never know. That type of retribution would be no surprise to anyone living within the USSR at that time.

Another outing for the company of Bolshoi dancers, on another free day in yet another city, involved the members of the company visiting the Ford Museum outside of Detroit, where we were all escorted to a cabin that had at one time been owned by Thomas Edison and later had been moved there. It housed many exhibits relative to Edison's inventiveness. When the tour guide made references to the lightbulb having been created by none other than Thomas Alva Edison, the Soviet administrator took umbrage and pulled me aside. They said, "Max, we are not here to have to listen to American propaganda. It was a Russian who invented the lightbulb. The company is very tired and we needn't waste our time here." He then announced to the company that this outing was no more than mere propaganda and that they must all return within a half-hour, if not sooner, to the buses awaiting them. I countered the administrator by saying, "I'm very tired, too, and, as a matter of fact, I don't need this at all. If you want to go back, it's fine with me. I couldn't be happier." The bus left an hour and a half later, as many of the company had earlier wandered off to view exhibits at their leisure rather than follow tour guides, and the remainder, knowing that there is strength in numbers, simply took their time reboarding the buses.

On earlier tours of the Bolshoi, for whatever reason, I found myself becoming very close to the prima ballerina Maya Plisetskaya. She was not only a great artist, but she was also very realistic and earthy. Maya has a very open and honest outlook on life. Among her idiosyncrasies is her love of shoes and gifts. While we were in Detroit dining in a restaurant following a performance, a gentleman in a wheelchair approached us from another table, excused himself, and told Maya how much he enjoyed her artistry and that of the Bolshoi Ballet. The man commented on the exhilaration and "lift" he had felt from seeing them perform, being otherwise restricted to his wheelchair. He said, "In exchange for the joy you and the company have given me, I would like to invite you to my place of business." Handing her his business card, which established him as a manufacturer of costume jewelry, he said, "I would like you to come and select anything that pleases you." Having an excuse to break away from the company the next day, since she had a damaged valise in need of immediate repair, we took a taxi from the hotel with the valise but instead of going to a repair shop, we directed the cab driver to go to the address of the costume jewelry manufacturer. I must say that on arrival, our host in the wheelchair was delighted to show us his headquarters, which looked like a cafeteria in which you took a tray and selected goodies from a huge steam table or salad bar. Maya, practically salivating, found she could use this item in this ballet, that in another ballet, and so on. Our host said, "Don't be shy, please. Take as much and whatever it is that you want." For the first time in my experience, I heard Maya say, "I'm uncomfortable with his generosity." However, the man continued by asking her to pick anything else she would find appropriate for the entire company, boys included. At that point she very seriously told him that she could not accept gifts on behalf of the troupe, as she had no authority to do so. I then stepped in and suggested that I could facilitate his gesture by receiving the gifts if they were sent to my room in the hotel, and that I would try to clear it with the administrators.

The baubles (gold necklaces with pearl pendants for the girls and bejeweled stickpins for the men) duly arrived. The next day happened to be the fiftieth anniversary of the USSR's founding. Usually we would have the company dine around two o'clock in the afternoon, but this day we were asked by its administrators to utilize the hotel's banquet room after the performance, instead. They wished to have a celebratory dinner party for the occasion. I spoke to the administrators and told them of the jewelry manufacturer and his generosity in appreciation of their performance and in honor of their government's anniversary. They resisted me, saying that they would not be used to advertise some commercial venture and that the costume jewelry man was using his generosity as just such an opportunity. I assured them that this was absolutely not the case and that his gesture was really so pure that he really didn't even care if his name was used. I was devastated by their quick reaction, when they looked at one another with great smiles of satisfaction and declared, "Oh, fine! Then we will give the jewelry to the company as our gifts." I brought the box from my room, and the administrators then placed a gift box on each dinner plate before the members of the company arrived to enjoy their party. I somehow got the true story around while everyone was dancing after dinner. The dancers understood.

Adding to my general level of discomfort surrounding that particular occasion was the necessity of being courteous, as well as diplomatically correct, with the company of dancers, their legitimate administrative staff, and the politically appointed staff. It was definitely a political occasion, and there were the requisite toasts with vodka and champagne to the fiftieth anniversary of the Soviet Union, Premier Khrushchev, and so forth. Knowing that members of the company shared my discomfort, I looked upon the whole scene as a kind of microcosm of the controlled Soviet society that merely demonstrated its general hypocrisy.

Generally, the People's Artists of the USSR, represented by Hurok Concerts, Inc., and Hurok Attractions, Inc., enjoyed the personal largesse of Sol Hurok. The noted artists who appeared under his aegis in North America would receive their regular paychecks at home in the USSR, and while they performed in the West they would receive an almost miniscule honorarium for each of their appearances.

The Soviet government would receive the greater portion of any fee paid for any of their soloists' services in the West. When David Oistrakh and Sviatislav Richter made a special for CBS-TV, they would receive approximately $160 each for such an appearance, while the actual fee paid for their extra services by CBS would have numbered in the thousands, paid to Hurok Concerts, Inc., which in turn would pay the majority of the fee to the Soviet ministry of culture. Hurok paid a similar sum to the artists for each of their concert appearances. Again, a greater sum was always paid to the ministry of culture. The Soviets rationalized this imbalance by reasoning that the artist was working for the Soviet people and not for his own individual benefit. Any such honorarium fees paid by Hurok to these artists were considered by the Soviet government to be their artists' "overseas pay," over and above what they still were receiving at home in rubles.

Naturally, the artists knew of the disparity in the income that accrued to them, but this was the only means by which they could ever hope to visit the Western world at that time. They accepted the conditions of their government, for the most part, but they were hardly averse to accepting the generosity of Hurok and others. Artists who are now legends benefited from Hurok's generosity and the image he created for them when he introducing them to the West. Mstislav Rostropovich and his wife, Galina Vishnevskaya, an operatic soprano, were the recipients of a fully equipped kitchen full of appliances and cabinetry made to measure and shipped by boat to their home in Russia. "Slava" Rostropovich and any number of other artists enjoyed the benefits of American dentistry courtesy of Hurok Concerts, Inc., and the talents of Dr. Jerry Lynn at his office a block away from the Hurok office in New York City. Hurok would pay for dental instruments to be carried by artists back to their own dentists in Moscow. Hurok's charge accounts at such refined purveyors of clothing as Saks Fifth Avenue and Bloomingdale's would skyrocket as formal evening clothes, shoes, and other wardrobe necessities were purchased so artists would look appropriate both onstage and in social circumstances, but also feel comfortable and appreciated. American surgeons were found who would have restored the eyesight of the legally blind conductor Yuri Fedorovich Fier, but he could not receive permission to have the necessary operation performed because the Soviet government did not want their medical limitations exposed as a result of the potential publicity that might be generated. The conductor was able to lead the orchestra when Galina Ulanova danced because he knew her tempos instinctively and she was comfortable with his collaboration. Nevertheless, Hurok had to engage the conductor's brother, who lived in America, to accompany him on the tour so as to accommodate his physical limitations, even escorting him by the arm into the orchestra pit at each performance.

In 1962, Ulanova, the foremost Russian interpreter of the role of Juliet in

Prokofiev's *Romeo and Juliet,* was traveling with the Bolshoi Ballet as a ballet mistress, along with her husband Rindin, a well-respected ballet and theater scenic designer. By nature, Ulanova was very controlling. When the company arrived in Chicago to perform at the Arie Crown Theatre at McCormick Place, the first thing she did was go to the theater to assess the stage. She had some concerns about the pacing of the ballets being performed in Chicago because she knew that the Arie Crown Theatre's stage was a very large one. Simon Semenov and I had accompanied her to McCormick Place. When we got there and she saw the stage, size became less important than the surface. Taking one look she said, "We are not performing here. This stage is covered in linoleum, and the Bolshoi Ballet will not dance on a kitchen floor." Semenov tried to persuade her not to be hasty and said that if she felt the risk of having dancers slip on the linoleum floor was too great, he had a solution. Disbelieving, Ulanova said, "Prove it."

Semenov, ever resourceful, found the stage porters and had them locate cases of Coca-Cola stored for use in vending machines. He had the porters fill three buckets full of Coke and proceeded to have them mop the stage with the liquid. When the linoleum surface dried it then had a slightly sticky film, which was enough to curtail any slipping by the dancers. Allowing the dancers to rehearse on the surface, Ulanova saw that Semenov's "Coke solution" worked. There were there no mishaps, not only throughout the rehearsal, but also during the entire run of the ballet, which garnered great reviews in Chicago. Ulanova commented on how much she had heard about American Coca-Cola, and how she now marveled at its versatile uses.

Under the terms of their contract, Hurok paid for the daily living expenses of all the Soviet artists performing under his banner, as well as transportation and myriad incidental expenses. Although he was not contractually obligated to do so, he always supplied Soviet artists with at least one major meal daily. Dancers, being athletes, posed a special problem. When Hurok first brought the Bolshoi Ballet from the USSR to tour in the U.S., there was a small daily food allowance for each member of the company. Approximately three weeks into the tour he found that many of the dancers were becoming ill. What was happening was that the funds allocated for food were instead being used to purchase much needed items that were difficult to obtain in the USSR and would be much appreciated when the dancers returned home. In order to survive, the dancers were cooking sausages, potatoes, and sardines in their rooms on alcohol stoves or portable hot plates and were slicing up cucumbers for their salads. That diet was not keeping up their strength. Finding that dancers were becoming ill and unable to perform, Hurok realized that they needed to be properly fed.

With the language barrier, together with the security problems imposed by their governmental watchdogs traveling with each company, feeding up to 150 persons was almost an impossibility. Expecting the dancers to fend for themselves at public restaurants in strange cities would have been impossible. Instead, the Hurok office resolved the problem by arranging menus and paying for a full meal to be served once a day, usually in the ballrooms of the hotels at which the companies were staying. The meal was served around two in the afternoon and was followed by a rest period until it was time for the well-nourished company to leave for the theater and their evening performance. The dancers were allowed to keep their daily stipend for food. The dancers' general health improved, and Hurok learned an important lesson about dealing with such companies. The dancers truly appreciated Hurok's concern for their welfare and all thanked him directly and sincerely. The Hurok daily meal continued to be served to all such companies appearing in North America under his banner.

However, on one of Hurok's trips to Moscow to scout new artists and negotiate contracts, the members of the Bolshoi Ballet greeted him rather distantly. This was highly unusual, and he could not immediately discover the cause of this sudden chill in his usual warm relationship with the dancers. He soon found out why they distanced themselves from him. Apparently, the administrators of the ballet reported back to the Soviet ministry of culture that in addition to their daily monetary stipend for food the dancers received a free meal from Hurok Attractions, Inc. Sensing an opportunity for further financial gain, the Soviets deducted a daily amount of $4.50 (at the time a relatively good sum of money for a meal) from each of the dancers' take-home pay at the conclusion of the tour. Gosconcert, the Soviet government agency that booked artists and attractions both within the USSR and internationally, was the official Soviet bureaucracy with which Hurok had all his dealings. Shocked, Hurok told his contacts at Gosconcert that their behavior was inexcusable. How could they dare to embarrass him with the dancers who understood their meals to have been Hurok's gift to them? Once at home they found they had been paying for those meals. He made it clear to Soviet officialdom that if they continued to make such deductions, he would not plan to feed any of their companies any longer. When the next company came, he did not feed them. After the first week with no meals, their administrators timidly asked Hurok's staff if they would not be fed as in the past. Having gained the attention of their administrators on the subject, especially since they also wanted to have their own free meals, Hurok made it emphatically clear that he would continue feeding the dancers provided everyone knew that it was to be his gift to them, and that should they go home to find monies were subtracted from their pay, it would be their own governmental agency that must be held responsible.

Given every assurance that this would not happen again, Hurok began anew his practice of feeding all of the Soviet People's Artists touring for him. There are countless other instances of Hurok's generosity. Naturally, he benefited as well, as the artists who appeared for him were not only grateful for the treatment they received at his hands but certainly willing to perform at their best for him.

Others expressed their appreciation of the Soviet People's Artists through their own generous gestures. Actress Natalie Wood, born in the U.S. of Russian immigrant parents, very much-admired Maya Plisetskaya and wanted to do as much as she could to demonstrate her warmth toward, and admiration of, the great ballerina. Maya had mentioned to Natalie the new and fourth Bolshoi production of the ballet *Spartacus,* in which she wanted to appear with a most luxurious head of hair. Unfortunately, Maya's hair could not be teased to produce the desired effect. Lo and behold, Natalie presented Maya with a wig that could be fashioned into the hairdo that Maya envisioned for her character in *Spartacus.* The cost of the wig in the 1960s was $1,500. Although Maya knew the cost of the wig, she unashamedly asked Natalie for a duplicate spare. Known for her graciousness, Natalie Wood had a second wig delivered to the Bolshoi's prima ballerina. As to the bouquets of flowers presented to Maya after performances, her suite was often so filled with them that there was no room to spare in the bathtub or, for that matter, sometimes the toilet. One thing she needed was her full cycle of sleep. If she couldn't disconnect her telephone, she would cut the wire. Otherwise, Maya was great!

In fact, Maya Plisetskaya was such a fascinating creature that she even attracted the attention of the attorney general of the United States, Robert F. Kennedy, during the Bolshoi Ballet's 1962 U.S. tour. By coincidence they shared the same birthday, which contributed to a sense of some sort of mutuality. Bobby Kennedy would call her in many of the cities in which the company was appearing. I would have to take the call, acting as interpreter while Maya and I shared the same telephone, our heads pressed together against a single earpiece. Their friendship seemed to be known within the Kennedy family, and later during the tour, a few of us were invited to Hyannisport the day before Thanksgiving Day. We were taken by private bus from Boston, where the company was appearing. Teddy Kennedy and a group of his friends who were also along for the ride hosted our bus trip. Someone played guitar in the back of the bus throughout the journey. I sat with Ted to interpret and Maya sat across from us. We all enjoyed a wonderful day at the Kennedy compound on Cape Cod. The matriarch Rose Kennedy came over to Ted's house to say hello to one and all. A wonderful and ample buffet of food and other refreshments were served. I was most impressed with the "real" cranberry juice served, which was so different from the bottled variety one finds on supermarket shelves. Ted and his former wife, Joan, proudly brought their two sons downstairs to meet us all, and later

Ted personally, and with great warmth and sentiment, showed us photos of his brothers and himself playing football games and enjoying other sports activities.

Still later that day, Ted took us to his father's house to show us the new swimming pool that had been installed for Joseph Kennedy's recuperation after his first stroke. He also showed us the projection room downstairs in the basement of his father's home. It could seat approximately forty people. What was also interesting about that room was a wonderful collection of antique dolls displayed in glass cases encircling the room. As some of the guests were looking at the dolls, Ted said, "Max, take Maya and come with me through this door." The door led into a laundry room. On one of the washing machines was a telephone with buttons. Ted, pressing one of the buttons, picked up the phone and was able to speak instantly to Robert Kennedy in Washington. Ted said, "Bobby, sorry you couldn't be here with us but say hello to Maya and Max," whereupon he handed us the telephone. The conversation was short and sweet. By the way, a little sailboat at that compound today is named *Maya*, which is the Russian word for the month of May. I don't know if that reference to Maya is just a coincidence.

The mood that day in Hyannisport was so pleasant that Ted wanted just five of us to come to his home in Boston after a performance a few days later. We were to meet in front of the Bradford Hotel, which was only a short walk from the theater where the company was performing. As our group of five walked together from the theater and was approaching the hotel, we noticed, standing to the right under the hotel marquee and doing guard duty, Tentuk, a short, sleazy creep. Then we also noticed to our left, across the street, Ted Kennedy sitting in his car. Ted was waiting for us to leave in our hotel rooms whatever items we had carried from the theater and then come right down, meet him, and be driven to his house.

As if there had been a total change of climate, suddenly everybody said, "Goodnight, until tomorrow" with a glance toward Tentuk. This meant all bets were off, and everybody disappeared into their rooms. I, not a part of this process, crossed the street to respond to Ted's query, "What's happening?" I said to him, "You see that little man standing over there? He's the watchdog doing guard duty. The Russians would not dare to go out with anyone as important as you without first getting permission and having a supervisor accompany them. It would change the whole mood of the evening, and instead of being relaxing, it would become very inhibiting." Ted's comment was "If I didn't see it with my own eyes, I would never believe it."

While the company was in New York, Maya and I and a couple of others were invited for late-afternoon tea and drinks with Jean Kennedy Smith and her husband, Stephen Smith, at their Fifth Avenue apartment. Expressing her desire to show Maya a New York nightspot after a performance, Jean invited Maya and me to El Morocco, which she thought might be fun for all of us. In order to do this and avoid the "monitors," Maya and I broke away from the company after a performance, telling them that we were going off for a sandwich together. Instead we met with Jean and Stephen on a given street corner on Broadway in the forties and headed by foot across town. It was about 11:30 at night, and as we passed one of the small grocery stores, an array of beautiful grapefruits caught Maya's eye. Since she marveled at them, Jean suggested that we stop in and buy a few. We ended up taking a large paper sack of grapefruits with us to El Morocco. Needless to say, Jean and her husband were expected and known at the famous watering hole. However, it seemed rather strange to be checking our coats along with a paper bag of grapefruit at such an establishment, though I'm certain stranger things had been checked in their cloakroom. We were seated at a table for four, and the conversation seemed to direct itself in a "getting to know you better" direction on all sides.

Jean asked Maya, "Do you have your home in Moscow?" which I translated for Jean to Maya.

Maya leaned over to me and said in Russian, though she could speak some English but was shy about it, "And what is she? An idiot?"

I asked Maya in Russian, "Are you speaking to me or do you want me to translate?"

She replied, "Tell her. Tell her."

Feeling somewhat uncomfortable, I tried to cushion the reply in a diplomatic way by saying, "The answer to your question 'Do you have your home in Moscow?' is "Quote, and what is she? An idiot? close quote."

Maya continued by telling of her two-room apartment, with each room approximately ten feet by fifteen feet, with a kitchen and a woman who cleaned and cooked and slept on the kitchen floor because both Maya and her husband were both busy professionals. Jean further asked if, as a People's Artist of the Soviet Union, Maya had a dacha. Maya's reply was "Yes."

Then, putting things into perspective, Jean said, "Oh, in other words, you have a 'pad' in Moscow near the Bolshoi, and you really have your home out of town."

Maya laughed and said, "No, it's just a wooden shack."

Jean became somewhat defensive and tried to explain by saying, "Please don't judge by what you've seen of my family because we are somewhat unusual even by American standards." Maya, trying to let Jean and Stephen know where she was coming from, said, "You know, I love to visit America. I find the American people very warm, very generous but very naive. I do not think of myself as a ballerina but as an athlete who is an artist. The one thing I do not take for granted is my health because without health the rest cannot be.

"My impression of the American people's naiveté worries me because, as with good health, I think they do not know what they have as a nation, and therefore they do not know what to protect and know not what they can lose. Jean, I appreciate your questions, which are also somewhat naïve, and that scares me because, after all, you are the sister of the president of the United States."

Rather than what one might think of as an evening of nightclubbing in New York, it was a rather poignant experience. However, drinks were served along with an enormous plate of shrimp cocktail to go around, and things did manage to lighten up a bit that evening.

The connection with the Kennedys did not stop there. Maya received a birthday gift from Bobby Kennedy. It was a charm bracelet with signs of the zodiac, acknowledging their mutual birth date. Word of this gift from the attorney general of the United States to Russia's prima ballerina and a People's Artist of the Soviet Union reached the Soviet administrators of the company. By some sort of osmosis, the Soviet embassy on 16th Street in Washington, D.C., also seemed to have been informed. Call it diplomacy or whatever, our White House received an acknowledgment from the Soviet embassy for the courtesy extended by the U.S. attorney general to its great artist. The Kennedys brilliantly kept the positive momentum spinning by extending an impromptu invitation for the entire Bolshoi Ballet Company to a tour of the White House to be personally conducted by Jacqueline Kennedy. Normally, such an invitation would have been handled directly by the Hurok office. In this case, the invitation was issued to the company through the Soviet embassy. Their administrators asked me to make the necessary arrangements, including bus travel, and since Sol Hurok was in Washington at the time, I felt obliged to mention this to him, as any costs involved would be charged to our office. Of course, the charges were not a problem, but Hurok had not been included in the invitation. The evening prior to our White House tour Mr. Hurok said, "So, you'll tell me what happened."

The following morning both President and Mrs. Kennedy greeted us all. She made an absolutely charming and warm welcoming talk to the assembled company about the pride she was taking in showing the White House, which she had just completed restoring and which now housed so much of American history. At just about that same moment, as Mrs. Kennedy concluded, in strolled Sol Hurok down the long White House corridor. Both Kennedys said, "Oh, Mr. Hurok, so nice of you to have come."

President Kennedy said, "Jackie is about to take everyone upstairs to start the tour. Would you like to go?"

Hurok in his warm and direct way replied with a shrug, "No, I came to see you."

The president hugged him and said, "Come on with me. We'll meet them in the dining room later."

We all proceeded up to the Lincoln Bedroom, where Mrs. Kennedy said that the president's and her first night in the White House was spent in that room, and legend had it that Lincoln's ghost would appear on that one night only for each new president. She chuckled and said, "After a sleepless night, nothing happened." She directed our attention to some memorabilia and on and on through the White House, including the Kennedys' own private quarters. We all later gathered in the dining room to chat with the president, and the dancers were invited to take souvenirs such as matchbooks and wrapped sugar cubes, since the tour had been arranged more or less on an impromptu basis, and more official kinds of mementos were not available on a moment's notice. This unofficial reception of the Bolshoi Ballet Company by President and Mrs. Kennedy is a good example of the Kennedys' superb personal diplomacy and brilliant sensitivity.

When we left the White House, Mr. Hurok asked me to accompany him back to his hotel in his limousine. After we were comfortably seated, he remarked to me, with great satisfaction, "You see, Max, if there's something that you want to have happen and it doesn't, you have to make it happen. I showed the bastards!" He had actually crashed the occasion, as he had not been officially invited and should have been. The "bastards" he was referring to were the flunkies at the Soviet embassy who hadn't included Hurok—the man who was paying the bills—in the invitation.

All this was occurring at the height of the Cuban missile crisis in 1962, involving forty nuclear weapons that were reported to have been targeted at the U.S. from inside Cuba. President Kennedy had ordered a blockade of the sea surrounding Cuba, intending to fend off further Soviet shipments of nuclear warheads there. Khrushchev now had a boat headed for Cuba loaded with even more missiles. Would he turn it around or not? This was, indeed, the question, and the crisis provided perhaps the most critical and tense moment of the Kennedy presidency.

THE FOLLOWING YEAR I WAS TRAVELING WITH DAVID AND IGOR OISTRAKH, who would make appearances together in concert, as well as separately. I would accompany one or the other, depending on the circumstances, to his next engagement. One of David's engagements was with the Montreal Symphony Orchestra under the direction of Zubin Mehta. Oistrakh was to play the Shostakovich Violin Concerto, a relatively new work that was performed in the Western world principally by David Oistrakh. At that time, it was even difficult to obtain the printed music for the Shostakovich work, and Sol Hurok had brought the score and orchestra parts from Russia himself in anticipation of these performances by Oistrakh in North America. Oistrakh arrived in Montreal for the rehearsals and concert, and there was very good collaboration during rehearsals between him and the then young Zubin Mehta. Since the work was still not standard repertoire, David Oistrakh, as soloist, insisted that the conductor's score be used for the actual concert. When he walked onstage the night of the concert, Oistrakh noticed that despite his specific request, the score had been removed. He had asked that Mehta use it in order to avoid any mishaps. Following the performance I stood in the wings as the last curtain calls were being made. I noticed that David Oistrakh was highly agitated, which was unusual for him. Since Oistrakh's German (the only common language he and Mehta shared) was limited and Zubin understood no Russian, I had to interpret while David vented his feelings to Zubin. He said, "Max, please tell Zubin, 'Your first priority should be to accommodate your soloist in order to make him comfortable. As your soloist, if I asked you to do something, it is for a reason, since I know the score is new to you. I should not have to worry about the conductor messing up, I have my own worries. When a conductor conducts a symphony, it's his show. But tonight your personal priority was to prove that you have a good memory at my expense. Okay, you have a very good memory, but I suggest you never do that again to me or any other soloist.'" At the moment, Zubin appeared to humbly accept the elder artist's rebuke, but I am not certain that he always adhered to the advice it contained.

In late November of 1963, I was with Igor Oistrakh in Orlando, Florida, where he was scheduled to give a recital on the evening of November 22. As that tragic day unfolded and the news of President Kennedy's assassination was broadcast from every radio and television, Igor's concert was canceled. With all sorts of speculation about who was responsible for the assassination, much of it focused on a possible Russian assassin, Igor and I were advised to remain indoors. We were told by Hurok's New York office to be extremely cautious, since we might find ourselves to be the targets of some vengeful maniac. In a relatively small town like Orlando, pre–Disney World, we presented a highly tempting opportunity for someone to "get back at the Russians."

The following day, Igor and I had to continue on to Washington, D.C. There we would meet up with David. A Sunday rehearsal would be coordinated with the Moscow Chamber Orchestra. That ensemble, under the direction of Rudolf Barshai, was touring the U.S. at the same time, and the rehearsal was to be in preparation for a concert several days later in Philadelphia. We found that there was no rehearsal space to be had in Washington that Sunday. A solution was to use the Soviet embassy's ballroom on 16th Street. In order to coordinate the logistics, I rang up Rudolf Barshai at his hotel and told him that the rehearsal would now take place at 5 p.m. that Sunday at the embassy. I suggested he talk with David Oistrakh about the order the works they would be rehearsing. Barshai surprised me by saying that he and David were not speaking. It was one more surprise Hurok had in store for me, as he had given me no warning. Before talking with David Oistrakh vis-à-vis the situation, I called Barshai once again and told him that David wanted to speak with him, so he should stay put and I would go to David's room to place the call. I then went to David's room in the hotel in which we were staying and said that I was in the process of coordinating the Sunday rehearsal. He looked blankly at me and told me that he and Barshai were not speaking. Being somewhat prepared for this nonsense, I continued with my improvisation, saying that I was aware of the problem but Barshai wanted to speak with him, and I had promised Barshai that I would call him from David's telephone to connect the two of them. I immediately proceeded to do just that. It worked. Each felt victorious over the other and they got on with the business at hand.

Off we went to the Soviet embassy at the assigned hour and entered the reception area of the building. I felt a real sense of accomplishment. An officer of the day greeted the group saying, "Welcome, comrades, you are at home again. Come upstairs and use the ballroom as much as you like. That is, everyone but the American." He meant me! I felt after all of that trouble I was getting a blatant rejection. I was told that if I wished to hear the rehearsal I could remain in the reception area and be seated there. Since I was being deprived of the opportunity of witnessing the reconciliation of Oistrakh and Barshai, I got up and happily took myself off to see a movie. Later, the artists were highly apologetic for the behavior of that officer of the day. His authority was not broad enough to have allowed any foreigner in the building on a Sunday, when no higher officer was available.

THE PUBLIC MAY PERHAPS FANTASIZE AND ENVISION A GREAT ARTIST enjoying himself after a performance by luxuriating at a celebrated restaurant with the finest wine and gourmet food available in New York City. So, on yet another tour in the late 1960s, the violinist David Oistrakh surprised me when, after a grueling day of videotaping three Beethoven sonatas with Sviatislav Richter at Alice Tully Hall in Lincoln Center, he declined my invitation to dine at either of two famous nearby restaurants, La Caravelle or La Côte Basque. Instead, Oistrakh's wife, Tamara Ivanovna, yelling "Oy! Oy! Oy!" as if she had forgotten something, hurriedly donned her coat and disappeared from their suite at the Essex House on Central Park South. Oistrakh looked at me and then shrugged his shoulders. We then chatted a bit, rehashing musical details of the televised concert, Richter's hatred of the lighting necessary for television, and so on. Later, Tamara Ivanovna reappeared with a huge paper bag containing many ears of corn on the cob that she had purchased at the nearby tiny Merit Farms takeout shop on West 57th Street opposite Carnegie Hall. With a simple, earthy, unpretentious kind of enjoyment we all partook of Oistrakh's reward for a good performance. As yet another American who took our land's bounty for granted, I marveled at hearing their expressions of how wonderful it was to be able to eat corn on the cob in the month of January.

During the 1966 tour of North America by the Bolshoi Ballet, the company was in Washington, D.C., for a series of performances. Maya Plisetskaya was to appear but, unfortunately, developed a fever, became ill, and could not perform. Her non-appearance was announced to the press, and we did not know when she would recover. I had a call from Robert Kennedy asking if he could come to the hotel to see Maya. I said, "Why don't I check with her and I'll call you back." Maya was none too happy at the prospect of having visitors, as she still had a fever and was perspiring and drinking tea, and preferred to doze off as often as possible without having to be presentable for company. I reported back to Bobby Kennedy that Maya thanked him for his concern, but perhaps it would be better to visit her on another day when she was feeling better.

Russians can always feel at home in a crowd of familiars. It was all right, therefore, for a couple of dancers in the company, along with Simon Semenov, to be with Maya that same day in her room, as they were considered "family." I later learned from a surprised Simon that there had been a knock on the door of Maya's hotel suite and that, unannounced, Robert Kennedy had come to visit regardless of Maya's wishes that he not do so on that day. They had a polite exchange, but under the circumstances he did not remain for long. I had no idea of how he had discovered which hotel suite Maya occupied, since such information was not allowed to be given out. However, given his authority, I am certain such knowledge was easily gained.

During the 1968 tour of the U.S. by the Bolshoi Ballet, I was supposed to escort Maya to Jackie Kennedy's Fifth Avenue apartment following a performance at the Metropolitan Opera House in Lincoln Center. The occasion was to be a rendezvous with Bobby Kennedy. I was not sure if I was simply supposed to deliver her, and if I would be able to find an appropriate time to make a discreet exit. I knew that Jackie was not planning to be there and, frankly, did not know whether the evening was to be just a continuance of their till then innocent flirtation or something more. I discussed this with Sol Hurok. His reaction was one of extremely serious concern. Ever conscious of the fragility of the Soviet-American cultural exchange program, he thought that in the event Bobby and Maya's relationship got out of hand, it could become an international scandal. The entire Soviet-American exchange, on which his entrepreneurial efforts greatly depended, could crumble at a moment's notice. His comment was that as far as he was concerned, and from the standpoint of his advanced years, the individuals involved were just "kids" despite their fame and power. His estimation of the situation was that it was not to be taken as a game and that serious consequences might ensue. Despite the courteous treatment Sol Hurok received from President John F. Kennedy and his wife Jacqueline in 1962 at the White House, Hurok was not reluctant to use his authority to bar Jackie from the backstage of the Metropolitan Opera House. Angered by what he considered to be Jackie's participation in the arrangement of the upcoming meeting between Maya and Bobby, when Jackie came to the Met's backstage entrance from the hall itself after a performance, Hurok saw her approaching from behind the open door where he was standing and slammed the door shut as she approached to prevent further contact with Maya. From that point on, Hurok made certain with the Metropolitan Opera House management that there were to be no visitors backstage during the Bolshoi run.

As the fates would have it, all of Hurok's concerns and precautions were unnecessary. Ironically, Robert F. Kennedy was assassinated in the early morning hours of June 5, 1968, just days before he and Maya were to have gotten together in New York City. On June 8, 1968, the day of Bobby Kennedy's funeral, most of the theaters and concert halls in New York City went "dark," closed in mourning and respect. It was decided that the Bolshoi Ballet Company would not shut down that evening but instead would dedicate that evening in honor of Robert F. Kennedy. The program would be changed from a full-length ballet to one consisting of ballet highlights. The most appropriate way to open such an evening would be for the great Plisetskaya to perform "The Dying Swan," which normally would close an evening's program to thunderous applause with stamping feet, and clamors for an encore of the three-minute work and Maya's sublime performance. This assignment created an emotional burden for Maya. She really did not want to dance that work that night. Unable to share her personal feelings about any of this with the Soviet administrators of the Bolshoi Ballet, she had to oblige them and perform as she was directed. Under the circumstances, I thought it was best for me to remain backstage in the wings. That turned out to be one of the most poignant moments I have ever experienced. Replacing the usual thunderous audience applause at the conclusion of Maya's unique interpretation of "The Dying Swan" there was a complete silence betokening the feelings of a mourning nation in the packed, cavernous Metropolitan Opera House. As Maya came off the stage in tears, she looked at me, raised her beautiful arms, looked upwards, and simply shrugged into the void and disappeared into her dressing room.

Reflecting on all of the circumstances, I recalled Bobby saying in one of the many phone conversations between Maya and himself: "Max, tell Maya I love her."

And, Maya to Bobby, through me again, "Tell Bobby I love him, too."

Bobby said, "Tell her she's crazy if she returns to Russia."

Her reply was, "I must return."

His reply was "Give me two reasons why."

She said, "One, were I to stay here for you, it would create a terrible international scandal."

He quickly responded "Give me another."

Her marvelous response was, "Need I remind you that it would be too much of an inconvenience to too many children," a reference to Bobby and Ethel Kennedy's nine, soon to be ten, children.

Whatever might seem implied by the cross-cultural relationship I witnessed between Robert F. Kennedy and Maya Plisetskaya, to my knowledge it was most definitely not, and certainly never became, anything beyond a truly innocent flirtatious and fun affair.

Another momentous performance of Maya Plisetskaya's "Dying Swan" took place on Sunday evening, May 8, 1966, on the occasion of the final ballet performance at the old Metropolitan Opera House just prior to its being razed to the ground. The evening of short ballet "bon-bons" danced by the Bolshoi Ballet was capped off by a coda performed by dance stars of the entire ballet world escorted by members of the Bolshoi Ballet in a grand promenade onto and off the Metropolitan's huge stage. Naturally, one of the highlights of the evening was to be Maya performing her breathtaking "Swan." The evening, however, was not complete without a demonstration of Isaac Stern's insatiable quest for visibility, no matter how inappropriate or inconvenient.

Sensing an opportunity to share the limelight during what would be a highly publicized occasion, Isaac imposed himself on the evening's bill of fare as violin soloist for Maya Plisetskaya's incomparable "Dying Swan." No matter that Saint-Saëns wrote his composition to be performed on the cello, or that the wonderful cellist Albert Catell had been the soloist for all of the performances at the Met that season. Moreover, Isaac Stern was unused to performing "The Dying Swan" and, surprising its ballerina, Stern suddenly wavered in his "treat" of a performance, becoming startlingly insecure. The performance had to be stopped, and Stern had to start again from the beginning. But Stern got his moment in the event's spotlight.

In the late nineties I spent three days at a retreat outside of Daytona Beach, Florida, where Mstislav Rostropovich premiered a new work by the brilliant Russian composer Rodion Schedrin with the London Symphony Orchestra. Both Schedrin and his wife, Maya Plisetaskaya, were in attendance as well. At the retreat Maya gave some ballet classes. Incidentally, surprising all outsiders, those sessions were observed by Rostropovich. His interest in attending any of the other arts seminars taking place at the time, it seemed, took less priority than viewing young ballerinas at work.

One afternoon, while Maya and I were having tea at one of the houses in the compound at the retreat and chatting about old times, she spoke of a book that she had been writing.

She said to me, "It is a shame you are so far away, Max, because I am sure you could remember more than I could."

I replied, "I think perhaps one day I will write a book of my own, since I have much that I would like to say."

Schedrin, reacting quickly, turned to me and said, "And, you'll write about Bobby Kennedy, too?"

We all laughed. Actually I do not really know what details Schedrin knows that perhaps even I don't know and probably never will. But in view of the fact that Schedrin was completely aware of the flirtation between Bobby Kennedy and Maya, I no longer have any qualms about sharing that story.

During the 1962 tour of the Bolshoi Ballet, Maya Plisetskaya made a guest appearance on the *Ed Sullivan Show* broadcast on CBS-TV on Sunday evenings. She appeared in her famous three-minute solo performance of "The Dying Swan." The fee for her performance, payable to Hurok Attractions, Inc., was $7,500. Ultimately, the majority of the fee was payable to the ministry of culture of the USSR and was entirely tax-free to the Soviets. The fee due to Maya for her services out of this money was approximately $160. This was the nominal sum allowed by the Soviet government for "overseas duty" by all Soviet artists, no matter their degree of stature or fame. As we were leaving New York City and heading for Montreal, Maya asked me, "Since we are leaving the United States, when do I get paid for the *Ed Sullivan Show* and from whom will I receive it?" She had been too shy to ask her own administrators. It seemed she wanted to purchase a woolen sweater for her husband. I assured her that there were marvelous woolen sweaters available in Canada. Joking with her, I said, "Rather than administrators, you would be better off having a manager with whom you can speak freely." Her marvelous reply to that joke was "If I had a manager, he'd get the $160, and I would get the rest of the $7,500."

Her arrival in Montreal presented the prospect of dancing for the local manager of the company's presentation, Nicholas Koudriavtsev, and it was not a happy one, as Maya held no warmth for the man. Nor was Maya going to suffer for him. Although, she was scheduled to appear for the opening performance of the Montreal engagement she preferred to find that a corn on her toe would prevent her from performing. By contract, she was obliged to consult a chiropodist. Since the wife of Koudriavtsev was a former ballerina and was familiar with such dancers' discomforts, she had recommended a specialist. Late in the afternoon Koudriavtsev came to Maya's hotel suite, asking in Russian, "Nu, Mayeschka!" and rubbing his hands together as if smugly satisfied, "Aren't you much better now?" Maya replied, in her direct way, "Thank you, I'm fine, but he cut too deep. So, I'm not dancing anyway." Were she not to appear in Montreal during the entire run, it would seriously affect the income at the box office. I had to telephone Mr. Hurok in New York immediately and inform him of the situation. He returned my call after a half hour and very strongly suggested that Maya remain in her suite and rest. I should keep her company as much as possible and order any needed room service. At around five o'clock the next day, he would be in Montreal along with representatives of the firm's insurance company. I was to ask Maya to be prepared to meet with the insurance gentlemen in her suite, preferably off her feet. There was no need for any exaggeration; she was merely to explain to them that she could not perform owing to the discomfort she was feeling. That next afternoon, Mr. Hurok arrived on schedule and made all necessary introductions. I remained with Maya and the insurance reps, who made some notes, and all was well. Later, it was suggested that if Maya was not going to dance at all in Montreal, she should stay put and not go shopping for shoes, which was what she really wanted to do. We had no idea who might be watching us from the insurance company.

Owing to the possible financial gain to Hurok, who would benefit from the non-performance of Plisetskaya, anxieties were muted but still ran high, awaiting the conclusion of the insurance representatives. Hurok remained his usual considerate, if somewhat Victorian, self. He excused himself to avoid subjecting Maya to any possible embarrassment in his presence should she have to expose her none too pretty dancer's feet. It was to be expected that she might be asked to do just that by the insurance company's agents as testimony to the physical injury she was claiming. However, he didn't mind my being subjected to any potential embarrassment and left me with them all. As I accompanied him and he made his exit through the door he whispered, "Call me when it's over. I can't stand it." I believe Hurok made more money from the insurance than he would have from only his usual share from that engagement.

Maya, although never promised any recompense for her inconvenience, received some sort of grateful acknowledgment for not making any shoe-shopping expeditions, which might have led to further questions regarding her incapacity in Montreal.

BOBBY KENNEDY WAS NOT MAYA'S ONLY AMERICAN MALE ADMIRER OF note. Longtime Hollywood bachelor and ladies' man Warren Beatty also showered the Russian dancer with his attentions. Warren wasn't going to depend on me to handle all of his conversations with Maya and began learning the Russian language. While his wooing of Maya took place during the filming of *Bonnie and Clyde,* his interest in the Russian language would prove useful when he undertook the filming of *Reds.* I recall receiving a note from a man who was not permitted backstage while a sold-out performance was in progress in Vancouver, British Columbia. The note read: "Can you let me in so that I can watch the 'Swan' die?" The note was signed "Warren B." Of course, we cleared him, and since there were no seats, I sat with him on the steps of the balcony, where he could watch the great Plisetskaya close the program with her incomparable interpretation of "The Dying Swan." An indication of the level of Warren's enthusiasm for this relationship was related to me by a member of the Hurok staff, Jay Kingwell, who had somehow overheard Warren in a rage trying to persuade Maya to remain in the West. Jay reported that Warren had smashed a lamp against a hotel room wall in his anger at Maya's reluctance to make such a drastic move.

AT THE CONCLUSION OF THIS TOUR OF THE BOLSHOI BALLET IN MIDSUMMER of 1966, all of the airlines in the U.S. suddenly went on strike. Hurok Attractions had originally obtained an excellent charter contract with Trans World Airlines to transport the entire company from Vancouver all the way to Moscow for a special low fee of $19,500. This was an advantage for TWA because at that time the airline was trying to penetrate Pan American's exclusive rights for routes to Moscow. In view of the strike, TWA was unable to fulfill the contract. We attempted to charter an aircraft from any of the other major foreign airlines, but it turned out that a special, last-minute Air Canada charter leaving at 2:30 a.m. from Vancouver to Montreal was the only way to resolve the very serious problem of returning the company as far as Montreal during the peak summer travel season.

That flight alone cost $15,000 and still left the company stranded in Canada for five days. The entire company still had to be fed and housed in Montreal, waiting from day to day for the arrival of two jet-assisted prop Aeroflot planes that Hurok Attractions finally had to charter for the flight from Montreal to Moscow. The planes had to be "deadheaded" (fly empty of passengers) en route to us, resulting in an outrageous cost of $46,000 for the round trip. I went to the airport in Montreal with the Soviet administrators of the Bolshoi to welcome the Aeroflot pilots and crew and bring them to our hotel. Amazingly, those pilots had no clue as to the nature of the passengers they would be carrying home to Moscow. Clearly, in the interests of "Soviet national security," they had not been told that they were to be carrying the Bolshoi Ballet Company. The pilots were delighted and I was totally puzzled. The logistics of this transportation nightmare being solved, pilots and crew had a night's rest, and the next day we were all to leave for Moscow with fueling stopovers scheduled in Newfoundland and Scotland. One plane would leave and wait for the other plane to arrive at each of the stopover points. We were about to leave the hotel in Montreal and were all seated on the many buses chartered to take us to the airport (I was traveling with the company to Scotland, which was as far as I cared to go); Maya was seated on the bus in her usual first-row spot diagonally across from the driver. Suddenly two Soviets boarded and gestured to her, politely saying, "Let's go" in Russian. They escorted her from the bus into a waiting private car, where she was purposely seated between the two men. Apparently, the official word was that Maya might defect. We all converged at the airport in a section reserved for passengers of chartered aircraft. That area was unbearably hot due to malfunctioning air conditioning. Maya used that circumstance to get permission to walk with me down to the area where cold drinks could be purchased. As long as her Soviet overseers knew where we were headed, they said "Alright." Maya took my arm and signaled to me by squeezing the arm several times as we walked, then said to me, "We will get a Coke and then you must make a telephone call for me at those telephone booths." Having said that, she then gave me a telephone number to call Warren on location in Texas. Taking the phone from me, Maya said her farewells to Warren. In a soft voice, as we walked back to join the company, Maya said, "He asked me to call if I could. Thank you, Max."

I had arranged with Air Canada to cater the Aeroflot return flights with all sorts of goodies and favorite alcoholic beverages and the requisite ice for drinks. After such a grueling, hot day I was certain that once we were aloft the company would be overjoyed to have cold drinks at their disposal. In those noisy, jet-prop planes we finally reached the altitude at which it was permissible to begin serving drinks to the passengers. From all of the surrounding seats, I heard dancers shouting, "Where's the ice?" Naturally, I asked the well-meaning, rather scruffy-looking stewardesses why they weren't serving the ice, which had been ordered for the flight. As it happened, they had proudly told Air Canada ground service that they had their own ice aboard and the supply ordered wasn't necessary. Believing they had economized for Hurok Attractions, they delightedly pointed out their ice-making equipment to me. I looked and beheld two home-sized refrigerators strapped in a crisscrossed manner against the bulkheads on either side of the plane. They said, "Don't worry. We'll have plenty of ice in two hours." The Aeroflot flights, representing the most expensive part of the journey for Hurok Attractions, yielded the least in creature comforts. It was more like traveling in a Waring blender. The irony of this Rube Goldberg–type adventure was that the Soviet administrators were spinning a web of propaganda around the whole trip. The scenario set forth for the dancers was that they could see for themselves the dissatisfaction of workers in the West, with all of these strikes. The capitalistic system was, therefore, chaotic and undependable. So, without disclosing the government's price-gouging on the flights, they characterized these return flights as their government's "rescue" of the company. Once again, I made certain that key members of the company who would keep the story straight for the entire troupe knew the complete picture.

The typical Soviet mentality of "Get what you can and from whomever, and don't look back" provided yet another incident I recall from the close of one tour. The watchdog Tentuk, whose presence had prevented us from visiting with Teddy Kennedy in Boston, came to see me in my hotel room the day before the Bolshoi's departure bearing a gift of a small, typically Russian painted wooden bowl. This offering was "in gratitude for everything you have done for us." Stating that his father was a tailor, he then said that he had one problem: he had completed all of his shopping for gifts to take home to Moscow but he had not located a place to buy professional tailor's shears for his father. I mentioned that the Hudson's Bay department store was located only two blocks away from the hotel. Undoubtedly, such scissors would be available there. He asked me to go there with him. I obliged, and after finding the correct department, we were offered top-of-the-line tailor's scissors that were priced at approximately $115 back then. The salesman suggested, however, a much broader availability of such equipment at a supply house that could be found at the end of the subway line. Although I could have taken a taxi, ignoring my own inconvenience, I deliberately chose to subject Tentuk to as much discomfort as possible and traveled there via the subway. We found the supply house, where there was a broad and low-priced line of shears available. What Tentuk chose was a pair of scissors at the surprisingly low cost of $13. However, giving me a somewhat pained and sad look, he said to me that he didn't have enough money to buy the shears. I asked, "Why all this travel when you knew you had no money?" It was understandable that Tentuk might not have had $115 for the price of the shears at the Hudson Bay store, but when he said that he did not have even $13 in his wallet for this inexpensive purchase I clearly realized that I was being manipulated. So, in a pleasant but deliberate tone, I advised him, "Since you've already spent your money for your wife and whomever else, I would suggest that on your next trip out of the Soviet Union you think of your father first rather than as an afterthought." We returned to the hotel, once again via the subway, empty-handed.

I remembered, as that tour had progressed, Tentuk would look more and more tired. One day I asked him, "Why are you so tired?" Although clearly not one of the performers, he said, "Tours are not easy." Knowing full well what his actual duties relative to the Bolshoi Ballet Company were, I said, "Why don't you get a good night's sleep? I see you sitting in the lobby most nights. You're never asleep when everyone else is." I never did elicit a response, but I think we understood one another.

I had been privileged to attend many brilliant performances over many weeks, but also subjected to the heavy cloak-and-dagger atmosphere surrounding the tour, and I really felt I needed a break. I chose to bid the company farewell at Prestwick Airport in Scotland, leaving with a warm feeling of admiration for their artistry, as well as dedication to their art. Then I took off with friends for London, Paris, Rome, and Venice. I don't wish to sound overly sentimental concerning my return to the U.S., but the sight of the American flag at the immigration check-in at JFK airport in New York City simply looked fantastic. As a first-generation American born in the United States to Russian parents, my respect and admiration for their courage in emigrating became truly meaningful. How lucky I felt. The flag now represented so much more to me that it might just as well have spoken the words: "Welcome home, Max!"

Chapter Six

DURING THE LATE SIXTIES, HUROK TOURED THE ROYAL DANISH BALLET in the U.S. I knew the exceptional *danseur noble* Erik Bruhn from previous acquaintance, and he and I became travel mates on that tour. This was not simply a matter of our friendship, it was a product of the other Danish dancers' resentment of Erik's fame and stature as featured star on the tour. Sol Hurok engaged him to enhance box-office draw. Erik had been dropped long ago from the roster of the Royal Danish Ballet. Far less well-known soloists were now performing the principal roles he had once performed at home in Copenhagen. So, generally the whole company gave him the cold shoulder. This company, accustomed to a socialist society's respectful treatment of them and their artistry, knew that whether they toured or not, they would still receive regular salaries. That they, without Bruhn, were a box-office risk for Hurok was of little or no concern to them. They simply resented Erik Bruhn's presence among them.

I had a rather curious, however flattering, personal experience during that tour with the Royal Danish Ballet. As a principal participant in the tour on behalf of Hurok Attractions, I was invited to an opening-night dinner reception for the company at the Danish Embassy in Washington, D.C. I was having a pleasant conversation speaking of my travels in Russia with a woman seated across from me at the dinner table, while the gentleman seated next to me sat quietly, not participating. He chimed in at one point, though, asking if he could join in the conversation, since I was speaking with his wife. We had been talking for quite a while when he said, "I find you very interesting." He asked how long the company would be staying in Washington, D.C., and I answered that we had three or four days remaining in our run there. He said, "Would it be convenient for us to get together once again? Could you come to my office?" I had no idea who the man was. Thinking he was a local corporate executive, I asked him where he worked. He laughed and said, "I am Dr. Charles Frankel, assistant secretary of state for Middle Eastern affairs, and my office is at the State Department." I found his governmental responsibilities fascinating and looked forward to visiting him in his office. So, the following day I went to the U.S. State Department office building and was ushered into a comfortable office to meet with him. Mr. Frankel, I discovered, was not only a gentleman, but he was also an exceptionally intelligent and direct person. The point of our meeting, it turned out, was that he wished to offer me a position in the State Department, suggesting that I could be doing a great deal of good there. I countered with my opinion that my position at Hurok Attractions, Inc., also offered me the opportunity to do good on an international relations basis. While his offer was indeed flattering, I told him that I could not leave the Hurok office. When I discussed the incident later with Patrick Hayes, the local presenter of the Royal Danish Ballet and most of the classical performing arts attractions in Washington, D.C., at that time, Pat said, "That's eighteen points." I had absolutely no idea what he meant. "Eighteen points," he said, "means the position he offered you pays $18,000 per year." That sum would have been less than I was earning at Hurok Attractions at the time, certainly another negative factor to Charles Frankel's offer.

As a result of the new familiarity with Erik Bruhn that I gained while traveling with the Royal Danes, I became his confidante by default. Reflecting on the success of Rudy Nureyev, Erik told me of his relationship with Rudy. It began when Rudy, having recently defected in Paris from the Kirov Ballet, arrived on Erik's doorstep in Denmark. Rudy said that Erik was his artistic hero, and that he wished to place his own artistic future in Erik's hands as a devoted student to benefit from his artistic influence. Rudy was already an acknowledged principal dancer. He played on Erik's own ego by assuming such a secondary role. Erik, admitting to his own gullibility, recounted to me that as soon as Rudy came to feel more secure in his new environment, their positions reversed to the extreme. Erik said, "Could you imagine, I ended up carrying his luggage?" In addition to their close artistic relationship, Rudy and Erik had a deep love for one another. Erik said he tried to understand Rudy in spite of Rudy's self-centeredness. He maintained that he would always care for Rudy.

Rudy could only have benefited from his relationship with Bruhn, both as an artist and a person. There are many today who still say that Bruhn was by far the superior dancer, whose pure, yet masculine elegance has yet to be duplicated by any other dancer. Rudy was not wrong in seeking to learn from this great Dane.

I also knew Yuri Soloviev, a principal of the Kirov Ballet from Leningrad. He was often cast as the Prince in the ballet *Cinderella*. Soloviev had been Rudolf Nureyev's roommate during the tour on which Rudy defected to the West at the airport in Paris. Upon Soloviev's return to the Soviet Union, he was required to adhere to the "party line" and make public statements as instructed. The official story he gave for public consumption in the USSR was that Nureyev had made homosexual advances to him, and his advances had been rejected. The story was that he could not accept such a rejection and therefore ran away from the company in Paris. Officially, then, he had not left the USSR for any political reasons, but entirely personal ones. It was unthinkable that a dancer would leave the Kirov Ballet for any reason. However, homosexuality was a major offense in the USSR, with severe legal penalties of long-term imprisonment or in some cases even death. Completing the scenario, Soloviev was instructed to find someone and to get married within the next year, which he did. Sadly, Soloviev took his own life four years later.

My travels with the Kirov Ballet showed me how detailed a knowledge Sol Hurok had of every aspect of the repertoire, the dancers, and their combined effect on box-office draw. I was in Rochester, New York, with the company when I called Mr. Hurok in New York City to tell him that we had arrived although it was snowing. It had been necessary, for this engagement in Rochester, to change the opening program to *Cinderella.* Normally, we opened with *Swan Lake, Sleeping Beauty,* or the Kirov's renowned production of *La Bayadere.* However, the heavy scenery required for those ballets had had to be trucked in advance to the next major city. *Cinderella,* for whatever reason, was not well received at the box office. One of its few selling points was in the proper casting of Cinderella's two ugly stepsisters. The ballerina Kaleria Fedicheva was a hit as one of those stepsisters. Her performance generated a certain magic with the public and at least would assure a satisfied opening night audience. This would help at the box office for the remainder of the run in that city. When I spoke with Mr. Hurok he asked me if Fedicheva was dancing for that night's opening performance in Rochester. I replied, "Yes. It's in the program." He insisted that I double-check it and call him back. I found that although Fedicheva was listed in the program, she would not be dancing. I was told that the reason was that she was menstruating and, according to the Kirov company's rules, was not obliged to appear. Not concerned at all about box office, the Soviets used such opportunities to have others gain more experience in principal roles. Much to my surprise, when Hurok was informed by me, he immediately replied, "That's not possible. She menstruated two weeks ago. Get Helen Gillespie and have her look, if necessary. Bring them both to the telephone and call me in a half hour." With the promise of one fur coat, Fedicheva's affliction magically disappeared, solving that evening's problem. She became the real Cinderella of the occasion. As if he were the owner of a racing stable, Sol Hurok knew which horses to run and when.

DESPITE THE CRITICALLY ACKNOWLEDGED, SUPERIOR LEVEL OF ARTISTRY exhibited by the Kirov Ballet on its American tour in 1967, the Bolshoi, with its more athletic and less aesthetic performance characteristics, remained the money-making Soviet ballet company in the West. The Kirov tour resulted in a huge loss for Hurok's office—approximately $200,000. He hoped for a better return on that company in any future tours of North America. His philosophy amounted to the feeling that he made it on the one ballet company, so he could lose it on the other. He was secure because the quality was of paramount concern to him. Within several weeks during the same season, the Moscow Art Theatre was due to arrive and perform at New York's City Center of Music and Drama for three weeks. Sol Hurok and I were reviewing a projection of local costs for the run in New York City when he strongly rebelled at the charges for one item on the list. He said, "The god damn Russians, no, no, I won't do it." I realized he must have been venting his frustrations at his enormous financial losses from the preceding Kirov tour and was now focusing his hostility on this one item, whatever it was. Much to my amusement and surprise, it was the cost for a dog to appear in *The Cherry Orchard* for twelve performances. The dog was to be paid $65 for each of his appearances, while his handler also received $450 per week. The description of the dog that was supposed to appear in the first and last act of the Chekhov drama was that it be a small white poodle. Mr. Hurok said, "Butch will do it. Bring him to the theater this afternoon."

The reality was that Mr. Hurok may have known very much about his ballerinas, but he had absolutely no knowledge of dogs. Butch happened to be my own pet, a very black, medium-sized spaniel of unknown and mixed origin, hailing originally from California's San Fernando Valley. After explaining this to him, I realized that any excuse for not involving Butch was falling on deaf ears. He said, "You'll bring him to the theater this afternoon anyway." The cast was comprised of actors initially chosen for their roles by none other than Stanislavsky himself, the youngest members being approximately in their seventies. I dutifully brought Butch to the theater, and although the company was shocked at the departure from casting requirements, they began to play with him, since they all seemed to have a fondness for dogs. This all took place onstage prior to rehearsal, and they found that Butch had comfortably sniffed all of the props and didn't relieve himself anywhere on the set. It was an unusual display of good manners on his part, for once, and he therefore passed his audition. Not knowing that Hurok had substituted Butch for the "real thing," they readily agreed to Butch's getting the role, provided that Hurok himself had no objection to the liberty being taken with the casting instructions. On opening night in New York City, Butch had been lovingly groomed and awaited his entrance, when he would be led in on a leash by the "Nurse," along with the rest of the cast. Their entrance depicted a family, newly arrived from the city, entering the magnificent parlor of their country estate. What had not been included, however, during rehearsals were the sound effects provided for the actual performance. These included the sounds of barking dogs, live sound effects provided by stage personnel rattling actual horse restraints festooned with bells, the recorded noises of horses, and so on. Additionally, an audience of thousands applauding the entrance of the large cast failed to have any sort of tranquilizing effect on Butch, who began to pant. At that point, I really wondered why I had allowed myself to become a willing participant in helping to assuage Mr. Hurok's disappointment at his financial losses from the Kirov Ballet tour.

The final scene of *The Cherry Orchard,* of course, is the one where the family, having lost its fortune, must abandon the estate. In sharp contrast to the upbeat, happy occasion depicted by the Act 1 entrance, the stage set is lit in blue, and the butler is left seated alone at the fireplace, as the nurse and the family dog become the last to leave. In order for Butch to cross over from one side of the stage to the other, I would direct him to "stay" at his entry side of the stage, which disengaged him from me. I then would run behind the stage set to the other side of the stage as Butch made his way across the stage. Butch would immediately miss me, though, and, midstage, would look up and around and over his shoulder, checking to see where I was. This had a profound effect on the audience because it looked as if the dog was taking his last fond look at the fabled country estate to absorb it all before he, too, had to depart this once happy scene forever. The applause that this moment drew from the audience was dramatic in itself. I have never submitted this achievement of yet another "Hurok first" to *Ripley's Believe It or Not*; however, Butch was the only American actor, as well the only as non-human, ever to be awarded the Stanislavsky Medal, as a charming and endearing acknowledgment of his thespian talents. He also distinguished himself as the only American-born individual ever to appear with that original Stanislavsky cast of actors. Unfortunately for Butch, he never was able to get the proper amount of press his newfound stardom might ordinarily have commanded. The major publicity surrounding his appearance in *The Cherry Orchard* was overshadowed by a tragic airplane crash on the day in which he would have made headlines (or at least a photo and caption in a centerfold) in every major newspaper in New York City. Photos taken of him in front of the City Center of Music and Drama are most probably lying dormant in the photo files of the New York dailies.

Sol Hurok and movie star Shirley MacLaine enjoyed a fun friendship, and Shirley would telephone Papa Hurok in New York City often. Whenever they were in Hollywood at the same time they got together. I recall being with them when we all attended a ballet performance together at the Hollywood Bowl. Shirley adored the ballet, and Mr. Hurok adored not only being seen by his audiences during intermissions, but on this occasion being seen with movie celebrity Shirley MacLaine as well. Once the last intermission of the evening was over, together with Hurok's intermission stroll with MacLaine — which constituted his own show — we once again seated ourselves in one of the front boxes. Just as the house lights went down before the curtain rose on the final act, Hurok rose up from his seat and said to us, "Let's go to Chasen's now before the traffic holds us up." Surprised, Shirley remained seated. She reached for his arm and pulled him down to his seat saying, "Sol, you took me here to see this show, and I want to see the whole damn thing." Hurok meekly acquiesced and stayed for the entire performance.

ANOTHER TIME IN LOS ANGELES, MGM MOVIE STAR GREER GARSON hosted an intimate afternoon tea party in the garden at her home in Bel Air for a few select guests from the Bolshoi Ballet, which was then performing in Los Angeles. The guest list included Maya Plisetskaya, Vladimir Vasiliev and his wife, Ekaterina Maximova, Sol Hurok, Shirley MacLaine, Simon Semenov, and myself. In my mind, not knowing her personally, I envisioned Greer Garson in her role as filmdom's Mrs. Miniver. Upon arrival at the magnificent English-style brick mansion she called home, we were greeted by our hostess, who actually still seemed to be the very incarnation of Mrs. Miniver, as she wore a wide-brimmed straw hat and carried a garden basket over her arm, as in the movie of that name. She had just finished placing flowers on the red-and-white checked cloths covering the tables that encircled the swimming pool.

We were welcomed into the house, and, naturally, the Russian dancers, particularly, wanted a good look around. Ms. Garson graciously escorted them throughout the mansion. Everyone finally gathered in the garden around the pool, enjoying the good weather that day, and we were made to feel exceptionally comfortable and relaxed. Having been invited to do so, we brought bathing suits with us, and the party became anything but formal. Shirley, Vasiliev, Semenov, and I were frolicking in the pool, joking about moviemaking, and had settled into the shallow end. Shirley was telling us about her experiences in France preparing for her role as Irma La Douce. Sol Hurok, more or less maintaining his poise, was standing poolside and eavesdropping on the conversation in the pool. As she delved deeper into her story about the requirements for the role of Irma, Shirley told us that in order to best understand the actual environment of a French brothel she had been advised to spend four days in one in order to see how business was conducted. She said that the girls in the "house" had been very nice and genuinely cooperative. So much so that they offered Shirley the privilege of peeking through keyholes as they went about their trade. Some of them were so proud of their work that they would tell her the number of minutes it would take them to service a client. They dared her to take a watch and time them, if she didn't believe their claims. Hurok kept edging closer and closer to our group in the pool, yet maintaining a distance. Shirley was getting more and more enthusiastic in her storytelling and, finding words not sufficient to illustrate all she had to say, ever the performer, began to pantomime some suggestive, seductive twists to illustrate the more lurid aspects involved. She then concluded by saying that perhaps God had not positioned her "privates" in the right place. At that point, it was more than Sol Hurok could bear, and, leaning over the pool, said, "Children, children! It's enough! Stop!" The contrast between the very proper "Mrs. Miniver" environment offered by Greer Garson and the realities provided by Shirley MacLaine's Irma made for a well-rounded, if titillating, afternoon tea.

Sol Hurok took a suite at the Beverly Hills Hotel whenever he visited Los Angeles. Hurok, the great impresario of ballet, and Stravinsky, the great composer for the ballet, knew one another quite well. Stravinsky resided in nearby West Hollywood, and *Life* magazine, knowing that Hurok would be staying on the West Coast for several days at one point during the sixties, wanted to do an article with accompanying photographs on these two Russian giants in America. Hurok suggested that the interview and photograph session take place at his hotel suite. Stravinsky thought it would be good to have the session take place at his residence. Much to the detriment of *Life* and its readership, no matter how anyone attempted to persuade either of the individuals to give in to the other, unfortunately the dual interview never took place.

I never could understand why Sol Hurok and Igor Stravinsky vied for some sort of one- upmanship, but that was their relationship. Only a year or so after the *Life* magazine fiasco, I was with Sol Hurok one evening in New York City when Stravinsky was hospitalized with thrombosis, which threatened possible amputation of a leg that very night. Hurok was so disturbed when I told him the news that he asked me to remain with him following a performance at the Metropolitan Opera House. We walked to the Plaza Hotel and dined on sandwiches there, and then I walked him to his Park Avenue apartment at 69th Street. The main theme throughout that entire evening was Hurok's compassion. He worried at the prospect of Stravinsky's possible loss of a limb. Stravinsky did not lose his leg, but, seriously ill, the composing genius died sometime later in New York Hospital.

Stravinsky was kept on life-support systems in the hospital for a number of weeks prior to his passing. Lillian Libman, Stravinsky's friend and sometime publicist, as well as a publicist for Hurok Attractions on occasion, told me of the frenzied need to revise, update, and copyright new editions of Stravinsky's creative output before what his associates and family knew was his imminent death. This was necessary since many of his works' copyrights would soon run out, and the royalties paid to his estate would also expire.

Stravinsky's funeral service was held at Campbell's Funeral Home on Madison Avenue in New York City. A long line of limousines, private cars, and taxicabs dropped off the invited mourners privileged to attend the Russian Orthodox religious service honoring Stravinsky in death. Hurok's chauffeur, Pernett Morgan, drove him to Campbell's in his limousine. There were four of us sitting in the limo with Hurok and Morgan while we waited for the cab in front of us to discharge its passenger. For some reason the taxi and its passenger were taking a very long time. Hurok, getting impatient with the long wait, said to Morgan, "Blow your horn. Blow your horn." Morgan turned around and politely said, "Oh, no, Mr. Hurok. One doesn't blow a horn at a funeral." Finally, the taxi passenger in front of us exited his cab and, shutting the taxi door in a grand gesture with his arm, grandly strolled into Campbell's. It was Leopold Stokowski who had been causing our delay. The service was being documented in its entirety by television cameras throughout, and, ever the showman, Stokowski seemingly had waited until a camera was in position for his exit from the cab and grand entrance into the funeral parlor. Noting a similar opportunity, and not wishing to be upstaged, Hurok suddenly improvised the choreography for his own emergence from the limousine with his entourage. He directed, "I will go first, George, you will go, next Martin, then Max, then Simon" (Hurok's stepson George Perper; Martin Feinstein, Hurok's publicity head; myself; and Simon Semenov). The service was very moving, indeed, and the sadness genuine, but I will forever remain puzzled why people behave as they do in life. Stravinsky's final resting place is in Venice, where notable colleagues such as Diaghilev and other artists are also interred. In death they were reunited. Although I was not privy to the moment when it was said, I understand that Stravinsky's wife, Vera, when asked why her husband was buried so far away in Italy, responded, "Where else? New Jersey?"

MY HIGHLY VARIED EXPERIENCES TOOK ME FROM BALLET TO THEATER TO the folk dance companies of Russia, Ukraine, and Mexico. The fabled Moiseyev Folk Dance Company, of which Igor Moiseyev was founder and choreographer, had a very deep impact on audiences and dance critics alike. A performance by the Moiseyev company was thrilling. There was rarely any problem encountered when touring with this very smooth operation. Although a strict disciplinarian himself when dealing with the dancers in his troupe, Moiseyev, who always spent his leisure time playing chess, was so reluctant to interrupt his backstage chess games that he was often remiss in taking the requisite curtain-call bows. However, we wanted to make his name and identity known to the public, in the same way that George Balanchine was known as the creative force and "star" of the New York City Ballet. So we did manage to convince Moiseyev to take his bows and give interviews during his first tours of the U.S., which brought acknowledgment by the media.

Years later, as the Soviet empire crumbled and Boris Yeltsin rode into Moscow on an armored tank, the Moiseyev company was literally en route to America on an airplane for yet another tour. I happened to be in Boston, where the company was appearing at the time, and attended a performance that was pretty much the traditional program with new and younger dancers performing the same traditional roles. I went backstage after the performance, only to discover that Igor had already returned to his hotel. His daughter recognized me immediately and said, "Momma is in Paris and Poppa just left for the hotel. Come with me, and we'll go to the hotel to surprise him." Much to my own surprise, a not very young woman answered the door to Moiseyev's hotel suite. Moiseyev and his wife enjoyed something of a "modern arrangement," even while on tour, and it was one of two former dancers in the company who had been Moiseyev's mistresses from way back who had answered the door. The rather elderly woman had recognized me immediately, although I didn't know her name. When I got over my own shock and settled down in the company of Igor Moiseyev, his girlfriend, and his daughter, we enjoyed reminiscing about our travels together. I broached the subject of the new change in his country's political system. Moiseyev commented that it all had happened while he was in an airplane, and he had no idea of what it was to which he would be returning. I noted to him that under the Soviet communist government his company was a highly useful propaganda tool throughout the world. It certainly justified the Soviets' financial support of his productions, the company's performances at home, his school of folk dance in Moscow, and the relatively high standard of living he himself enjoyed. I asked whether he thought Yeltsin's new government would be interested in supporting such creative enterprises any longer.

To Moiseyev's creative credit, they are truly archival. In America, once a show has been seen, despite the occasional revival with changes in choreography and direction, its destiny, fortunately or otherwise, is to be shut down, be it *A Chorus Line, My Fair Lady,* or whatever. Moiseyev looked at me blankly and said, "You know, I never thought about that." In reminiscing that evening, we spoke of the troupe's trip to America back in the sixties, following the assassination of John F. Kennedy. The one thing they felt they had to do at that time was to go to the Kennedy grave in Arlington, Virginia, to pay their respects. Although the gravesite was not yet the completed monument we know today, nor even open to the general public, Moiseyev, the company, and the members of his family traveling with them were granted permission to visit, escorted by two U.S. marines.

COMPETING WITH MOISEYEV IN THE SOVIET ARTISTIC HIERARCHY, IN A way, was the Virsky Ukrainian Dance Company from Kiev. Owing to the success of Moiseyev, Hurok felt it was time to introduce the folk dance troupe representing Ukraine. A government-sponsored school, together with a museum exhibiting the priceless, hand-embroidered folkloric costumes, musical instruments, and other related artifacts, was devoted to this art in Kiev. Choreographically a more conservative representation of folk dance than that offered by the Moiseyev company, the Virsky troupe was nevertheless very well received on its first North American tour and was acknowledged to be an attraction of the highest level. I traveled with the Virsky company as its company manager during its initial visit to Canada and the U.S. The tour was designed to fly from city to city, except that the leg from Calgary to Saskatoon would be taken by bus. The morning after the performance in Calgary, while checking the company out of its hotel there, I was approached at the desk in the lobby by the Royal Canadian Mounted Police. They asked if I was Mr. Gershunoff, and one of them said, "I have bad news for you. I understand that as soon as you load up the bus, you are heading for Saskatoon. You will pass your scenery and costumes truck on the way there. It was on fire and completely burned down."

That truck had left the previous night after being loaded with the company's properties following their performance in Calgary. The police were unable to establish what had caused the fire. Sabotage was a very real possibility, in the minds of the Canadian police. That area of Canada was home to a very large segment of émigré Ukrainians who might best be described as rabidly anti-Soviet. The police said that they would continue to be in touch and that the truck would be placed under armed guard until lab results and other evidence could determine the actual cause of the destruction. They told us that we could take nothing from the truck, although there was literally nothing left to take and we would see that for ourselves as we passed it on the highway. Regardless, the company had to be boarded on the bus, and we left for Saskatoon. As the police had described, there really was nothing to be salvaged from the forty-five-foot trailer truck when we finally caught up with it. What remained of the copper tympani was melting, dripping copper, as the heat from the fire was still strong enough to produce molten metal many hours later. Upon viewing this disaster, the women of the company all began crying, and the forty-five American musicians traveling with the company seemed bewildered. We still had nine weeks of touring ahead of us. Following Saskatoon we were to continue on to Vancouver, Seattle, San Francisco, Los Angeles, Chicago, and beyond. While still on one of the buses, the Ukrainian conductor of the folkloric orchestra brought to our attention the fact that he had taken the orchestra's scores with him, and they were not on the destroyed truck. Amazingly, this was a positive "ray of light" since the music could not be bought in stores anywhere. With the exception of two unique accordions that were not available in North America, these scores were the troupe's only physical properties that could not be duplicated. The traveling American musicians, not only feeling the emotional impact from viewing the smoldering remains of the show, but realizing that there were nine weeks of potential canceled employment owing to the "act of God" cancellation clause in their contracts, immediately offered to copy by hand their individual parts from the salvaged musical score. When one musician would complete his copying, he would pass the score on to another.

To build on this expression of goodwill and cooperation, Virsky, Semenov (Hurok's dance coordinator and general factotum), Jack Kopera and Stephanie Cherutan (American wardrobe supervisors), and I had a very serious meeting to determine how much we could salvage of the remainder of the tour. We decided that with hard work it would be possible. With all that in mind, a most important problem had yet to be resolved. I had yet to break the news to Sol Hurok, who was in Los Angeles promoting the imminent appearance of the Virsky Ukrainian Folk Dance Company there. I made the necessary telephone call with trepidation that the news might give him a heart attack, as he was not a youngster at that time. In carefully choosing my words, I prefaced it all by saying, "Mr. Hurok, I have bad news to report. However, no one was hurt and everyone is in good spirits." He then said, "What happened?" I said "There was a terrible fire in the truck en route to Saskatoon and everything burned down." At that point, Hurok asked, "Is there anything left?" I replied "Nothing." There was dead silence on the other end of the telephone. Some moments passed as I kept saying, "Hello … hello … hello." Finally, Hurok responded in a quiet, yet confused tone, "I don't understand. If everything burned down and there's nothing left, why is everyone in good spirits?" With that reply I felt he was over the initial shock.

I then told him that we had already had a constructive meeting at which we determined that the show could be restored if given one dead week without performances in Vancouver, where we could work up to twenty hours a day. Girls' blouses and skirts would be purchased and, to create the illusion of the traditional embroidery, would be hand-painted by the women dancers themselves. The male costumes, while not perhaps the most accurate replications, could be achieved through the use of ski pants and tee shirts of varying colors. Caps approximating Ukrainian headgear could also be easily found. Much of what was needed was to be located in the local J. C. Penney and other distinguished emporiums, such as Woolworth's. However, we would have to send two people back to Kiev on a round trip with an immediate return to replace the two special accordions and some additional specialty paraphernalia that they could bring back with them. Emergency visas would have to be applied for and serviced. After describing all of this to Mr. Hurok, I concluded, "If an American company was stranded in the USSR, we would not be happy to be sent right back. I think the Ukrainians really would like to be able to complete the tour as originally scheduled." Hurok said, "You're the captain. If you feel you can do this, and you and everyone involved are willing, then I will back it."

The representatives of every department met in my hotel suite in Vancouver each night at midnight for the week. All reported what they had accomplished that day and what yet remained to be completed. We reviewed all of this daily, covering each performance number of the program. The two company members who had traveled to Kiev back brought the accordions by the end of that week; the American musicians copied all of their parts; and, though feeling as if we were skating on thin ice, we had the first rehearsal onstage and in the orchestra pit. When the sounds of the overture to the performance rose from the orchestra pit, while in our minds we still had the very fresh image of the burnt truck, we all felt that we had accomplished a minor miracle in resurrecting the show. That moment's emotional quality is difficult to describe. There was a mixture of tears, laughter, joy, and pride as we realized we had done it! The remainder of the tour was now going to be completed. In actuality, the attendant publicity surrounding the news of the fire and the restoration of the show generated additional interest with audiences throughout the balance of that tour. It perhaps turned a negative into a positive.

It was eventually determined, after the truck had been placed under guard for three weeks, that no sabotage had been responsible for the destroyed vehicle and its contents. The culprit had been burnt-out bearings transmitting heat through the axle of the trailer that started the conflagration. The fire erupted in spite of the fact that the temperature that night in Saskatoon had been thirty degrees below freezing.

Chapter Seven

THE PHILADELPHIA ORCHESTRA CONSISTENTLY ENGAGED SOVIET ARTISTS represented by Sol Hurok. Once, when I toured with pianist Emil Gilels, he and I needed to go to Philadelphia, where he was to record a Chopin piano concerto with the orchestra, conducted by Eugene Ormandy. Rather than fly the short distance from New York City to Philadelphia, making the trip via the Pennsylvania Railroad was more advisable. While waiting at New York City's Penn Station, we heard the announcement that our express train to Philadelphia would be departing in ten minutes from track number 11. Much to my surprise, Emil asked whether there was any other train going to Philadelphia and, if so, when. I found that there was a local, which would be leaving from track number 18 twenty minutes later and would take forty minutes longer. In a very relaxed manner, Emil said, "We're in no rush, let's take the local. The recording is to take place tomorrow morning." I said, "Fine." We took the local, arrived in Philadelphia, and checked into the Bellevue Stratford Hotel on Broad Street.

For acoustical reasons, the Philadelphia Orchestra's recordings were not made at their home, the Academy of Music, but rather in the main ballroom on the mezzanine of the Broad Street Hotel in North Philadelphia. The following morning, after it had started, the recording session had to be stopped because of a knocking noise coming from the heating system. A forty-five-minute intermission had to be called for the heating system to be turned off and allowed to cool down. The recording executives were none too happy, since this increased the cost for the sessions. However, they ordered coffee or other refreshments for everyone and proceeded to start once again after the intermission. Temporary lights had been strung across the ceiling of the ballroom so that the orchestral musicians could to read their music. Unfortunately, one of those lights came crashing down, without causing any harm to anyone, but glass was scattered everywhere. Another break in the session was called so that the hotel porters could clear away the glass. I was in the control room with the recording engineers while Gilels remained seated at the piano keeping his fingers warm by playing whatever came into his head. He beckoned to me to come out of the booth and to come sit with him on his piano bench. Moving over to accommodate me, but still just noodling away at the piano, he leaned over to me and said, "Today will be a catastrophe. But, I have uncovered the solution. I know our enemy. Do you see the orchestra trunks lined up against the wall? Don't tell anybody, but if you could ask one of the porters to remove trunk number 92 from this room, we'll have a good recording." I concluded that Gilel's brain had sorted out a combination of numbers that totaled the number 11, as with the train on track number 11 the previous day. I asked him about it, and he said that, indeed, he did have a thing about that number which he traced back to an incident during World War II. The trunk was removed, and the recording session actually went quite well thereafter, with conductor Eugene Ormandy showing unusual patience throughout the difficulties surrounding that day.

During this same tour, Emil Gilels performed at Clowes Hall in Indianapolis and was invited to the campus of the University of Indiana at Bloomington, where he was escorted around the university's music department. In seeing the many practice rooms available to students, he was shocked to find that there were about 1,500 piano students enrolled at that school. He simply couldn't imagine the eventual professional involvement of so many music students. He asked, "What are you going to do with all of these people? What are they going to do with their lives?" Traveling with him was a problem in hotels of modern construction where the windows were sealed and no outside air could get into a room. Air-conditioning ducts had to be taped with a plastic sheet to seal them, or Emil was not happy. At performances, no visual intrusions, including stagehands, were allowed on the stage, to ensure that there would be no visible distraction. He was highly competitive in his artistry and felt that his major competition was none other than Sviatislav Richter. One time, while in Rome, I attended a recital given by Gilels in the Italian capital. Visiting with him after the concert, I found him to be in an unusually grumpy mood. I couldn't really decipher with whom he was angrier, the local presenter or Gosconcert. Gosconcert had booked him to appear in Rome on the same night as his major competitor, Richter. Richter's recital was broadcast on Italian radio, as well, to add insult to Gilels's injury. A very conservative man, he usually dressed in a dark suit. Members of the Hurok staff attempted to loosen him up, at least in his choice of garments. We took him shopping at Saks Fifth Avenue in New York City and suggested that he try on a sports jacket in a medium-brown shade. He became very animated, admiring himself in the mirror, and we ended up purchasing a whole array of more casually tailored clothing in autumnal colors, rather than the forbidding black or navy blue he normally favored.

One of the concerts scheduled for him in the New York City area was at the C. W. Post College on Long Island. This facility was a multipurpose building with one-half devoted to a theater/concert hall and the other to a gymnasium. At the time Gilels's concert was scheduled there, the building had not been completed. A series of dressing rooms were yet to be installed between the two facilities. The day after that concert, Mr. Hurok was unhappy to find that his artist was inconvenienced the previous night, the reason being that during the intermission Gilels felt that it was improper for the soloist to relieve himself in the same facility as the audience. Hurok was highly upset about the situation, not only on behalf of Gilels, but also for other artists who were scheduled to appear in the same hall a number of weeks later. He called the local presenter, Robert Bernstein, and told him that he was canceling the next pianist three weeks hence, who happened to be Artur Rubinstein. Bob Bernstein panicked. He had a sold-out audience at very high ticket prices for his Rubinstein concert. Bob felt he had a solution, however. The women's committee for the local concerts would set up a temporary dressing room backstage, and he could rent a Porta Potti. Hurok didn't know what a Porta Potti was, but it was explained that it was similar to the restrooms on airplanes. At that point in my life and career, it was my mission to go all the way out on Long Island to inspect and approve the improvised dressing room and toilet facility. If I did not approve, the concert was to be canceled. As I jokingly say, this was the most important assignment of my career. I found, surrounded by antique screening, a lovely, improvised parlor created by the women's committee with a wicker couch and chairs, a potted palm, antique pitcher and wash basin, hand towels, and the "Holy Grail," the Porta Potti itself. I gave it all a "green light." Artur Rubinstein played that engagement with great success. However, Bob Bernstein was decidedly annoyed because no one had used the $600 Porta Potti rental. So, before leaving the hall that night he said he was going to get his money's worth and, opening the door to the rental unit, went in and proceeded to relieve himself. Many years later, after a particularly heavy snowstorm, the roof of that facility collapsed from the weight of the snow, and the entire building had to be rebuilt.

ONE OF MY MORE PLEASURABLE DUTIES AT HUROK CONCERTS WAS OBTAINING engagements for young Soviet artists and helping them to become acclimated to the differences in our societies. One such youngster, whom I also accompanied on his debut tour of the United States, was the twenty-three-year-old violin virtuoso Viktor Tretyakov. Included in his first tour of the U.S. was an appearance with the Philadelphia Orchestra with music director Eugene Ormandy, a former violinist himself, conducting. Rehearsals went very well. The next evening, arriving at the Academy of Music for the actual concert, Eugene Ormandy beckoned me into his dressing room. As he started to speak, his wife interrupted saying, "Eugene, don't! Eugene, don't!" But he said, "Max, I have a present for your artist." Again, I heard, "Eugene!" The present was handed to me, and it was a spray can of underarm deodorant. Ormandy declared, "All of the Russians play very well, but they smell." Actually, I thought this gesture to be very cruel on Ormandy's part. I knew that Tretyakov was meticulously clean, showering three or four times a day and changing his shirt at least twice a day. I thought that the most discreet thing to do was not to discuss it further with Ormandy and not to give it to Viktor.

I began to conclude that Eugene Ormandy was not a very nice person. This impression of the maestro was further reinforced by another incident. David Oistrakh, Eugene Ormandy, and I were seated in the empty Academy of Music, with a young Zubin Mehta seated in the row behind us, attending a rehearsal of the Moscow Chamber Orchestra. The orchestra was to appear that evening with David's son, Igor, as soloist, and I was interpreting for the parties. Ormandy questioned David wondering why Sol Hurok didn't book his major artists with Ormandy's Philadelphia Orchestra. That question made no sense to me because so many on Hurok's roster of Soviet artists did, in fact, appear with the orchestra. The thought occurred to me that Ormandy was trying to influence someone of David's stature to encourage Gosconcert to direct more Soviet artists to Columbia Artists Management, Inc., (CAMI) rather than Hurok Concerts, as CAMI was Ormandy's longtime representative. Ormandy further said that he felt Hurok preferred the Soviet artists to appear in recitals, where he would most benefit from the total box-office receipts, rather than from the fees obtainable through orchestral engagements. At that point, I had to step into the conversation, not as an interpreter but in order to confront Ormandy with the reality that he was to have had Rostropovich appear with the Philadelphia Orchestra the preceding season, but the cellist had become very ill in Austria and the engagement to perform Strauss's *Don Quixote* in Philadelphia was necessarily canceled. I told Ormandy that Mr. Hurok had asked me to go to Rostropovich's hotel in New York City, where Slava wished to write a letter to Ormandy expressing his regret at the cancellation and his hope that Ormandy would invite him at another time. Therefore, I was puzzled by the question he had addressed to David regarding Mr. Hurok.

I got up, left the auditorium, went backstage to Ormandy's office, and asked his secretary, Mary, "Do you remember receiving a letter from Rostropovich addressed to the maestro?"

Mary went to a filing cabinet, took out a sheet of paper, and, handing it to me, asked, "Is this the letter?"

I said, "Yes, may I take it to the Maestro?"

She said, "Yes, and if he says he never saw it, he's a liar."

I did bring it to Ormandy and gave it to him in the presence of Oistrakh. He looked at it thoughtfully and then commented, "Mr. Hurok is most fortunate to have someone in his organization such as yourself."

I FIRST MET RUSSIAN CONDUCTOR YURI TEMIRKHANOV, THEN A CONDUCTOR with the Leningrad Philharmonic, while I was in the employ of Hurok Concerts and we were presenting that orchestra on tour in the U.S. At the time I joined Columbia Artists Management in 1972, Gosconcert, the Soviet concert agency, began to shift artists from the Hurok agency to CAMI, owing to the sale of Hurok Concerts, Inc., first to a holding company and then to General Electric. Sol Hurok had remained on solely as paid president. So, Yuri Temirkhanov was on the roster of CAMI under Ronald Wilford's division there. His first engagements in the United States were to include appearances with the Cincinnati Symphony Orchestra and the Philadelphia Orchestra. Apparently there were problems in Cincinnati with rehearsals that were held with an interpreter. The interpreter was an academician in the Russian language but not familiar with musical jargon. Yuri felt that he was wasting rehearsal time explaining musical concepts to the interpreter, when he should have been using that time to work with the musicians. He spoke with Ronald Wilford, explaining that he wanted me to join him in Cincinnati and accompany him to Philadelphia, where he would be more comfortable with a fellow musician at rehearsals. He said, "If I stop the orchestra, Max will know right then and there why it was I stopped. We can work in unison, like one person." At rehearsal in Philadelphia, I sat right beneath Yuri for the three days of rehearsal. Yuri was correct; no time was wasted as I conveyed his wishes to the orchestra. Actually it became a joyous experience for all of us, as almost half of the musicians in the orchestra had been schoolmates of mine at the Curtis Institute of Music. Yuri Temirkhanov was very, very well received both by the local critics and the musicians in Philadelphia. He was so well liked, as a matter of fact, that Eugene Ormandy, music director of the Philadelphia Orchestra, did him the unimaginable honor of allowing Yuri the use of his own dressing room, which was off-limits to any other guest conductor. All was going well for the evening concerts, with a matinee on Friday yet to come. It came as news to Yuri and me that the expected mode of dress for the conductors of matinees was striped trousers and morning coat. Yuri showed me what he thought he might be wearing, which was a brown blazer and tan slacks. In discussions of the situation with the orchestra's management, they emphatically said that the brown/tan ensemble would be out of the question. While at Hurok Concerts, I could proceed to act independently using my own judgment, but with CAMI being more rigorously structured, I felt it best to call New York and speak directly with Ronald Wilford before solving the problem. In so doing, all I heard from Ronald was "If you think I'm going to spoil those damn Russians like Hurok did, forget it. Let him solve his own problem."

I said, "Ronald, he only gets $160 and hotel. If you want to capture the Soviet market away from the Hurok office, why are you going to treat the Soviet artists in this manner? Since the Soviet ministry of culture gets the majority of their artists' fees, without the imposition of any U.S. taxes, the artists have little or no motivation other than being allowed to come out to the West for short visits."

Ronald offered no authorization to spend any funds, nor any solution to the quandary. Having gone to school in Philadelphia and knowing the Center City area quite well, I took Yuri and we walked the streets looking at wedding tuxedo rental establishments. Finally we found one that could provide Yuri with proper garments for his Friday afternoon concert, and a proper fit, at a rental cost of fifteen dollars. After Temirkhanov's success had been established, and he was under the management of an English firm well connected with Gosconcert, he was invited to conduct at the Boston Symphony Orchestra's Tanglewood Festival in Massachusetts. Ronald Wilford maintains a summer home nearby, since he has long been the manager of the Boston Symphony's longtime music director, Seiji Ozawa, as well as any number of the famous guest artists appearing there annually. I was up at Tanglewood for the event, and Yuri said, "Guess what? Ronald Wilford has invited me to his home here for lunch." I asked, "Are you going to go?" Yuri replied that he had accepted the invitation after making it very clear to Ronald that if they were to lunch for the purpose of pleasant conversation that would be fine. However, if it were for the ultimate purpose of asking Yuri to sign on exclusively with CAMI, the answer would be no. The reason for Yuri's negative reaction was the fifteen-dollar rental cost he had had to pay in Philadelphia for the morning coat and striped trousers during his debut season in America a number of years earlier.

Ironically, Yuri Temirkhanov at the time of this writing is the music director of the Baltimore Symphony Orchestra. While Yuri and I were in Philadelphia for those debut performances, on our first evening in that city, since there was nothing of any interest to do locally, we took a train to Baltimore. There we went to hear the Baltimore Symphony Orchestra. So it was that the first orchestra Yuri heard as a member of an audience in the U.S. was the Baltimore Symphony. I also took Yuri to my alma mater, the Curtis Institute, a few blocks directly down the street from Philadelphia's Academy of Music, then the home of the Philadelphia Orchestra. I showed Yuri where Fritz Reiner had taught, where I had received my private academic tutoring, where I had roomed as a student and where Leonard Bernstein had done the same, and regaled him with local stories of Philadelphia.

Fortunately for its students, Yuri has been invited to conduct the Curtis Institute's Symphony Orchestra many times since.

Still later, when I had opened my own offices in New York City, Yuri would always call whenever he came into town, and we would get together socially. One year, I knew that he would be arriving shortly, as he was scheduled to conduct the Philadelphia Orchestra the following week. Surprisingly, I received a call from him a week earlier than his schedule called for. He was very excited and asked me to come over right away. I explained that I still had much work to do that day and that I would see him around 6 p.m.

He said, "I wanted to tell you that I'm here a week earlier because I will be conducting the New York Philharmonic this week."

Upon hearing this, I said, "Yuri, that is not good news. I will be right over and I will explain."

Taking a cab, I was at Yuri's borrowed digs on Manhattan's West Side within fifteen minutes. Once I got there, Yuri explained that he would be substituting for Gennady Rozhdestvensky, who had canceled his engagement. I had already heard the reasons for that cancellation, which, in fact, included not only the New York Philharmonic but all of Rozhdestvensky's engagements in the West, which had been booked by the Soviet concert agency, Gosconcert. Rozhdestvensky had openly rebelled against the system of having Gosconcert receive 90 percent of his Western fees. He felt he could no longer tolerate this system and its inefficient, bureaucratic posturing. He would simply stay home. To prove his point and expose the musical ignorance of his Soviet handlers, he had deliberately submitted to Gosconcert a program comprised of nonexistent works, which was unthinkingly forwarded "as is" to an orchestra in Scandinavia. After receiving the "dummy" program, the orchestra called Rozhdestvensky directly, asking him if the program that Gosconcert had sent them was some sort of a joke or was he crazy. He now had proof positive of the exploitative inefficiency of Gosconcert. This scenario had already been written about in all of London's newspapers. Undoubtedly, the New York press was merely awaiting its own opportunity to print the story because it might now include Yuri as a fellow Russian unsupportive of his musical colleague's rebellious gesture.

Explaining the situation and the risk to Temirkhanov, I asked him how he could be willing, under the circumstances, to dilute the impact of his colleague by filling in for him. Yuri would appear to be a total "puppet" of one of his government's bureaucracies. At that moment in time, no one had any idea that the Soviet system would ever collapse. But, somehow, presciently, I argued that if it did, much as had happened with Germany's questionable collaborating artists after World War II, Yuri's popularity and career would be in jeopardy in most of the West. The very weak excuse given to Yuri in order for him to conduct the New York Philharmonic at the time was that Gosconcert did not wish to punish the New York musicians because of its "in-house conflict." I laughed when I heard that one. I explained to Yuri that the musicians of the New York Philharmonic were hardly children hungry for musical nurturing. They were sophisticated and rather jaded adults who didn't necessarily care which conductor the orchestra management had engaged. They knew they had to play for whoever was assigned to the podium. After a few moments' reflection, Yuri called his manager, Anthony Phillips, in London, and said that he would not be conducting the New York Philharmonic that week but would be returning the scores that had been provided to him. Anthony told Yuri that if he did not conduct in New York that week he would never speak to him again. Yuri's reply was "That would be your decision." End of conversation. Yuri turned to me, hugged me, and said, "Now I feel my face is clean." The following day I saw Yuri again and he said, "Guess what? Anthony called me from London and said that he had just spoken with Rozhdestvensky and had to convey a one-word message. The word was *spacebo* [thank you]." That week of concerts was finally taken over by an assistant conductor of the New York Philharmonic, and the opportunity of the press to elaborate on the Rozhdestvensky dilemma with Gosconcert at Temirkhanov's expense passed.

WHILE ARTISTS SUCH AS YURI TEMIRKHANOV WERE ALLOWED OUT OF their country by the Soviet government to perform in the West, their families were held hostage, as a form of security, back home in the USSR. Being allowed out at all was a form of privilege, and was considered to be "overseas duty" for the people of the Soviet Union. The "hostages" were family members or, as in the case of the then young virtuoso pianist Alexander Slobodyanik, someone else at home who could act as a human "bond" guaranteeing that the artist would return home. For Slobodyanik's first trip to the West, that human bondsman was none other than his mentor, Sviatislav Richter. At the time of his Western debut, Alexander Slobodyanik was not married and had no children, and his parents were separated so they weren't considered suitable to serve as hostages guaranteeing against possible defection. Richter volunteered in their stead so as to advance the career of his protégé.

I FREQUENTLY TRAVELED WITH DAVID OISTRAKH, HIS WIFE, TAMAR Ivanovna, and their son, Igor, since David and Igor played the Bach Double Violin Concerto with orchestras desirous of that father-and-son combination. Then, they would go their separate ways and perform individually with other orchestras. Because many Americans knew of the difficulties associated with Soviet artists traveling abroad and the risk of their possible defections, I was asked on many occasions how it was possible for the entire Oistrakh family to be traveling together in the West at the same time. But actually, it wasn't the entire Oistrakh family. Igor's wife and children remained in the USSR to ensure his return. Also, David was so enamored of his grandchildren that everyone at home knew he would never abandon them.

As in the case of ballerina Maya Plisetskaya, with all of the incentives the Western world offered, at home were her husband, famed composer Rodin Schedrin, and traveling with her and the Bolshoi Ballet Company were her uncle, the illustrious ballet master Asaf Messerer, and her two brothers, who were also dancers in the company. (Her younger brother later joined Alicia Alonso's Ballet de Cuba.) Had Maya defected at any time she would have placed not only her husband, but also her uncle and two brothers in serious jeopardy. They could have been dismissed from the company and generally deprived of a livelihood.

Violin virtuoso Leonid Kogan traveled with his wife, although their son Pavel remained at home attended to by relatives. Kogan's wife was the sister of pianist Emil Gilels. Her potential defection could have possibly reflected on Gilels under the Soviet bureaucracy's twisted standards. It was said that Leonid Kogan held a high position in the Communist Party. Kogan had seriously wooed my cousin Lily, daughter of my mother's sister Ida, to the point of a marriage proposal. Lily was a cellist who had attended the Moscow Conservatory along with such classmates as Mstislav Rostropovich and was well known among her contemporaries in Moscow's musical community. Lily became aware of Kogan's reputed position in the Party and was so repulsed at the idea of marriage to him that she rejected his proposal forthwith. Knowing how her parents had been so cruelly maltreated in jail by Soviet officialdom, she was simply disgusted. Later Kogan married Emil Gilel's sister.

Leonid Kogan knew of me long before I knew him as a result of his pursuit of Lily. When I joined the Hurok office, I had to be in Boston, where Kogan was performing a guest engagement with the Boston Symphony Orchestra. Doing my duty as a representative of Hurok Concerts, Inc., Kogan's U.S. management, I went to the concert and, afterwards, to his dressing room to introduce myself. No sooner had I walked into the room than Kogan, looking at me, said, "Max." I was literally stunned. I asked, "How do you know me?" Replying, he said, "Your photograph sits on your cousin Lily's piano at home in Moscow. I've seen it very often." Regardless of politics, we got along very well.

Along the same lines as the questions about the Oistrakhs traveling together, I was asked about the freedom Rostropovich seemed to be enjoying as he traveled with his wife, soprano Galina Vishnevskaya. Only those ignorant of the fact that two daughters of the famous pair remained at home being looked after by relatives asked such questions.

Rostropovich is a profound and very versatile musician. The entire world has acknowledged his talents on the cello. He would accompany his wife on piano for her vocal recitals, and he has been able to conduct orchestras despite a somewhat limited "stick technique." Nevertheless, he has communicated his musical instincts to the musicians of many symphony orchestras and produced exciting concerts.

Early in Rostropovich's exposure to the Western world, Sol Hurok wanted to make this artist feel welcome. In the Russian culture you can do so only by inviting your guest to your home rather than even the finest restaurant. So, Hurok invited Slava to his ten-room Park Avenue apartment for dinner. Upon learning that Slava had never sampled a soufflé, Hurok raved to him about the wonderful live-in French couple who cared for his culinary and other household needs. One specialty of a menu at Hurok's table was a soufflé as prepared by this French couple. With three more weeks of touring left, Slava and I were invited to dine at Chez Hurok the Saturday night his tour ended. Hurok felt that having me join the party would make the experience more comfortable for Slava, since he and I were closer in age. The French couple were taking a two-week vacation in France. However, they never returned and were quickly replaced by a couple from Spain. This left Hurok in a quandary. He couldn't be certain that the quality of a soufflé prepared by the new help would live up to the enthusiastic praise he had heaped upon their predecessors' creations. So, in order to avoid losing face and having an embarrassing disappointment befall him when Slava dined with him, he held an "audition" dinner. On a Tuesday, the exact menu that was to be served to Slava four days later would be duplicated. I was invited to help "audit" on Tuesday evening. The new help passed muster with flying colors. On Saturday, Hurok held secure and comfortable sway over the evening's repast. I've enjoyed a chuckle with Slava in years since over this story. Attention to detail under all circumstances was a Hurok specialty.

Also on the lighter side, although not another soufflé story, one of my more memorable exchanges with Rostropovich came when he asked me to introduce him to a somewhat notorious colleague of his, the cellist Charlotte Moorman. Charlotte had toured for me as a member of the Manhattan Concert Orchestra, a Community Concerts attraction led by conductor Harry John Brown, later music director of the Milwaukee Symphony Orchestra. Charlotte had made headlines around the world when she appeared topless in a concert "happening," the word coined for some of the events staged by the avant-garde of the sixties.

Slava had heard of the bare-breasted cellist and wanted to meet her. Coincidentally, following a recital given by Rostropovich at Carnegie Hall, I was on my way backstage to his dressing room when I heard someone calling my name from the long line of fans waiting to meet and greet the evening's star. Who should it be but Charlotte Moorman herself. I grabbed her by the hand, took her out of the long line, and said, "Come with me." We reached Slava's room before the onslaught of the autograph seekers was allowed in, and I introduced Charlotte by name. Slava politely said hello, since he only knew of her as the "bare-breasted cellist" and not by her given name. Then, in Russian, I said, "Slava, you asked me to find her, and it is she standing in front of you, the cellist who bared her breasts for all the world to see." He practically jumped with joy and immediately became most effusive, his wish having been granted, albeit by sheer accident.

Although he is known for his predictable trademark Russian bear hugs and kisses, which some may question as merely superficial or comic, Slava exhibited his real sensitivity and compassion on one occasion while on a recital tour in the U.S. Simon Semenov was escorting him as the Hurok representative and interpreter. Semenov was the father of six children, and he was an exceptionally close friend to Sol Hurok. Their friendship went back many years to the days of the Ballet Russe de Monte Carlo, when Hurok had been that company's representative in North America during the thirties. Semenov had been a leading character dancer with the Ballet Russe, among other companies. So, his dancing career over, he often traveled with the Soviet artists and troupes imported by Hurok, performing myriad tasks as a coordinator. He was particularly well liked by the Soviet dancers. He knew their art, could speak their language, and was a great deal of fun to be around at most times. Semenov's oldest son was attending university in Athens, Greece, when he was tragically killed on a motor scooter. We had to telephone Simon requesting that he leave Rostropovich in Washington, D.C., immediately, on the very day of Slava's concert there, with the excuse that Mr. Hurok wanted Semenov in New York City at once. Actually, Sol Hurok was in Moscow at that time, but we did not want to shock Simon with the news of his son's death until it could be communicated in person. Unfortunately, the task of telling him fell to me. We had telephoned Slava in Washington before even calling Simon so that Slava would know the whole story and would not feel abandoned. Slava would have to shift for himself for the remainder of that day, including his concert appearance. He would return the following day to New York City on his own. The office immediately made arrangements for Simon to travel to Athens the following night in order that he be able to handle his son's burial arrangements in Athens. Back in New York City, Slava was supposed to come to my apartment around 2:30 the next afternoon, when he, Simon, and I were to meet. It was thought that after Simon had dealt with the tragic circumstances in Athens, the best therapy for him would be to continue on to Moscow where he could join Mr. Hurok. There he could grieve with the young dancers in Moscow, who adored him and he them. This was not so easily accomplished because a Soviet entry visa for an American passport holder entering the USSR via Athens could take forever to get approved, if it got approved at all. Slava, using the influence of his position, telephoned Mikoyan, the Soviet ambassador to the U.S., in Washington, explaining the circumstances, and was able to accomplish the miraculous, whereby Simon could pick up a visa days later at the Soviet embassy in Athens. Following that telephone call, Slava turned to Simon and said, "Promise you will not refuse me a favor." Not knowing what it was, Simon agreed. Reaching into his jacket pocket, Slava, said, "When you left me yesterday in Washington, I already knew of your tragedy before you knew. I played last night's concert like I have never played before. That was for your son." He then finally pulled an envelope from the pocket. Handing the envelope to Simon, he said, "This envelope contains my fee for last night's concert. I want you to take it with you and use it to buy a headstone for your son's grave." Once again, the fee paid directly to a Soviet artist at the time approximated all of $160.

Many years later, when Slava was music director of the National Symphony Orchestra in Washington, D.C., I was with him in a small, private, denlike area beneath some stairs that he used as a private hideaway at the Kennedy Center. This followed a concert I had attended, and two or three familiar people were sitting around and enjoying some cognac and conversation. At one point, Slava asked me if I would do him a favor and write out a check he had to give someone because he couldn't write the check in proper English. Conductors have a tendency to exercise control, whether it is over the woodwind, brass, or string section, or someone writing out a check, regardless of the conductor's own capabilities in that particular area. Handing me his checkbook and a pen, Slava stood over my shoulder as I filled in the check for the amount he requested. It was for one thousand dollars. As I wrote, Slava attempted to phonetically pronounce the number "thousand," and what came out sounded like "*tao-who-zand.*" He went on to approve by saying "Verry gooed, verry gooed, Max." I turned and looked up at him with surprise, knowing he was incapable of the task himself, and that I certainly did not need his approval of my check-writing abilities. Knowing of his recent enormous financial successes in the West, I said, "Slava, if you'd rather, I can write the word 'million.'" Knowing that I knew him when, he understood my humor, and we both had a good laugh.

Chapter Eight

In 1969, Sol Hurok, the sole owner, sold Hurok Concerts, Inc., and Hurok Attractions, Inc., at a time when corporate takeovers were very popular. Hurok always told his key employees, "This will always remain the 'Tiffany's' that it is for you boys." Martin Feinstein, Hurok's head of publicity, heard that the business had been sold. Hurok denied the rumor. The very next day Martin brought the morning newspapers announcing the sale to Hurok in his office and angrily said, "And you denied this only yesterday." The reality was that, without discussing the matter with any of us "boys," he had sold his companies to Transcontinental Investing Corporation (TIC), a holding company. Unfortunately, certain older financial commitments had been outdated by inflation, such as an agreement with the Bolshoi Opera contracted five years previously. Hurok now found it personally more practical to divest himself of his corporations by converting them to cash. He could and did remain on as a paid president for the new owners and no longer had enormous personal financial risks. TIC would, in turn, quickly spin off its recent purchase to General Electric.

Several days later, during an evening with Mr. Hurok at his apartment, we discussed the sale. He related to me one of its prime requirements: owing to his age an "heir apparent" must be named. He was rather gleeful in explaining the master plan that he had structured. With all seriousness, he had conceived something consistent with an old-world Russian melodrama. Like a previous ruler of a different empire, Louis XIV, his attitude now was: "Après moi, le déluge." He believed that the enterprise he had built would not and should not survive without him. In order to have his vision truly play itself out according to his devising, he would appoint a successor who could not possibly handle either the scope of the business or the stress it would impose. He had deliberately named such a person, a former employee on whom he wished to wreak his very own form of revenge, Sheldon Gold.

Now Hurok, in high spirits, said to me with delight, "Let them all break their heads against the wall and, especially, I hope it falls on the heads of Shelly and the wife with the poison kisses." (Each time Shelly's wife Michaela—

"Mickey" — greeted him and kissed him, Hurok, unembarrassed, would wipe the kiss from his cheek). He told the buyers that Columbia Artists Management currently employed Gold and that TIC would have to woo him away from CAMI. Hurok made it clear to TIC that he would not back any individual for the position who was then in the employ of Hurok Concerts unless TIC first approached Shelly Gold at CAMI. Marketing maven that he was, he bolstered the man's image by implying that Gold would possibly be very expensive. Hurok was thoroughly aware that intimating the need to offer Gold a large salary would impress the buyers. Better still, it would no longer be coming out of his pocket. Hurok, during the course of relating his scenario, wanted to reassure me by saying, "Don't worry, Max. I will not let you down." Despite his wanting to assuage any personal trepidations I might have been feeling, I nevertheless realized that what was about to come into play was a most unhealthy situation.

I replied to Mr. Hurok that I was not concerned with his letting me down personally, but that, in fact, what he was about to do was to let us all down. It was the first indication to me that perhaps Mr. Hurok was accepting the reality of his age and wished to have it all his own way. He wanted an "out" that provided him not only a material profit but also an outlet for satisfying his anger at someone who had not only attempted to destroy him and his life's work, but had offended him perhaps as deeply as anyone was ever capable of doing.

Gold accepted TIC's offer, but CAMI elected not to release him before his contract with them expired. As a form of retribution, CAMI kept him on ice by removing all current business from his calendar but making him report to work daily until the end of their agreement. Gold would then subsequently be named president of Hurok Concerts, Inc.

What Hurok interpreted as a deeply offensive breach of ethics lurked behind his vendetta. The previous year, upon Hurok's return from a trip to the Soviet Union, I met him as usual at JFK airport with Mr. Morgan, Hurok's chauffeur. Upon returning from a trip to the USSR, he would normally arrive somewhat like a proud Santa Claus having secured a big bag of "goodies" that he could now distribute to performing arts centers and universities throughout North America. His "goodies" always included the best of the best, as well as any new artists emerging from behind the Iron Curtain. This time, however, when he got into his limousine he seemed agitated and very anxious to tell me something. It wasn't long before he started by saying, "I'll get the bastard! I'll get the bastard!" I looked at him questioningly. He relaxed momentarily and said, "After all of these years, instead of them being grateful, this was the first time I ever had to qualify myself to the Soviets." He related the entire story of how Sheldon Gold had carried out a mission to Moscow on behalf of CAMI. Then Hurok told of his own latest encounter with Gosconcert. Hurok learned that Shelly Gold had attempted to undermine his usually harmonious dealings with the Soviet concert agency.

Several years earlier, when Gold, then an employee of Hurok Concerts, Inc., was about to get married, realizing that marriage might involve financial responsibilities beyond his scope at the time, he asked Sol Hurok for a raise. However, instead of simply asking for a raise he threatened to quit and go to CAMI if an increase was not granted. Hurok took offense at Shelly's tone and at his threat and told him not to come back the following morning, saying that, as far as he was concerned, Shelly could "go to Columbia or go to hell." Shelly then successfully sought employment at Hurok's competitor, CAMI.

While the U.S.-Soviet Cultural Exchange Agreement was in effect, CAMI was making an enormous effort to build goodwill with Gosconcert and the Soviet ministry of culture. CAMI had hopes of possibly being able to start importing to the U.S. some of the artists and attractions that had proven so profitable for Hurok Concerts, Inc. Shelly Gold had gone to the USSR to open doors for CAMI, and as a former employee of Hurok Concerts, Inc., he had used inside information, however inaccurate and incomplete, to cast suspicion on and thereby sabotage Hurok's relationship with Gosconcert. He reported fee differences between what Hurok was paid for engagements by Soviet soloist artists and what he thought Hurok reported and paid to Gosconcert for the services of those artists. After Gold's visit, Hurok arrived in Moscow to confer with the Gosconcert administrators about future North American performances. But Hurok now found himself in the unusual circumstance of having to reestablish his credibility in the Soviet officials' eyes. The Gosconcert representatives accused him of questionable financial dealings that had been brought to their attention. He asked them who had told them "all of this nonsense." Their reply was "A former employee of yours." He asked them, "Was it Sheldon Gold?" They answered in the affirmative.

Unaccustomed to having his personal integrity attacked, he was literally shocked to the depths of his being. He was emotionally devastated. The majority of his whole life's effort had been devoted to furthering Russian culture and enhancing the careers of its great artists. However, Hurok was famous for never exposing his emotional reactions. Gathering his wits, Hurok, a very proud man, turned the tables and started to ask questions of the Gosconcert officers: "Did Shelly tell you anything about my losses, about which I have never cried crocodile tears to you people? I make money on some companies and am willing to risk losing money on other groups in the hopes that one day they will make money. Profits counterbalance losses, if I'm lucky. That is what 'risk' is all about. The Kirov Ballet was a total financial disaster. Shelly wouldn't know anything about our business involving group attractions. He was merely a salesman in the booking department and, on occasion, traveled with Vladimir Ashkenazy. The pennies Shelly talked about with you are not even worth our time in discussion."

When Sol Hurok died, Sheldon Gold did assume the mantle of leadership of the corporation that still bore the Hurok name, but it had been sold again. The corporation would crumble into failure as its last owners finally sought bankruptcy. As a means of rescuing the careers of artists who had been left floundering, and at Isaac Stern's suggestion, Marvin Josephson, head of ICM (International Creative Management), soon formed a management group. A new concert division was established at the large entertainment agency, and Shelly Gold now became president of the new enterprise, called ICM Artists, Ltd.

Sol Hurok would often comment that Isaac Stern should practice at home rather than meddle in arts management. But it was at Hurok's suggestion that Stern had seriously entered into a form of arts management when he led the battle to salvage Carnegie Hall. Hurok believed that an artist, rather than someone from management, should head the efforts to save this historic public auditorium. He believed a profit-making manager would be suspect. Isaac Stern was instrumental in saving Carnegie Hall, and he supervised its renovation and resurrection as a premier performance venue.

Stern's efforts contrasted sharply with Hurok's lone attempt to save the old Metropolitan Opera House on Broadway at 39th Street in New York City. In 1966, a group of prominent, concerned New York citizens, operating as the Telemann Society, had been formed to wage a last-ditch attempt at preventing the destruction of the dowager building, a gem in its own right. The committee had been rebuffed in its efforts to reach Sol Hurok by telephone. I received a telephone call at home from a representative of the group. The gentleman explained their difficulties in reaching Hurok and asked me to intercede in their behalf and connect them with Hurok. When I broached the subject, Hurok told me that he thought saving the old Met was, if anything, a long shot, but it was definitely worth a try. At that time, he believed he could provide a schedule at the old Met that would fill out a complete season with his ballet companies and other attractions. The committee then arranged a meeting between Hurok and Sir Rudolf Bing, then head of the Metropolitan Opera Association. However, the grim reality of the real estate value of the land on which the old Met stood was apparent. The construction of an office building on the leased site of the old Met would produce a substantial annual income to the Metropolitan Opera Association. If the old opera house were accorded New York City Landmark status, as proposed, the Metropolitan Opera Association would receive virtually no truly substantial income from the property.

Hurok would rent the Metropolitan Opera House annually for many weeks in the spring, at the close of each opera season, for a ballet season. This venue was an important outlet for the Hurok organization. At that time using the Radio City Music Hall for such a purpose would have been considered a vulgarity. Because saving the old Met meant financial loss for the opera association, Sir Rudolf Bing told Mr. Hurok, "If you win your fight to save the old Met, fine. But, if you lose your fight, I will see to it your office will never be allowed any rental rights at the new Lincoln Center Metropolitan Opera House." This threat constituted too much of a risk for Hurok to assume. It would have affected too many ballet companies, and the entire scope of the Hurok operation. Hurok had to accept defeat.

Being a native New Yorker myself, and seeing how the surrounding areas of Times Square and 42nd Street were transformed in the nineties, it is clear to me that the old Met, only three blocks away, could have been a crown jewel in that transformation today.

OTHER THAN THE RESCUE OF CARNEGIE HALL, ISAAC'S INVOLVEMENTS IN artists management affairs sometimes created problems for Hurok because of Isaac's preferences for specific artists. In one instance, Hurok found himself caught in a minor dilemma because Isaac strongly objected to the addition of another famous violinist to the Hurok roster of artists. Hurok felt obliged to accommodate a favor requested by pianist Artur Rubinstein, who was perhaps even more important to Hurok than Stern. The violinist was Rubinstein's fellow Pole, Henryk Szeryng. Hurok's dilemma was related to a major risk factor involved in his subscription series, both in New York and Los Angeles. Invariably David Oistrakh, Leonid Kogan, or another Soviet violinist was included on those series. Owing to fragile Soviet-American international relations, a last-minute substitute of equally stellar quality might be needed to replace an Oistrakh or a Kogan. The great violinist Nathan Milstein, whom Hurok also represented, had a deserved reputation for canceling his concert appearances and, in addition, could never be counted on to serve as a last-minute substitute. Also, he would only travel from his home in Europe via ocean liner, never by airplane. Stern, though based in the United States, might be busy performing anywhere when a substitute was needed. It would be useful for Hurok to have Szeryng available. Hurok was obliged to try to appease both Stern and Rubinstein. So, if Rubinstein was granted the favor of his request, Hurok had to grant Stern's desires with respect to focusing attention on Israeli musicians to the ultimate disadvantage of non-Israeli Jewish artists. This focus excluded Szeryng, since he was a Polish Jew. In response to Stern's coercion, and to provide a counterbalance for Szeryng, Hurok agreed to give a generous annual stipend for three years to the young Israeli violinist Pinchas Zukerman, planning to recover the costs of this stipend through young Zukerman's future bookings in the following three years. Szeryng was aware of the hostilities surrounding his acceptance to the famous Hurok roster of artists. Only after twelve years of Szeryng being on the Hurok list did Isaac Stern and Henryk Szeryng start speaking to one another.

Interestingly, in the second year of the Zukerman stipend agreement, there were very few bookings for the artist, and the stipend funds could not be recovered as originally expected. When this was discovered, following a booking meeting in his office, Hurok came to see me in my office. I was busily at work engaging orchestra musicians for an incoming ballet company. Hurok shouted, "Put the bastard in the pit! Put the bastard in the pit!"

I asked him, "Who?"

He said, "Zukerman. Let him work for the money. Put him next to your friend Guy Lumia." (Lumia was the concertmaster for the ballet orchestra.)

Under the circumstances I didn't think this was a good idea. Hurok had too deep an artistic commitment to Zukerman via Stern. He then said, "Well, put the girlfriend in the [orchestra] pit." He was referring to the flutist Eugenia Rich, who later married Zukerman.

I said, "Mr. Hurok, she is not prepared. She's familiar with the concerto repertoire, and is not at all experienced in the ballet repertoire. In any case, she insists on playing first flute. She doesn't come anywhere near Paul Dunkel or Ransom Wilson, whom we use as first flutists. They are experienced orchestral players. While she is learning at the needless extra expense of costly rehearsal time, you will have an irritated conductor. The overtime will cost you more than you think you are losing at this juncture." Hurok accepted the logic of my arguments and started venting his anger at Isaac and Vera Stern.

Stern had imposed frequent and uninvited "arts management" intrusions upon the Hurok operation. However, as president of the Carnegie Hall Corporation Stern was on a precarious footing in his dealings with the new management company, ICM Artists, Ltd. Carnegie Hall engaged many artists from ICM's roster of artists, and Stern's influence in both arenas was unquestionably weighty. He could have been vulnerable to accusations of a conflict of interest.

He could not hold any official position in a top commercial artists management firm and still be president of the nonprofit Carnegie Hall Corporation. Former president George H. W. Bush put it well when he frequently used the unforgettable phrase "It wouldn't be prudent" in reference to some course of action he did not favor. As it happened, prudence was not always in evidence, and other managers of exceptionally fine artists began complaining that there appeared to be an imbalance in the exposure of artists presented on the series run by the Carnegie Hall Corporation, slanted toward too many of the ICM artists.

Another incident that raised ethical questions involved ticket sales for a concert by pianist Vladimir Horowitz at Carnegie Hall. Hopeful ticket buyers lined up overnight before tickets went on sale for the Horowitz event. When the box office opened, however, many of the hundreds of prospective purchasers found that there were no tickets left to purchase. Naturally, there was an uproar. The box-office clerks were at a loss to explain why tickets were missing from the racks. Apparently, a block of hundreds of tickets had been arbitrarily taken from the box office. The seats were to be sold to raise funds for the American-Israeli Cultural Foundation. Vera Stern was a member of its board of directors. Blocks of tickets for the Horowitz concert had not been offered to any other nonprofit organization. *Time* magazine covered the incident and, referring to Isaac and Vera, remarked that Carnegie Hall could be considered a "Mom and Pop" operation. Vladimir Horowitz scheduled a second recital to placate his disgruntled admirers who had been deprived of hearing him in concert.

Ultimately, as Hurok had predicted, the pressure of Sheldon Gold's responsibilities took their toll on him. Shelly died of a heart attack in 1985, still a young man in his mid-fifties. I believe Shelly never knew that Hurok's cynically generous endorsement of him as successor was meant to ensure Shelly's failure. Hurok's scenario of retribution, straight from a Russian melodrama, was played out exactly as he had choreographed it, as if it all had been directed from his grave. Shelly and his supporters did not suspect that they were merely playing a role in the Machiavellian scheme of vengeance that Sol Hurok had perfectly plotted years before. Upon Shelly's death, Lee Lamont, who had served as Isaac Stern's private secretary, stepped into the role of president of ICM Artists, Ltd. Former secretaries were stepping into managerial positions, and Isaac Stern suggested that Lamont, an individual who would acquiesce to his wishes, be brought into the new firm.

PRIOR TO THE SALE OF HUROK CONCERTS, INC., AND BEFORE IT WENT into a tailspin, General Electric had fantasies of filming concerts featuring the world's greatest classical artists, to be shown on closed-circuit television and projected on movie screens in theaters throughout the country. Some great artists such as Artur Rubinstein and Andrés Segovia simply had "handshake" or oral agreements, as they are legally known, while others had written contracts for their representation by Hurok. It was very much to the advantage of both TIC and General Electric to maintain the presence of Sol Hurok as a security blanket for all of the famous artists on his roster, as well as for his highly developed, ongoing relationship with the Soviet ministry of culture. Keeping the artists happy and on the roster was an important part of any future development of the corporate entity by General Electric.

To add to a more alluring sense of "glitz," by General Electric's more commercial standards, it opted to move Hurok Concerts, Inc., from 730 Fifth Avenue at the corner of 57th Street to twentieth-floor offices in a newly completed building at 1240 Sixth Avenue on the southeast corner of 56th Street. I was assigned a corner office there on the southwest side of the building, while Sol Hurok was given a more impressive and commodious corner office facing the northwest. The new offices occupied the entire twentieth floor of the building. My commute to work had been lessened by one full block, and I now had less than two blocks to walk to work from my apartment at 145 West 55th Street, where Simon Semenov had an apartment, too. New York City Ballet star Edward Villella, composer Hugh Martin, Broadway choreographer Michael Bennett, and other show business icons had apartments in the same building.

Performances by Soviet artists were often the targets of protests, which could take place inside or outside of the theaters. Outside, artists could encounter picket lines, while inside, the protesters who had purchased tickets were planted in seats near the stage, where they could disrupt performances. At the old Metropolitan Opera House, the Virsky Ukrainian Folk Dance Company was covered with blood from raw chicken livers that were tossed at its dancers during performance. White mice were released from small containers during a recitalist's performance. Flyers were tossed from balconies on still other occasions. A fire-bomb was thrown into the orchestra pit of the Auditorium Theatre in Chicago. The protesters were well organized, and their efforts extended to every major city of the U.S. The protests were based in part on the fact that Jews were not being allowed to emigrate from the USSR. With the creation of the state of Israel, all Jews throughout the world had citizenship rights in Israel. However, Jews in the USSR were not allowed to claim these rights, as dual citizenship was not permitted under Soviet law. Since the Soviet government spent money educating its youth, it was not considered a wise investment to educate an individual who might in later years choose to leave. As a result young Soviet Jews were not being given the same educational and employment opportunities as other Soviet citizens. The word "Jew" was stamped on birth certificates and identity papers, including passports. On one of my visits to the USSR, I questioned my official interpreter as to the reasoning behind this categorizing in official documentation of Soviet citizens. The reply I received was the canned response that must have been drummed into the interpreter, as I got a very casually voiced "Oh, that is for statistical reasons only." In the beginning of the Soviet-American cultural exchange program, Jewish artists including Emil Gilels, Leonid Kogan, David Oistrakh, Maya Plisetskaya, Kiril Kondrashin, and many others of the older generation were sent out worldwide to represent the culture of the Soviet Union. (An interesting side note is that most of the instrumentalists were natives of Odessa, in Ukraine, and, therefore, should not even have been considered "Russian." Jews had not been permitted to live in Moscow or St. Petersburg since the era of the czars. The tradition of educating young Jewish musicians had been kept alive in the famed Ukrainian seaport city.) As time went on, the younger artists who were used by the Soviet Union as cultural performers were not Jewish. The younger Jewish artists were no longer exported on performance tours to use as propaganda tools. The Western media and cultural organizations had placed too much focus and attention on the "Jewishness" of the earlier artists.

A complicated system in the USSR decided one's status as "Jew" or "Aryan." Through four uninterrupted generations of intermarriage, an individual would be "cleansed" and no longer be considered of Jewish origin. The traditional anti-Semitism of these Slavic peoples prevailed regardless. If a Jew in the USSR requested to emigrate, he immediately lost his job. If he was refused permission to exit, his employable life in his own country ended. A person was damned if he did, and damned if he couldn't.

The protesters at the performances of Soviet artists were mainly representatives of the Jewish Defense League, headed by Rabbi Meir Kahane. He and his followers, often the very young and highly idealistic, hoped to direct the attention of the world via the American media to the anti-Semitic practices prevalent in the USSR. One can appreciate Kahane's efforts but hardly his methods. In order to get the attention of the world, it is not absolutely necessary to resort to threats and violence as he and his followers did. Kahane's most devastating form of protest tragically resulted in the death of one young Jewish woman, Iris Kones.

The Hurok office normally opened at 10 a.m. However, employees sometimes arrived before 9 a.m. On one such morning in January 1972, Sol Hurok was in his office early, as were a number of other employees, including a receptionist. Scotty Boland, who worked in the mailroom, also had the routine morning responsibilities of turning on the lights and lamps in the reception area. The reception area, located immediately in front of the bank of elevators, formed an access barrier to the actual offices. That morning, two young white men distracted the receptionist and casually planted an incendiary device in a container. Soon after they departed, the container that held the bomb exploded. The staff members who had arrived earlier were now trapped because all exits led to the reception area. Hurok stayed in his corner office, and others ran to the offices furthest from the reception area. The entire office was being darkened by smoke, and fire was consuming all of the oxygen. Three women went into my corner office and lay down on the floor, where the smoke was less dense. Hurok remained in his corner office. He had access to a sink in his private lavatory, and his chauffeur, Mr. Morgan, assisted him in wetting towels through which to breathe. He also possessed a bronze bust of President John F. Kennedy that he kept on the grand piano in his office. He used it to smash through one of the sealed windows surrounding his corner office. Hurok's and Morgan's quick thinking saved both of their lives.

The young women in my office were not as quick witted and did not have the foresight to break a window. Others in offices along the south wall of the building's twentieth floor were also able to break windows to get fresh air. The fire had been so intense before firemen arrived and put out the flames that typewriters and other pieces of office machinery were later found melted into balls of metal. Many of the interior partitioning walls had evaporated, and bare concrete was exposed on ceilings as well. Virginia Proodian, Myra Armstrong, and Iris Kones, who had sought refuge in my office, were overcome by smoke inhalation. They were rushed to a local hospital in ambulances after the firemen had gained control of the blaze and rescued them. Hurok, too, was admitted to a hospital but soon recovered. Virginia Proodian and Myra Armstrong also survived the ordeal; young Iris Kones did not. She succumbed to having breathed in the smoke for too long a time. Virginia and Myra and several other staff members were hospitalized for a couple of weeks. Whether true or false, it was reported that Sheldon Gold had escaped the episode, knowing where to find the building's fire exit and using it to leave as soon as the bomb exploded.

That morning I had not gone in to the office early. I approached Sixth Avenue and saw that the police had blocked it off and that fire trucks surrounded our office building. I also saw Rosemarie Buxhovedon, my secretary, standing on the corner. She said, "Max, look up." As I did, I saw office windows being smashed and glass cascading down nineteen floors. I invited the members of the staff who had arrived and been blocked from entering our office building to come up to my apartment. We set up a temporary camp for communication purposes. We fixed pots of coffee, waited for word about the conditions of our coworkers, and discussed how we could continue to conduct business. Concerts had been scheduled all across the United States, and local presenters needed some form of temporary pipeline. As word of the bombing spread, artists called from all over the world expressing their concern and confusion. We relocated almost immediately to our old offices at 730 Fifth Avenue, which, fortunately, were still unoccupied. Adding to the general melee, within the next twenty minutes on that January morning the Jewish Defense League had planted a similar device in the offices of Columbia Artists Management at 165 West 57th Street. The device was wrapped as a package and addressed to Ronald Wilford, president of CAMI. CAMI's receptionist was not at her desk at that hour, and the young men tried to give it directly to Mr. Wilford. However, not permitted past the building's entry area or the elevators, where they could have gained access to Wilford's office on the top floor of the building, they left it on the receptionist's desk and hurriedly departed. Fortunately, no one was in the area when the package exploded, but the reception entry hall was torn apart. The two incidents created an almost nightmarish situation for New York City's fire department and police force. They had to cope with two almost simultaneous bomb explosions within two blocks of each other in midtown Manhattan at rush hour.

JDL leader Meir Kahane, who had resided in Israel for several months prior to the Hurok and CAMI bombings, condemned the incidents as "insane." Later identified by the police as having been the actual perpetrators of the criminal bombings, several JDL members were charged with Iris Kones's murder and brought to trial. The prosecution, unable to supply witnesses due to legal technicalities, saw their cases against the JDL members dismissed. With no legal retribution, the result of the bombings was that public sympathy went entirely to Hurok and Iris Kones's family. The JDL and its causes soon slipped into the background and never came to the forefront again, except some years later when Meir Kahane was murdered in New York City.

THE CORPORATE ENTITIES TRANSCONTINENTAL INVESTING CORPORATION and Tomorrow Entertainment, Inc. (a General Electric subsidiary and the official purchasing organization of the Hurok corporation from TIC) had not anticipated the reactions of some of the leading Hurok Concerts, Inc., employees, myself included. For example, we were all given a book of rules and regulations for General Electric employees. We quickly began calling it "Chairman Mao's book." There were also questionnaires to be answered. Observers from GE would come and sit with us and interrupt our work with questions, which clearly reflected their complete ignorance of the concert world and its inner workings. We had to explain to them that these prolonged sessions seriously interrupted the purpose of our being there. Their lack of knowledge was reflected by the "job you are doing" judgments they were making. These observers had no way of evaluating the marketplace network that had been carefully built and the various outside individuals involved. Our job was to book artists. The observers thought that the booking staff was comprised of "order takers." They had no concept of the trust and "give and take" that was built up between "buyer and seller," particularly when developing new and unknown talents that depended on endorsements based on our musical knowledge and values. They were sure that anyone with a calendar and a list of fees could book concert artists. After all, didn't everyone know who Artur Rubinstein was and want him to appear in their community? The responsibilities we were being paid to carry out did not include taking time to educate them as to the principles, practices, and standards inherent in the concert artists management profession. Anyway, given the extent of their ignorance, that would have taken a lifetime. General Electric was especially guilty of putting in place a corps of observers who had no idea whatsoever of what it was they were there to observe. Their assignment may have fascinated them personally, but it was highly disruptive to our work process.

The questionnaire required that we provide such data as how many sick days we had used during the previous three years, or how many vacation days had we taken during that same period. I had not used one sick day in the course of twelve years and, though entitled to a paid month's vacation each year, had not taken any vacation time for the previous four years. My devotion to my job was not due to any heroics. It was the result of my interest in what I was doing and in what was occurring around me.

Finally, I took the questionnaire to Mr. Hurok's office and I said, "If these people see that I took no vacations in four years and was not reimbursed for my time, they will conclude that I am some sort of a moron. Their questions clearly show that their standards are completely different from ours. If these facts pertaining to employees involved monies that were being accounted for regarding the corporation's final sale settlement, then they are going to conclude that I have worked for a third of a year for no salary because I haven't used my vacation time." Hurok said, "Ach. Don't pay attention."

I replied, "You can afford to say that because you got your money. I regret to say that since you sold out, I no longer feel that I have any need of loyalty to you personally, and do not wish to be employed by General Electric."

I tore up the questionnaire, placed it in his wastebasket, and never again spoke with this man I had so admired. Thereupon, I immediately left the employ of General Electric's newest acquisition, Hurok Concerts, Inc.

Hurok's stepson, George Perper, telephoned me on two occasions and asked me to speak to Mr. Hurok. On the second telephone call, he said, "Mr. Hurok wants to speak to you. He's here in my office."

I replied, "I'm glad that he's there, and I would like you to tell him for me that in all the years of his life, I am sure that he has learned many lessons, but one lesson he has yet to learn. He cannot buy friendship and I am not for sale."

Saying that hurt me very deeply, but I felt it absolutely necessary to clearly state my position. By that time, I really knew Sol Hurok like a father but felt that he was not being supportive of longtime employees. His only interest seemed to be highly selfish. Now, I hoped he would understand me and my position.

"Fifty-Seventh Street," as New York City's classical music profession is known throughout the world, had viewed my relationship with Sol Hurok as almost that of a "crown prince," which is how Henryk Szeryng referred to me. I never enjoyed being thought of this way, but, in fact, I did have a favored status with Hurok. It was well known that I spent a great deal of personal time with him. He treated me as a surrogate son, devoted to the business to which he was devoted. In turn, I treated him much like a surrogate father and truly enjoyed the time I spent with him. When he had free time in New York City in the evenings, he would often call me to dine with him at home or at one of his favorite restaurants, usually La Côte Basque but occasionally Le Caravelle. The public associated him more with the Russian Tea Room, but it was not one of his preferred dining spots. The Russian Tea Room served more as a way to make the concert-going public aware of his presence, particularly after a performance by one of his better-known artists at Carnegie Hall next door.

I was not the only member of the Hurok staff to resign at that time. Martin Feinstein also left. Martin headed publicity for the office for many years and could most ably have taken over the entire administration of Hurok's businesses. Martin would have preserved the outstanding reputation the Hurok enterprises had always maintained. He went on to head the Kennedy Center's performing arts program and eventually the Washington Opera at Kennedy Center.

Harold Shaw, who had operated as an independent booker and artists' manager within the framework of Hurok Concerts, Inc., refused a salaried position with General Electric, which would not even have come close to his prior annual income. He abandoned his previous arrangement with Hurok and opened his own concert management company.

Harold already had a number of artists such as guitarists Julian Bream and John Williams who, while appearing on the Hurok roster of artists, were signed to Harold's personal direction. Other artists, such as violinist Henryk Szeryng, though under Hurok's personal direction, chose to sign on with Harold's new enterprise away from Isaac Stern.

James Murtha, who worked in the publicity department under Martin Feinstein, also left Hurok's employ and established a public relations and management firm operating as Gurtman and Murtha that survives to this day. Also working in the Hurok publicity office was Peter Gelb, son of Arthur Gelb, managing editor of the *New York Times*. He joined Jimmy Murtha's new organization, which, as a PR firm, profited enormously through its employment of Peter. Peter was not only Arthur Gelb's son, he was also the godson of the famous pianist Vladimir Horowitz. He was able to measurably increase his value to his employers by adding his godfather to the roster of artists they represented. Eventually feeling he had proven his worth to his bosses, Peter at one point asked for a raise. When he was refused, he joined Shaw Concerts, Inc., and brought his godfather to that roster. Peter went on to head a video division at CAMI and then to head publicity at the Boston Symphony Orchestra. He now heads SONY Classical Records and soon will assume the administrative helm of the Metropolitan Opera.

When he heard I had left Hurok, Ronald Wilford, president of Columbia Artists Management, telephoned and asked if I would join their organization as a full-fledged artists' manager. I would be assigned artists from their current roster. CAMI had been Hurok's main potential competitor. It was a strange turn of events for me to accept employment there, but then again I had to face the reality that the dynamics of the whole profession had changed as a result of Hurok's sale. I accepted Wilford's offer.

Of course, there were differences in office procedures. At Hurok's I had my own secretary for correspondence, Rosemarie Buxhoeveden. At CAMI, I shared Randi Greenberg with Sir Rudolf Bing, who had the office next to mine. Whereas at Hurok's our secretaries typed our correspondence, at CAMI we spoke into a microphone and dictated letters to a "communications center." The completed letters, numerically coded for filing purposes, were delivered to my office at the end of the day for my signature. Any enjoyment derived from letter writing was completely eliminated through this antiseptic means of correspondence. Other similar differences unfolded in due time.

There was an artist I had intended to bring onto the Hurok artists roster who had been introduced to me by pianist Alexis Weissenberg, whose career I had helped enormously. In the hopes that I could accomplish much the same as I had for Weissenberg, the artist and I had lunch together in New York in an effort to get to know one another. I had told him that he would be hearing from me about having his name eventually added to the Hurok list. I now had to write to this artist in Hamburg, Germany, to let him know that Hurok had surprised everyone by selling his corporation and, whatever my reasons, I was no longer with Hurok. I was now an artists' manager with CAMI. If this artist still wanted me to help him, I would do what I could for him in my new position at CAMI.

Months passed, and I had not received an answer to my letter. Then one day a memorandum arrived on my desk addressed to all of the managers at CAMI announcing that a new artist had been added to the Ronald Wilford Division of Columbia Artists Management, Inc. When I saw the name of the new artist, I realized that my correspondence was being monitored through the communications center. Wilford was now managing the artist with whom I had been corresponding in Germany. Years later I visited this artist backstage after a concert. This was the first time I saw him since he had joined the CAMI roster under the direction of Ronald Wilford. I told him I was surprised that he had never answered my letter. He said, "I assumed that there had been communication between Wilford and yourself because he wrote to me two days later. I then presumed that the courteous thing to do was to reply to the president of CAMI, rather than to respond to your earlier letter." In hindsight, we both laughed, and I said, "I think you lucked out, as your career has unfolded into something far beyond the fine pianist that you are." I said this to Christoph Eschenbach, the

Bolshoi Ballet principal dancer Sergei Radchenko and I finally made it to California's Disneyland. The fantasy amusement park was always a big attraction for Russian performers. Even Khrushchev visited Walt Disney's Magic Kingdom. (Collection of Maxim Gershunoff.)

With the great Russian violinist David Oistrakh and his son, violinist Igor Oistrakh. A portrait photographer snapped this candid shot for me. (Collection of Maxim Gershunoff.)

Yousuf Karsh

David Oistrakh explaining to me why he chose to phrase a few bars of music the way he did. We often enjoyed such discussions. (Collection of Maxim Gershunoff.)

A rarely seen candid photo taken at the wedding in Israel of the exceptionally talented English cellist Jacqueline du Pré and the Argentinian/Israeli pianist and conductor Daniel Barenboim. (Collection of Maxim Gershunoff.)

With members of the Moiseyev Russian folk dance company in June 1965 as they place a wreath on the grave of President John F. Kennedy in Arlington National Cemetery, accompanied by members of the United States Marine Corps. (Collection of Maxim Gershunoff.)

An autographed Hurok Attractions publicity photo of Mstislav Rostropovich. (Collection of Maxim Gershunoff.)

Pianist Alexis ("Sigi") Weissenberg's autograph indicated no shortage of ego on his part; he claimed to be the "leading man" of those I represented at Hurok Concerts, Inc. (Collection of Maxim Gershunoff.)

A Hurok Attractions publicity photo autographed by Russian violinist Leonid Kogan. When we first met he recognized me from a photo displayed on my cousin's piano in Moscow. (Collection of Maxim Gershunoff.)

Boris Goldenberg

Ukrainian pianist Alexander Slobodyanik as he appeared during his first concert season in the U.S. I was later able to add him to my roster of artists when I opened my own artists management office. (Collection of Maxim Gershunoff.)

With my first and primary trumpet teacher, Harry Glantz, in the mid-eighties at a gathering of brass instrument players who were honoring him. (Collection of Maxim Gershunoff.)

During what turned out to be our final meeting, Lenny Bernstein showed me a photo he kept in his wallet of his latest amour, a dolphin he swam with in the Florida Keys. (Photograph from Henry Grossman.)

Henry Grossman

Royal Opera House

Covent Garden London WC2E 7QA
Telephone: 01-240 1200
Cables: Amidst London WC2
Telex: 27988

Mr. M. Gershunoff,   3rd June 1982
Maxim Gershunoff, Inc,
Delmonico's,
502 Park Avenue at 59th Street,
New York,
NY 10022,
U.S.A.

Dear Mr. Gershunoff,

Sir Frederick has asked me to thank you very much for your letter
and to apologise profusely for taking so long to reply but he has
been away from London a great deal during this last year.

Sir Frederick said he is so sorry he did not have the opportunity
of seeing you when he was in New York but he was extremely busy
with the Ballet Company and he simply did not have the time to
get in touch, which he would so much like to have done. He said
that nowadays at his "advanced age" he does get very tired and
cannot undertake so much as he once used to do.

He said it was so nice to hear from you and please forgive any
seeming discourtesy on his part.

He sends you his love and best wishes.

Yours sincerely,

Iris Law,
Royal Ballet Company

An indirect response from the ever polite but aging Sir Frederick Ashton to a note I
had written.

Van Cliburn International Piano Competition "loser" and Russian defector, pianist Youri Egorov in snapshots taken in 1978. *Left*, aboard my yacht, *Donna Mia*; *right*, outside a New port, Rhode Island, mansion prior to an appearance that summer at the Newport Music Festival. (Collection of Maxim Gershunoff.)

Russian conductor Yuri Temirkhanov and me getting together once again at his hotel suite in New York City. During the 1980s he always called upon arrival in New York, and we would meet and "catch up." (Collection of Maxim Gershunoff.)

An early Hurok Concerts, Inc., publicity photo of cellist Yo-Yo Ma taken around age sixteen. (Collection of Maxim Gershunoff.)

man who is now the music director of the Philadelphia Orchestra and was then music director of the Houston Symphony Orchestra.

In spite of the great financial loss that the Kirov Ballet represented to Sol Hurok, CAMI considered it quite a coup when they acquired the rights to present the troupe in the United States. Sam Niefeld, a senior manager at CAMI, was handling the projected tour by the Kirov. I was called into Ronald Wilford's office one day, where I was asked questions regarding programming and logistics for the Kirov. The Kirov had proposed that they would tour with five different programs: *Swan Lake, Sleeping Beauty, Giselle, Don Quixote,* and an evening of ballet highlights. I had commented that such a tour would require seventeen to nineteen forty-five-foot trailer trucks, hotels and meals for the company, an American orchestra, and countless other arrangements, as had been necessary to tour the Bolshoi Ballet. CAMI was already committed to a contract with the Kirov for a tour, but the parties had not yet settled on repertoire. At this point I felt Wilford and Niefeld were panicking due to their inexperience.

They asked, "What if we do three ballets instead of five?"

I said, "For purposes of box office, it would depend on who was being featured as soloists."

Niefeld asked, "What if we do only one ballet, like *Giselle?*"

I pointed out that *Giselle* is a very short ballet and certainly could not constitute enough programming for a tour.

Defending himself, Niefeld said, "Well, *My Fair Lady* is one program and it tours. We could be touring *The Kirov.*"

With that absurd remark, I found myself in the position of having to somehow suppress my amazement at the ignorance being exposed so guilelessly before me. Fortunately, I had the experience necessary to try to assist them.

"Ballet audiences," I told them, "rely on repertoire. To tour such a large company, you need a run of performances in each city whereby the same audience will buy tickets for different programs. You can't afford to do just one-nighters."

When Ronald Wilford and I spoke about possible soloists, he asked me if I hoped CAMI would send me to Russia to select ballets and soloists for them to present. I told him that having been to Russia so many times and knowing the Kirov Ballet as well as I did from having traveled with them, I had no personal interest in making such a trip.

Wilford added, "Max, you're a very conservative guy. I'll bet if you went into a restaurant, you wouldn't order anything on the menu that you hadn't tasted before."

I replied, "Ronald, there's just about nothing I haven't tasted, but I will never recommend to a friend something that I myself have not tasted."

CAMI initially enjoyed a run of good luck as regarded the Kirov Ballet. Then, however, there was a sudden break in Soviet-American relations, and the cultural exchange program was interrupted. The Kirov fell victim to the hiatus, and their projected tour under the CAMI banner was canceled. It was a stroke of luck for the Kirov, since CAMI had absolutely no idea at the time of the magnitude or the complexity of this project to which they had so happily agreed with Gosconcert and the Soviet ministry of culture.

In the second year of my three-year contract with CAMI, I found that the artists assigned to me were not particularly to my liking and did not meet my musical standards. During the early seventies, there were so many artists on and off of CAMI's roster that those whose careers I had been entrusted with were, for the most part, rhinestones, while I was accustomed to selling diamonds. It was quite difficult for me to recommend these artists with any enthusiasm to those people who were accustomed to trusting my endorsements. In discussing my reactions with Ronald Wilford, I asked him if I could bring in at least one artist whom I believed to be a major talent. I had started this young artist's career. His father had great trust in me. He knew that I had left Hurok and was at CAMI and would consider moving with me. Although the young man was attending Harvard University at the time, we had many telephone conversations relating to such a move.

Wilford said, "Max, you cannot act so freely as you did at Hurok's in bringing him fine artists. Here at CAMI, everything has to be 'committee approved.'"

Having no other option, I agreed, and said, "As an objective exercise, submit my suggestion when the committee meets and let's see what happens."

The meetings usually took place every few weeks on Tuesdays. Ronald reported to me after the meeting at which my request had been submitted, letting me know that my suggested artist had been rejected. I had a serious talk with him after that.

I said, "Ronald, if this is a barometer, it's not a good sign for me. I have a solution for you, and I can make a lot of money for you next year."

Ronald said, "Great! How, Max?"

I replied, "By leaving. Let me out of my third year of our contract, and we will remain friends."

He did, and we are. The artist whom I requested we add to the CAMI roster, and who was rejected by its committee's decision, was the great cellist Yo-Yo Ma!

Chapter Nine

OF THE ARTISTS ASSIGNED TO ME FOR MANAGERIAL RESPONSIBILITIES BY CAMI, there was one whom I held in highest esteem for his artistic talents and sensibilities. That individual was the Israeli pianist David Bar-Ilan. David's career had been hindered by the necessity of caring for his family financially. He accepted as many engagements on CAMI's Community Concerts circuit as were possible. Thus, the managers of symphony orchestras did not bandy about his name with any regularity because the number of his performances with orchestras became fewer and fewer as a result of his being occupied with Community Concert performances. Managers of symphony orchestras regularly speak with one another, as did the local organizers of Community Concerts presentations. They were quick with praise for artists who pleased and charmed their audiences and just as quick to banish lesser lights to even further obscurity. David Bar-Ilan was a hit of no small proportions on CAMI's Community Concerts series throughout the North American continent. Although highly profitable to both Bar-Ilan and CAMI, the Community Concerts series provided no help in the process of achieving a major career for the artist. He and his family were able to live well in an apartment on New York City's West End Avenue due to this success. But, he was not playing with the major symphony orchestras, where his talents deserved exposure on a regular basis. David's father was very active politically in Israel at the time it became a nation and was instrumental in establishing Hebrew as the official language of the new country. Ultimately, David's priorities changed, and he returned to his homeland, where he practiced journalism and eventually became the managing editor of the *Jerusalem Post* before engaging in politics there on a full-time basis.

David's best man at his wedding to his wife Beverly was Benjamin ("Bibi") Netanyahu, who, years later, was elected prime minister of Israel. When Netanyahu became prime minister he enlisted David Bar-Ilan as one of his most trusted advisers, and David was a principal spokesman for Netanyahu's political administration in Israel. An exceptionally well educated and highly articulate gentleman, David served his friend and his country well in his official capacity.

Although David knew that he would be losing me as a manager, since I would soon be leaving CAMI, he asked to meet with me. At that meeting, he piqued my interest by telling me about the dilemma of the two émigré dancers Valery and Galina Panov. They had become a worldwide symbol and focal point of the plight the Soviet Jews who wished to emigrate and were not being permitted to leave the USSR. Instead, they lost their jobs and all other rights applicable to Soviet Union citizens. They were virtually trapped, and the fear of such entrapment prevented other Soviet Jews from requesting official permission to immigrate to Israel.

Clive Barnes, then dance critic of the *New York Times,* had used his position to develop a publicity campaign enlisting famous performing artists throughout the world to "Free the Panovs." He was joined in this endeavor by his wife Patricia and her sister, who lived in Britain and was connected with the dance world there. Clive Barnes claimed that Valery Panov was one of the greatest dancers of Leningrad's Kirov Ballet. Similar laudatory references were being bestowed upon his wife Galina Panova as well. Adding to their tragic circumstances was news of a miscarriage suffered by Galina. A photograph of Valery with his head shaved had been widely published when he was released from prison after an arrest in Leningrad.

David suggested that with my background and knowledge of the dance world I could be of enormous assistance to the Panovs upon their release from the Soviet Union and immigration to their chosen land of freedom, Israel. Since I would soon be free of commitments, I found the potential of such a project highly appealing. I subsequently met with Clive and Patricia Barnes at their apartment in Manhattan, and we discussed the various avenues for possible performances by the Panovs, particularly in the U.S. I also met with the dance critic Walter Terry and sought his views as well. It was decided that I would have to travel to Israel to gain a complete picture of what would be needed to establish a career for these artists outside the Soviet Union. I was offered no funding whatsoever toward this project but was willing to undertake all expenses necessary on my own.

I flew to Israel, where I met with the Panovs for the first time. Much of our time together was spent simply getting to know one another. Their new friends in Israel were among that country's wealthiest citizens. Wealthy Jewish citizens of other countries, including tax havens like Switzerland, who maintained homes in Israel as well and were large contributors to the state of Israel wanted only the best for Israel's newest citizens, Valery and Galina Panov. The Panovs were being housed in a penthouse apartment quite luxurious by Israeli standards. Their immediate financial needs were obviously being looked after. While there I found that the highest echelons of Israeli society and officialdom were treating them as national heroes, as was the general public. If we ventured into a theater for a concert or other event, the entire audience would rise as one and applaud the Panovs as they entered an auditorium. It became abundantly evident to me that for the Israelis and their sympathizers these were not only dance artists but symbols of a larger and very special cause. Putting the political situation aside, I decided to go and watch the Panovs take dance class. The Panovs insisted sessions be kept most private.

A level of cloudiness in discussions of what dance repertoire the Panovs would be most comfortable performing began to dim their glamour for me. They actually could not provide any concept whatsoever as to what they as artists might be capable of performing in public together. The Panovs appeared to me to be thinking that their sudden world fame equated to their having "arrived" and that little more was expected of them than simply their celebrated existence. They were, at least momentarily, satisfied with being the recipients of the largesse showered upon them in Israel by their wealthy well-wishers. They were being neither creative nor imaginative.

So, with virtually no creative input from either Galina or Valery Panov, I concluded that they were very limited and we would have to invent a more or less "cosmetic" program. I recalled other dance duos in concert programs of ballet excerpts interspersed with orchestral ballet music. The best suggestion I could possibly imagine for musical input would be to engage the services of conductor Robert Zeller. He had been responsible for the musical elements of very successful concert dance programs of Alicia Markova and Anton Dolin. He had extensive experience conducting for the Royal Danish Ballet, the Royal Ballet (including in its earlier incarnation as the Sadler Wells Ballet), and the Stuttgart Ballet. Zeller was also very well known in the symphonic world and was regularly engaged throughout Europe and the U.S. to conduct in that capacity as well. I returned to New York to discuss the matter with Zeller. He and I returned to Israel to meet with the Panovs.

"Cosmetic" is the proper word for what had to be accomplished in order to get the Panovs on a Western dance stage. Despite the emotional praise heaped upon them by Clive Barnes as dance artists, the Panovs, from what I had observed in their dance classes, were of less than stellar ability. I felt it best to proceed more or less cautiously and thereby limit their first tour of the United States to only four cities. This would be a "welcoming" tour symbolizing freedom. Philadelphia, emblematic of American liberty, would be the first city in which a performance by the Panovs would be scheduled. San Francisco, Los Angeles, and, finally, Washington, D.C., would follow in that order. All agreed, and a contractual agreement was signed between us, establishing me as impresario for the Panovs. Shaw Concerts, Inc., in New York City would be the booking agent for the project, and I, in my role as impresario, would pay for all of the rentals and royalties for orchestral scores and parts, as well as new orchestral arrangements, a lighting designer, transportation, hotels, publicity representation, and myriad other incidentals. Shaw Concerts would receive its normal 20 percent commission, and the Panovs would receive a guaranteed fee per performance. A program was devised after consultation between the Panovs, Zeller, and myself. The Panovs in no way had to compensate either myself or Zeller for our consultation services, which truly rescued them from a potential artistic disaster. I was responsible for all of the expenses incurred by Zeller in the process.

When consulted, both Clive Barnes and Walter Terry approved the format we had collectively created. Among the ballet divertissements decided upon, were a grand pas de deux from *The Nutcracker,* a scene from Stravinsky's *Petrouchka* that Valery would dance, and a solo from *Don Quixote,* performed by Galina. They also added a dance from their repertoire entitled *The Lady and the Hooligan.* Colorful, rather upbeat orchestral interludes would allow the dancers brief periods of rest in which to change costumes. When the program was finally and definitely established, Valery insisted that he had a costume designer he wanted. The designer, an English woman, was brought to Israel for conferences, body measurements, and scheduling purposes. Price seemed to be no object to the Panovs, since I was paying, and her fees for the costumes, all of her travel expenses, and so forth were part of my financial responsibilities. Time was also a factor. The Panovs were scheduled to break in the show and actually debut the program with the Israel Philharmonic in their new homeland at Tel Aviv's Frederick Mann Auditorium. My overall investment could either benefit me financially or result in a partial or even complete loss of my funds. The Panovs, on the other hand, had a complete financial guarantee, and additionally guaranteed to them were all of the elements above that I had provided to them, which constituted the "tools" of their trade." I was creating a path for their careers to get launched in the West. I was willing to take the risk.

AFTER ALL OF THIS GROUNDWORK HAD BEEN LAID, VALERY PANOV SUDDENLY started on a campaign for a place to rehearse other than in Israel, although every studio in the country was available to him. He argued that no studio in Israel had ceilings high enough to accommodate his "gigantic leaps," though nothing in the program to be performed required any such leaping. I began to sense that he was creating an excuse to get out of Israel as soon as possible. With great resentment, he often commented about the legal requirements for new Israeli citizens, which obliged him to attend Hebrew classes and imposed other demands on all émigrés, even the Panovs.

Owing to the phenomenal publicity these "freedom fighters" had received, the Western world was excitedly anticipating the opportunity of seeing the Panovs live in performance. Thinking in a positive vein, and in the hope that if they were provided with excellent studio facilities they would improve, I approached Clive Barnes, who worked out a solution. Clive found accommodations with which the Panovs could not possibly find fault. He arranged with the Stuttgart Ballet's new director, Glen Tetley, for the Panovs to be hosted in Germany for their rehearsal needs. All of the dancers' expenses would also be covered for a one-month rehearsal period there. At the conclusion of their month in Stuttgart, the Panovs returned to Israel.

Clive asked me to speak carefully with Valery about the meaning and use of the word "diplomacy," as I once again was departing the U.S. for Israel with Robert Zeller. We were making the trip so that the dancers could begin rehearsing tempos with their musical director. Seeing that he had not made himself very clear, Clive explained that it had come to his attention that Valery was sabotaging his host, Glen Tetley, by promoting himself to the company in Stuttgart as potentially a much better director.

This was another new and negative dimension that now began to unfold and one that was completely contrary to the publicized image of the artists that the world had been so desperately trying to rescue from the USSR. I couldn't help but remember what Igor Stravinsky had told me years before, "Max, don't believe everything that you read ... Ach, young writers and young critics do not want to hear the truth. If you tell them truth in an interview, is not interesting."

I began to realize that I had better get to know Valery somewhat better. In conveying Clive's request about "diplomacy," one of my first comments to Valery was that I was somewhat puzzled by his overtures to the dancers in Stuttgart, since I understood he publicly professed that he wanted to become an Israeli citizen. I deliberately pointed out to him that Stuttgart was in Germany and not in Israel. Valery then made it quite clear to me that I had been right. He had no particular desire to live in Israel and wished to get out. He would often say, simply, "the whole world is waiting for me." I asked him what it had been like to be jailed by the Soviets. He confidentially said that he had not been jailed for political reasons at all, though his incarceration had been made to seem so in all of the publicity disseminated in the West surrounding that arrest. He informed me that actually he had physically beaten his wife's mother, and that was the reason he had been taken into custody by the police in Leningrad. Galina's mother did not have sufficient income credits for a full pension and needed her daughter's assistance to support her in her old age. She would not sign a release forfeiting her rights to a pension from the Soviet government. Such a release form would have allowed her daughter Galina to emigrate. The Soviet government would not allow even Galina, a non-Jew, out of the country without her mother's formal release. Valery said he had beaten "that selfish old bitch. She should have died in the first place.

Her life is behind her, she should realize we have our lives ahead of us." Upon his release from the jail in Leningrad, he had shaved his head, giving himself the appearance of a somewhat gaunt creature who had suffered. His altered appearance was merely a deliberate bit of theatrical makeup designed to enhance the role he was now playing for the Western media.

His claim to being Jewish also became a relevant topic between us. According to Jewish religious law, an individual can only lay claim to being Jewish through having a Jewish mother. I learned that Valery's mother was not Jewish, although his father's name, Schulman, was quite Jewish. The fact that his father was Jewish is irrelevant in terms of Jewish Orthodoxy. In the Soviet Union his father's name had been most inconvenient to him, as it easily identified him as Jewish. To circumvent prejudice, in his earlier Soviet days Valery had adopted the surname of his first wife, "Panova."

In addition, I learned that Valery had never been a principal dancer with the Kirov Ballet, but was, however, a fine featured character dancer in that company who was often singled out for praise of his acting abilities. As he approached his mid-thirties, he realized his career would now be on the wane and he would easily be replaced in the Kirov company. He thus switched roles to become the "oppressed Jewish dancer." He used this ruse to gain the attention of such leaders of the Western dance world as Clive and Patricia Barnes. In this self-promotion, his dramatic abilities were used to their highest level of artistry. When he arrived in the West he and Galina would be assured of achieving major attention, such as was the case with those other famous defectors from the Kirov Ballet, Nureyev, Baryshnikov, and Makarova.

It was true. He had managed to extract every bit of notoriety possible. The release of Galina and Valery Panov from the USSR and their arrival in Israel was noted in every capital of the Western world and in all the Western media. I even found myself to be part of the hype when I was interviewed in Israel for a BBC-TV documentary, and still later when we all arrived in the U.S. All of the interview hosts sought time with the Panovs.

Once Robert Zeller had set the tempos with the Panovs for their newly established program, he and I flew home to New York aboard an El Al jumbo jet. Although the entire flight was coach class, the front part of the aircraft was reserved for VIPs only. Apparently due to our involvement with the Panovs we were accorded the utmost courtesy and were seated in that forward area of the plane. Once aloft, the very special persons in our section were offered drinks. I was seated next to Robert Zeller four rows from the front of the seating area. Knowing Zeller as I did, I knew that the mere sight of a martini glass would be enough for him to become somewhat expansive in his behavior. His very resonant voice was especially effective while conducting rehearsals with a symphony orchestra of one hundred musicians, but it was totally unnecessary in the small upper cabin of a jumbo jet. I could hear him very well, as I was seated beside him. The courtesy of the aircraft's crew, the whole ambience of the flight, and the thought of getting back to New York City for the fourteen limited days we had before having to return to Tel Aviv encouraged Zeller to vent his emotional relief. His venting, unfortunately, was greatly aided by his having imbibed just one cocktail.

One of the flight attendants politely leaned over to us and requested that he lower his voice, as it was very disturbing to a passenger in the front row who was very tired. Zeller blurted out in his alcoholically emancipated full rehearsal voice, "Tired, tired? I'm tired." Indeed, we both were fairly well exhausted by our sessions with the Panovs. He said, "If he's that tired, he shouldn't be flying. I'll relax my way." On hearing that note of further abuse, the gentleman in question, without looking back, simply arose from his seat, walked directly forward, and freely entered the cockpit of the jumbo jet.

I noticed some scurrying back and forth by some of the stewards a while later as they began to create some sort of a sleeper accommodation similar to a Pullman berth with blue curtains. When the changeover had been completed, the same gentleman who had gone into the pilots' cabin was escorted out and directed to the newer facility. Since we had not seen the face of the man until that moment, it was devastatingly embarrassing to me to realize that it was General Moshe Dayan, whom I now easily recognized due to his black eye patch. My mortification was such that if I could have fallen 38,000 feet, and dragged Zeller with me, I would have. Regardless, by then Zeller had unwound so completely that he was fast asleep and suffered no discomfort whatsoever. Both the gracious crew and the seemingly forgiving General Dayan never mentioned the incident.

ZELLER AND I RETURNED ONCE AGAIN TO ISRAEL FOR THE PANOVS' FINAL round of rehearsals and their debut In Tel Aviv. The Panovs seemed fully refreshed. The full array of new costumes I had paid for had arrived. All the other participants involved, including the entire Israel Philharmonic Orchestra, were ready to go. There was a constant barrage of requests from the media for exclusive interviews. Arrangements had to be made for a variety of international television coverage, and it was all dealt with fairly smoothly. The Panovs' debut performance in the Mann Auditorium was completely sold out. When the performance was about to begin, Frederick Mann, a part-time resident of Tel Aviv, after whom the auditorium was named, asked me to go out onstage with him. He then presented me to the audience, expressing deep gratitude to me for literally getting the Panovs on their feet once again. Then the debut performance began.

My concept worked, and the Panovs enjoyed a striking success. If their technical abilities were limited, an enraptured audience participating in a highly emotional event forgave all. I received no compensation whatsoever for the performance. I have no idea what the Panovs may have received. Perhaps they contributed their performance, as I had contributed on my part. Almost immediately following their debut, we flew to New York City via London, where there was much press coverage of the Panovs' arrival, made very colorful by the presentation of many bouquets of flowers.

After they arrived in New York, new demands began to surface, and the Panovs virtually became the "property" of possessive American supporters of Israel. The Panovs were a highly useful "tool" for extracting large-scale donations for Israel. Without being consulted beforehand, they were expected to appear at fund-raising events the United Jewish Appeal in New York City had scheduled in advance. There were also other events planned by organizations connected with Israel. The National Press Club in Washington, D.C., had scheduled a luncheon in the Panovs' honor as well. The Panovs became so exhausted from the round of events, and so concerned for their forthcoming performance, that they canceled the one thing they should have attended, the luncheon with the National Press Club. In my attempt to control the situation, I was viewed as an uncooperative ogre by some who were less than understanding and concerned only about their own goals.

There was a private dinner held at a restaurant feting the dancers that was attended by such New York celebrities as Isaac and Vera Stern and Leonard Bernstein. I was seated at the table with the Panovs when Vera Stern approached me and asked me to bring the Panovs to the table at which Bernstein and the Sterns were seated. Knowing all of the personalities and egos involved only too well, I knew that Lenny was asserting his elevated artistic position and wished to have the Panovs pay homage to him. I found it necessary to point out to both the Panovs and Vera Stern that the party was in the Panovs' honor. I had the Panovs remain seated. I assured them that Leonard Bernstein would get up from his table and come to properly greet them, if only to have his photograph taken in the act. Of course, I was correct and he did.

In addition to the many favors already bestowed upon them in Israel, the Panovs were now the recipients of American generosity. Among the myriad parties in their honor or to which they were invited as honored guests, and around which funds were being raised for Israel and other Jewish charities, the UJA's event at the Hilton Hotel in New York City was especially memorable. The Panovs' presence lent pathos to the ongoing efforts of the United Jewish Appeal, and surprisingly large amounts of money were contributed. Similar events by the UJA were being planned for the Panovs' appearances in San Francisco and Los

Angeles. All of this was with complete disregard to their requirements as artists to have proper rest periods and necessary rehearsal time. In my effort to respect their needs, I sensed that I was becoming polarized from these philanthropic organizations, since I felt that the Panovs' availability for these fund-raising events should not be taken for granted by anyone. The Panovs themselves were happy to accept the gifts practically being thrust upon them. These included everything from their personal wardrobes to a Mercedes-Benz automobile. But they were hardly anxious to attend all of the events for which their presence was enlisted to assist in fund-raising. It was necessary for us all to focus on their American debut in Philadelphia. So, off to Philadelphia we went and encamped at the Barclay Hotel on Rittenhouse Square. Frederick Mann's presence was much felt, as he was now at home in the apartment he maintained at the Barclay as his U.S. residence.

Two days prior to their expected appearance at Philadelphia's Spectrum Arena, Valery Panov abruptly complained of a leg injury. I inquired as to the seriousness of the injury, and Valery said that it was serious enough that he could not dance. I asked about his getting help from a doctor and was surprised to discover that, without consulting me, Frederick Mann had driven him to a doctor in New Jersey who confirmed the fact that Valery could not dance. Therefore, I would have to cancel the Philadelphia performance.

I felt bad for Valery and worse for myself. It seemed somewhat suspicious, however, that this situation, including the visit to the doctor, had not been shared with me until after the fact. As matters further unfolded, I was informed that any future dealings were not to be conducted directly with the Panovs but with an attorney, Ellis J. Friedman, in New York City. His role would be attorney/manager of the Panovs. This new development completely disregarded my contract with the dancers and failed to recognize my financial investment in the Panovs.

While I had been busily occupied with the Panovs' scheduling and with fending off those who would occupy them in other than artistic endeavors, it seems that the dancers were listening to advisers who were planting suspicions about my possible profiteering. Displaying absolutely no trust in or loyalty to me, or gratitude for my efforts on their behalf, the Panovs, with their Soviet mentality and its attendant paranoia, believed these advisers' slanderous accusations.

I now knew that Valery's leg injury had been feigned and found it necessary to take the issue to court. It was my belief that Valery was instructed to create such an excuse to justify the Philadelphia performance's cancellation. He would thus never appear under my aegis. I claimed malicious interference by Ellis J. Friedman and breach of contract by the Panovs. Later, Valery unintentionally bore witness to my belief that he had faked his injury. When he was asked in court to point to the leg that had been hurt, he pointed to the wrong limb, in direct contradiction to the New Jersey doctor's letter. He was then "led" by his attorney, who asked, "It wasn't the other leg?" Valery said he couldn't clearly remember, and the judge let pass an objection to that response by my attorney. As the trial progressed it became evident that with each postponement or delay, the case was being handled "by rote," and a new judge was assigned to the case each time. As it turned out, practically every judge in the New York State Superior court who presided in the matter was Jewish, and there were at least four of them. In the end, the Panovs walked off with my format for their performances and my payment for their elaborate costumes and musical arrangements, as well as a wealth of further publicity. In the courtroom, as well as the media, I was being portrayed as taking unfair financial advantage of the Panovs, but in actuality I felt I was being robbed at pen point. Due to the contrived cancellation, they never actually worked for me, as was their attorney's intent, and I was certainly not guilty of having profited at their expense. Even if I had, it is not a sin in a capitalist society if one profits on an investment. At one point, one of the Jewish judges on New York State's Superior Court admonished my attorney not to have anything negative said regarding the state of Israel in his court. My attorneys had advised that we not place an injunction but rather allow the Panovs to perform. Otherwise public opinion would automatically turn against me, which it did anyway.

Regardless of the ensuing controversy, many anxious presenters took advantage of the Panovs' availability. The Panovs then earned in excess of one million dollars in their first year of performing outside of the USSR. I later learned that Ellis J. Friedman was charging a commission on the Panovs' performances as manager, in addition to a percentage on the same performances to be applied to his services as attorney "in the Gershunoff matter." Those commissions certainly amounted to more than what Harold Shaw would have charged for his role as booking agent. Any monies coming to me, as impresario, would certainly have been appropriate in my role as an American businessman and investor. Certainly, my investment both in creating and bankrolling a presentation format for the artists, acting as a direct liaison to the media for them, and hiring press representation among other duties involved deserved remuneration. Friedman, as it turned out, had to sever his association with the legal firm with which he had been associated. His associates in the law firm did not wish to expose themselves to potential losses. My charges must have had enough validity to make them wish to disassociate themselves from their colleague. The Panovs eventually ended up at odds with Friedman when they found that they would have to pay him. It seemed that they "wanted it all." They may have been getting it all, since contributors covered their legal fees.

Earlier, Isaac Stern had entered the picture when he heard that I planned to take Friedman and the Panovs to court. He chose Martin Feinstein, former head of press at the Hurok office, as his emissary. Martin visited me at the Shaw office, where I was temporarily headquartered for the project. Martin stressed that the Panovs were highly valuable as a focal point for fund-raising for Israel, which was desperately in need of funding to attract a large mass of immigrants from the Soviet Union for expansion of its new settlements. My legal suit would have the potential of exposing the Panovs as blatant opportunists who had only used their drama of immigrating to Israel as their excuse to be released from the USSR. Further, it might reveal that they were not even Jewish by religious standards and had no genuine feelings for Israel whatsoever. I knew they were "cardboard heroes." Their selfish behavior now working against me, I really wanted the truth to be exposed. I no longer had any desire whatsoever to participate in furthering the Panovs' distortion of history and their blatant opportunism. I had been duped by the pathetic story these "heroic dancers" bandied about in the international media, as had others whom I respected, such as David Bar-Ilan, never dreaming that it would become the nightmare it did. There were some, however, who did not wish to have the public's illusions shattered. Stern, then, however the funds were made available to him, authorized Martin to offer me a sum of $35,000. This was to be applied toward the monies I had already expended on the Panovs' behalf. In effect, it was "hush money" for me not to blow the whistle by dropping my suit against the Panovs and Friedman. Revolted by Isaac's suggested trade-off, I declined his offer and would not speak to Stern again for twenty-five years. However, two years prior to his death, I was in New York City attending the annual publication party for the *Musical America International Directory of the Performing Arts.* Isaac, after giving a short speech, approached me with a flattering remark about my "never changing." I was complimentary about the remarks he had just made, and our mutual estrangement was officially ended.

Although never guilty of any wrongdoing with regard to the dancers, I eventually lost my suit against the Panovs and Ellis J. Friedman. The one lesson I learned was never to sue an attorney in New York State. The Panov story is now just a historical footnote. Valery and Galina Panov, in the ensuing thirty years, have gone through many dance companies in Europe and even Australia and have never been accepted anywhere long enough to find an artistic home. They have never been able to live up to the hyped-up artistic reputation that Clive Barnes and a parroting media conferred upon them. Ironically, the duo is divorced, and Valery is now permanently ensconced in Israel, the country he did not wish to call home. There he has been able to elicit support for a dance company of his own creation.

Chapter Ten

DURING THE SUMMER OF 1976, I ONCE AGAIN BEGAN TO REPRESENT AN artist. I was contacted regarding a recent émigré from the Soviet Union by the name of Albert Markov. A concert violinist, he was in serious need of representation in order to get started on a career in the United States. He had a wife and two young sons, both also musicians. Alexander, the youngest, was a violinist like his father, while Pavel, the elder boy, was already an accomplished pianist who was capable of accompanying his father in recitals. On a couple of occasions the three appeared in recital together. Though Albert Markov enjoyed a modicum of success when he first came to the U.S., his career never took off after he left my management. His son, Alexander, is also highly talented and has enjoyed some success since becoming a full-time concert artist. Pavel, the older son, did not wish to pursue a career as a musician and had been accepted as a scholarship student to Harvard University. Before he could enter Harvard, however, he died in a fall from the rooftop of the apartment house where his family was living at the time on Manhattan's West Side.

By September of '76, I had accumulated enough of an artists list to be able to publish a roster of those artists in the annual *Musical America International Directory of the Performing Arts* published for the year 1977 and released in December 1976. I seemed to be a magnet of some sort for any recent émigré musician from the Soviet Union. The musical community in Moscow knew of me through my association with so many of the artists who had performed in the U.S. under the Hurok aegis. Also, my relatives in Moscow were musicians, who bandied my name about among their colleagues. The émigrés would arrive in New York City and when visiting the Hebrew Immigration Assistance Services would tell HIAS's social workers that I might be a source for potential employment.

I would interview and audition many such musicians fleeing from the USSR and seeking to reap the rewards of the good life in the U.S. As I was to learn slowly but indelibly, each and every one of them unfortunately brought with them a lifetime of indoctrination into the good life as it existed in the Soviet Union. There, they had all been provided with an excellent free education in their chosen art form. The Soviet system had identified their talents as musicians early in their development, and their government nurtured such talents. If they had achieved a certain recognition at home in the USSR they were rewarded with better housing there than most others. As performing artists, they received an annual income from the government that could be augmented by teaching or performing in countries outside of the Soviet Union. While their government always received the majority of any fees paid for their services outside of the country, they were, nevertheless, compensated with extra honorariums for each such service. The government concert agency, Gosconcert, paid for any printed materials, photographs, and even the evening clothes required for performance on the concert stage. They were truly the "children" of the USSR. As a matter of fact, on my many visits to the Soviet Union, it often seemed like I was visiting an entire country comprising a "kindergarten" for adults.

Like children, these artists were totally unaccustomed to the ways of the Western world. They had no idea that they had to provide glossy photographs, printed flyers, publicity packets, and other tools of their trade in order to pursue a career in the United States. Culture shock prevailed. They balked at the idea that in addition to the commissions that went to the managers who obtained employment for them, there were also many other charges. The result was that a manager could spend almost as much time explaining the ways of the West to such artists as attempting to gain engagements for them.

These émigré artists had no idea of how competitive it was in the West in terms of performance opportunities. At home in the USSR they had been the recipients of annual incomes no matter the number of performances they gave. In the United States and Europe, fees for engagements would differ depending on the circumstance. One concert hall might hold 500 seats, while another would have a capacity of 2,500 seats. The artist's ability to attract an audience would have an effect on the ticket prices. Innumerable variables had to be considered. These "naifs" from the USSR had to be exposed to all of the variables and commit these as well as musical scores to memory. But, the ancient memory of basically being looked after could not be erased. It was their cultural conditioning that the more these artists could milk from any given situation the more highly they regarded it.

These former Soviet artists came from a very close-knit community. They all knew one another in Moscow, or at least knew of each other, and all were keenly aware of the rewards available to successful performing artists in the West. I met up with one such Soviet émigré artist at a leading piano competition.

I have never been a fan of the competitions for musical instrumentalists. Panels of judges choose the winners, who immediately upon the conclusion of the contests become competitors for the ever-shrinking concert opportunities

136

available in the classical music world of today. Each judge contributes a score based on his or her personal view of performance standards. The resultant winners are the homogenized results of such scoring schemes. The years have proven that very few winners of these competitions have become household names or survived within the "marketplace" after the initial excitement and resultant publicity have faded. Van Cliburn, winning the Tchaikovsky Competition in Moscow during the Cold War of the late 1950s, was an anomaly. No other winner of a musical competition has ever been afforded the extremes of hyperbole surrounding his victory, including a ticker tape parade down Broadway in New York City. Cliburn's win had as much to do with the international politics of the era as it did with his potential musical talents. He was the national hero of the moment in the United States. For Texans he became a lifetime hero and icon.

Van Cliburn has lived alternately in Louisiana, Texas, and New York; however, his residence of choice has always been Texas. It is no wonder, because there he is lauded in the extreme and surrounded by highly influential and admiring friends. They have been supportive of him ever since his win in Moscow and have established a foundation and a quadrennial piano competition bearing his name. In recent years, the foundation has provided a managerial and booking service for the winning participants in its competitions.

In its beginning, however, the Van Cliburn International Piano Competition did not include such managerial and booking services, and it invited major concert managers from all over the globe to attend its contests. Hurok Concerts, Inc., managed most of the first winners of the Cliburn competition in the U.S. When I set up my own independent artists management in late 1976, I became eligible for an invitation to audit the competition for potential artist clients.

So, in the fall of 1977 I was invited for the first time to attend the Van Cliburn International Piano Competition, held that year once again in Fort Worth, Texas. The chairperson for the quadrennial event at the time was an energetic woman by the name of Martha Hyder. As usual, Van Cliburn himself was in evidence throughout the contest. I arrived in time to hear those performances that would assist the judges in selecting the finalists of the competition. Among these semifinalists was the young Russian pianist Youri Egorov, who had recently defected to the Netherlands. Among the judges in '77 was a pianist from the Soviet Union, Nikolai Petrov, who apparently was doing his best to unnerve Egorov. Egorov had been a prize pupil of Jakov Zak at the Moscow Conservatory, as was Petrov. Zak had recently died of a heart attack. I had known Jakov Zak well from my days at Hurok Concerts and had accompanied him on a tour of the United States. Zak was a highly cultivated individual with a well-developed sense of spirituality and a poetic approach to his pianism. He had imbued Egorov particularly with this poetic sense. At the competition, Petrov had said to Egorov:

"You killed our teacher by defecting. You were the cause of Zak's heart failure." Such an accusation had indeed reduced Egorov to tears, he later related to me.

To me, Youri Egorov's sensitive, individual style of performance stood out among a strong group of pianists that year, including Steven de Groot, Santiago Rodriguez, and Alexander Toradze, a contender from the Soviet Union. However, with a reduced score from the Soviet judge, Egorov did not make the finals of the competition. I was angered by the injustice of such a phenomenal talent having been eliminated. Others attending the competition were of a similar mind and felt that something should be done on Egorov's behalf. I suggested to these like-minded audience members that I had a solution.

At this point, Martha Hyder, the chairperson, asked me, "Now that the six finalists have been announced, which one would you pick to sign up?" My reply was that after hearing them all, I was not interested in any of them because the most interesting and poetic one was not even in the finals. There were two days remaining before the announcement of the gold, silver, and bronze medal winners. The gold medal cash award was a sum of $10,000. I later conferred with my fellow objectors and explained my possible resolution of Egorov's rejection. If I could have their combined guarantees totaling $10,000 toward a New York debut for Egorov, I would see that he got his well-deserved recognition in that manner. I had suggested that exact amount because it equaled the cash award of the Cliburn competition's gold medalist. My group of fellow malcontents mustered up the courage of their convictions and they agreed upon that sum of money.

I then proposed to Martha Hyder that the Van Cliburn Foundation accept $10,000 toward Youri Egorov's career, since I wanted to present him in New York City. My artists management firm would be responsible for any of the costs of Egorov's New York presentation that exceeded $10,000. Martha objected, saying that it would be making folly of the competition and its jury. She also asked why I had selected the sum of $10,000. My reply was, that was what the first prize was. If the foundation's first prize had been $2,000, that is the sum I would have asked for and also would have paid the difference of the cost of a New York debut for Egorov, regardless.

I asked Martha to rethink her priorities, since the foundation should be responsible for all participants — winners or losers. Were I to propose this formula for a nonparticipating pianist, her objection would be understandable. In this case, however, she would be avoiding the foundation's overall responsibilities. I also pointed out to her that we didn't need the foundation's approval. If we did not have it, we would proceed with Egorov's New York debut anyway. I said, "You are possibly damned if you do, and damned if you don't."

Martha was avoiding a decision in the matter. The Cliburn competition had come to its conclusion with Steven DeGroot having been announced as its gold medalist. Martha was the hostess for the competition's closing night party, always a traditional high point. Since I was scheduled to depart for New York the following morning, I felt it imperative to get Martha to focus on the subject of Egorov. Realizing that there was no convenient moment, I took Martha aside and simply said, "Martha, it's time that I have an answer regarding Egorov, and we must have a pow-wow, now!" She gathered together several people whom she felt she wanted present, and we adjourned to one of the many upstairs bedrooms in her home. Following a reasonably lengthy discussion, my suggestion was deemed acceptable to the Van Cliburn Foundation, with a proviso that we would not present Egorov in New York City sooner than seven or eight weeks after the Cliburn first-prize winner had his debut under the Cliburn aegis.

In the end, Steven DeGroot had two debuts in New York City. As a previously selected artist on the roster of Young Concert Artists, a nonprofit artists management and presenter based in New York City, he had been scheduled earlier to make his New York debut on the Young Concert Artists Series at the Kaufman Auditorium in the 92nd Street YMHA. The Young Concert Artists management would not concede its privilege of presenting their artist for the first time in New York City, and Steven DeGroot, first-prize winner of the 1977 Van Cliburn International Piano Competition, made his New York City debut under the Young Concert Artists banner. He received excellent notices but little of the hype usually surrounding a winner's New York debut. This was because not all of the city's music critics were able to attend the 92nd Street Y concert. Their editors felt that DeGroot's upcoming Carnegie Hall debut was far more worthy of coverage. The Carnegie Hall concert was the presentation of the Van Cliburn Foundation.

Like many young artists, DeGroot had a limited repertoire. He had put his best foot forward at the 92nd Street Y. At Carnegie Hall, he would be playing an entirely different program, most of which would probably be new to him, or at least not as frequently performed as the pieces he had performed at the "Y." Unfortunately, the Carnegie Hall program did not consist of his best "party pieces." The natural excitement that should have ensued from the large audience, consisting of most of New York City's music mavens, just did not happen. Too many had missed the earlier performance, and now they questioned what all of the fuss was about.

In the meantime, my office had been preparing for Youri Egorov's debut at Alice Tully Hall, a 1,100-seat recital facility at Lincoln Center for the Performing Arts. The Cliburn foundation graciously sponsored a postconcert reception at the apartment of their New York publicist, Mary Lou Falcone. The press had been alerted to the story surrounding the sponsorship of Egorov's debut and was on the lookout for reasons either to reject this pianist who had failed to be recognized in Fort Worth or to hear for themselves the reasons that a number of people had come to Egorov's aid. A number of his supporters from Fort Worth and even one from Canada flew in to New York for his debut. Youri Egorov triumphed with the press in New York, eliciting rave reviews and "buzz" from the managerial professionals in the city.

Not long after, Chicago's leading impresario, Harry Zelzer, telephoned me, asking if "that pianist you're raving about" was available within a few days to replace an ailing Murray Perahia on his Allied Arts Piano Series. It was a Wednesday afternoon, and Harry needed a replacement quickly for that following Sunday afternoon's scheduled recital in Chicago's Orchestra Hall. Owing to the relative anonymity of Egorov, Harry was not willing to pay more than $400 for Egorov's services as a recitalist. Knowing there was an enormous difference between $400 and what would have constituted a fee for the well-known Perahia, I had to realign my thinking very quickly. Since the invaluable benefits of potential rave reviews for an unknown artist's performance in Chicago's Orchestra Hall do not come that easily, I had to "bite the bullet." I did not want to risk playing games with Harry. I explained that the airfare alone, not to mention hotel expenses, would eat up his miserly $400. Then, too, since Egorov did not speak very much English, it was incumbent upon me as his new manager to fly to Chicago at my own expense. Harry generously came up with an additional $200 to complement his offer. It was still a joke. Needing whatever rave reviews could be gathered quickly in order to build Egorov's career from that of a "loser" at the Cliburn competition, I agreed to Harry's final exploitative offer.

I immediately telephoned Egorov in Amsterdam, where he had returned only weeks before, and asked him if he was willing to accept both the low fee and the emergency circumstances. The fee would just about cover his airfare to and from Amsterdam. I encouraged him to accept this engagement in a major city, as it would mean reviews from a couple of America's leading music critics. Egorov agreed. He flew to Chicago and arrived on Saturday, performed on Sunday afternoon and again garnered great press.

The following season I had booked him at Dartmouth College in New Hampshire, and Thor Eckert, then the music critic for the *Christian Science Monitor,* made a special trip from Boston to hear the twenty-three-year-old prodigy. Eckert also praised Egorov's artistry. To help solidify Egorov's increasingly excellent reputation, I booked Carnegie Hall for a recital to be given during the annual conference in New York City of the Association of College, University and Community Arts Administrators (ACUCAA), America's presenters of student entertainment on college campuses. To introduce and showcase this young pianist, the ACUCAA membership was issued invitations to attend Egorov's recital. I arranged that the concert be recorded as well. An up-and-coming label at that time, Peters International, undertook that task and hired a producer who came from the Netherlands to record Egorov live in his Carnegie Hall debut. We hired the famous artists' photographer Boris Goldenberg to capture Egorov's image during the concert, and a color photo of the artist taking a bow on the Carnegie Hall stage was used as album art. Rave reviews once again topped off the event. It had been such an enormous success with the audience that one person, forgetting himself during the concert, upon hearing a particularly well-executed phrase shouted "beautiful!" in full voice. That musical phrase was the only set of notes that had to be rerecorded prior to the album's release. The album made the classical "best seller" list when it was released.

Because so many of the ACUCAA attendees had missed out on hearing Youri Egorov in his first outing at Carnegie Hall, I immediately booked the hall for another Egorov recital the following December, making for a third consecutive recital under my aegis in New York City. My office paid for each of Egorov's two recitals at Carnegie Hall, as well as all of the expenditures over $10,000 involved in his Tully Hall debut recital. Because the audiences for these performances by Egorov were largely invited guests, the box-office receipts covered only a limited amount of the expenses involved. With each season the young pianist's bookings increased accordingly.

Like many youngsters flush with success, Egorov attracted a group of young hangers-on both from Amsterdam and New York, and they turned out to be exceptionally bad influences on the young pianist. When he toured the United States, his stay would be lengthy because of the significant number of engagements we were able to gain for him each season following his triumphs with the press in 1978. He kept a loft apartment near Greenwich Village year round. To provide him with the initial funds needed to secure the apartment, we advanced him $12,000 against his fees for that season, so substantial had his income become. A large amount like this paid up front to obtain a lease on a desirable apartment was called "key money" and was over and above the cost of rent. Two or three of his "groupies" would join him in New York City and crash with him for weeks or months at a time. Egorov and his friends became habitués of late-night haunts that flourished at the time, such as the legendary Studio 54. Egorov, being a regular, did not have to wait in line to gain entry to Studio 54, where hallucinatory drugs were very much a part of the scene.

As one of his first major orchestral engagements, we had been able to secure an appearance for Egorov with the St. Louis Symphony Orchestra. He was to perform a Rachmaninoff concerto as a provision of his contract there. However, a week prior to his scheduled arrival in St. Louis, he notified us that he wanted to change to a different concerto. Under no circumstances did he wish to play the work that he had been contracted to perform. The administration of the St. Louis Symphony Orchestra responded to this information with a firm rejection of any change of program. If anything, they would find another pianist to perform the planned concerto. They said that if Egorov did not play as contracted, they would never engage him again. He did not want me to know it, but he had failed to prepare himself to perform the required concerto. His ego having been pumped to gigantic proportions, he now thought himself indispensable. Egorov believed that the St. Louis Symphony Orchestra would simply acquiesce and accept an alternate work. His gamble failed. The orchestra concluded that he had broken the contract and asked us to tell him to stay home. They quickly found a substitute pianist to fill in for Egorov.

At that stage of his career, reviews of performances with symphony orchestras were needed. As noted, his recital performances had accrued an excellent number of raves. The lack of orchestral reviews would deeply interrupt the momentum we were establishing in his career toward eventually establishing him as worthy of performing with the New York Philharmonic, the Philadelphia Orchestra, or the Boston Symphony Orchestra. He was becoming anxious to have such performing opportunities. These major orchestras book their guest artists up to three years in advance.

In general Egorov's behavior was becoming more and more irresponsible as he basked in the admiration of his so-called friends. We also noticed that in his reviews there seemed to be constant references in varying cities to Egorov "seemingly fighting a cold." I had no idea that this young artist was nurturing a serious drug habit. His sniffles at the keyboard during recitals were apparently being brought on by a cocaine habit. My serious attention was drawn to his condition when I received a telephone call from a concert presenter in the Midwest who was alarmed that Egorov had not shown up at the airport that day as scheduled for a concert that very evening. I immediately telephoned the apartment Egorov had rented in New York City for the season and was told by one of his friends that they had no idea where he was. Naturally, his concert in the Midwest was canceled. He had not even left New York. Egorov turned up later that day. He had blacked out in a New York City gutter, having ingested too much of one or more drugs while partying the previous night.

Following that incident, I had a long discussion with Egorov about his behavior and the resultant problems. As a good actor, he appeared appropriately contrite, seemingly acknowledging the dangerous path he was embarked upon. However, like most addicts he actually remained in a state of denial. He had merely been attempting to assuage my fears regarding his personal as well as professional conduct. To aid him in his denial he began to listen to the advice of both his hangers-on and a provincial artists' manager from Amsterdam, who all encouraged his state of denial. Youri even had the manager from the Netherlands visit me to outline his dissatisfaction regarding the state of his career. I had no recourse other than to let him proceed to work under other management. I had predicted that he would be performing under even more stringent circumstances if he chose to change management. It turned out exactly as I outlined. He was appearing in communities with organized audiences that were far from the major venues in which he had thought he should be performing. He was to go through three more major managements before his career in the United States completely dissipated. The classical music world is a very small and close-knit community. Word of Youri's misconduct and his addictive illness had gotten around.

Tragically this young artist from the 1977 Cliburn competition was to contract AIDS. Conductor Paul Strauss told us he had heard in Europe that rather than die a slow and painful death, Youri Egorov chose to have a formal farewell dinner party at his home in Amsterdam. After his guests left he had a doctor administer a lethal injection.

Ironically, the freedom Youri sought through defection from the USSR literally was the contributing cause of his demise. His social emancipation with no self-disciplinary constraints was his undoing. Youri's entire circle of male friends in Amsterdam all succumbed to this dread disease. Coincidentally, Steven DeGroot, the gold medalist of the '77 Cliburn competition, also reportedly died of AIDS.

In an era of celebrity adulation as a national pastime, we are too often witnesses to the negative effects of success, particularly upon the young and inexperienced. The temptation to believe that they are indestructible, that their success exempts them from the rules that apply to everyone else, is often too great to resist. An ego is a necessary tool for a performer, but, as exemplified in Youri Egorov's career, belief in one's own indestructibility can result in the artist's downfall and demise. Perhaps the sound of applause is even more of a narcotic than cocaine.

I have had occasion to interact with Martha Hyder many times over the course of the years since 1977. I was once invited to stay at her vacation home in San Miguel de Allende in Mexico and enjoyed her hospitality very much. She has been an active supporter of the Van Cliburn Foundation for many years and was particularly supportive of one the first-prize winners from Russia, Vladimir Viardo. When Viardo received first prize in Fort Worth in the early '70s, Martha became very expansive and, getting somewhat carried away, showered him with gifts. Rumor has it that when he showed interest in Levi jeans, Viardo was the recipient of something like fifty pairs of the denim trousers. He was to be endowed by Martha with other goods from such purveyors of luxuries as Neiman Marcus, as well as an automobile that was shipped to Moscow. As first prize winner, Viardo was obliged to return to the United States to perform concerts scheduled in advance of the actual competition for the contestant who placed first, whomever it might be. After a heroic return to his homeland, the Soviet

Union, the higher priorities of the Soviet government took hold. The generosity of the Western world could prove highly tempting, posing a risk to the Soviets that Viardo might defect if he were let out to meet his obligations as a Cliburn winner. So, he was forced to remain at home in the USSR for years, with his wife and two sons, and could not fulfill those initial engagements in the U.S. During the years he was obliged to remain in the USSR, he constantly received still further evidence of the Martha Hyder's largesse.

I attended the Tchaikovsky Competition in Moscow in 1986. Also attending was Susan Tilley with members of her family. Susan was the successor to Martha Hyder as chairperson of the Van Cliburn International Piano Competition. Richard Rodzinski, who had just been appointed executive director of the Van Cliburn Foundation, was also attending the event. Aside from attending the Tchaikovsky Competition, Susan had two favors to carry out while in Moscow. One she had promised to do for Van Cliburn, while the other was for Martha Hyder. The Cliburn favor had to be delivered first, and time was growing short, as flowers were to be in place prior to the opening event of the competition. Van had authorized an expenditure of up to $1,000 for a floral presentation of roses to be placed beneath the statue of Peter Ilyich Tchaikovsky, which is situated on the street in front of the Moscow Conservatory. Susan enlisted my help, as our small group of Americans was quickly beginning to discover that the simplest of tasks became a most complicated effort in the Soviet Union. I found out that one could not place anything in a public space without first obtaining official permission to do so. Even the content of any printed message on a floral arrangement had to be approved in such a circumstance.

Remembering my acquaintance with the president of the Union of Soviet Composers, Tikhon Krennikov, when I had been in the USSR with Franz and Lella Waxman, I telephoned his office. He was able to help facilitate our needs in obtaining both flowers and permission to fulfill Van's request. Flower shops were few and far between in Moscow. We were directed to a shop that was on the outskirts of the city. Only that shop could create the kind of significant display required. Roses were entirely out of the question owing to the heat of the city during that time of the summer. Red carnations were the recommended alternative. As for the printed message on the ribbon, the long poem suggested by Van had to be reduced to several words with his name beneath. As to the price of the flowers, I was pleased to save the sum of $900 for Mr. Cliburn. The final problem was that the arrangement was much too large to fit within the confines of a Moscow taxi. In desperation, I asked Krennikov's office for some sort of vehicle to convey Van's flowers to the Moscow Conservatory. They soon let us know that a vehicle would be waiting to pick us up at the Conservatory at around 5:30 that afternoon. Much to our surprise, it was on time. More to our pleasure, we found that it was a huge, empty, air-conditioned, fifty-passenger bus. We were "home free" on this task and, gathering up the flowers, brought them back to the Moscow Conservatory and placed them at the base of Tchaikovsky's statue. This favor to Van had consumed an entire ten hours of the day. We were on to our next assignment.

We had a bit more time in which to grant Martha Hyder her request. We had several days until the end of the competition in which to carry out her wishes, which involved transporting more gifts for pianist Vladimir Viardo. Susan Tilley had conveyed the gifts in her and her family's luggage to Moscow. They included enormous decorative pillows that were up to two feet square in size and a number of posters. The pianist was not in Moscow but was staying at his house, or dacha, in the countryside outside the city. He could not be reached by telephone. The only solution turned out to be enlisting the cooperation of another Soviet pianist and personal friend of mine, Alexander Slobodyanik, and the additional assistance of his wife, Natasha.

We gathered together in the evening after the final event of the Tchaikovsky Competition, in the Tilley family suite in Moscow's National Hotel situated opposite the Kremlin. Seated on the half landing of each floor of the hotel was a concierge (watchdog) assigned to observe the activities of hotel guests. Placing the pillows in valises would not solve the problem of getting them out of the Tilley suite. There could be no logical reason for a group of people going out with valises unless they were checking out of the hotel. We all joked about not even being able to steal a lamp out of the hotel with the watchdogs everywhere. We came up with a "master plan." It would appear perfectly normal for us to take a short walk out of the hotel together at around 10:30 at night. Natasha was supposed to leave first and get her automobile. She would drive around past the hotel and remain with the car at an idle on one of the side streets a block or two away. We would join her separately with pillows stuffed under our jackets. Each of Susan's children also was involved, all stuffing pillows under their outer garments, including shirts worn loosely outside of skirts and trousers. Leaving in groups of two or three people at a time, we casually slid past the concierge and down the stairs, through the lobby, and onto the sidewalk. As we approached the corner and looked up the side street, Natasha awaited us as directed. However, there were two policemen conversing with her. Our entire party was petrified.

The policemen had noticed her sitting in the parked car and wanted to know why she was not moving. Somehow, Natasha convinced the policemen that her car had overheated and she was simply waiting for it to cool down before proceeding on. They apparently believed her and went about their business elsewhere. In the meantime, we had walked on and now doubled back to see if Natasha was okay and the coast was clear. With nervous relief, we quickly loaded up the car with the mountain of pillows. Alex and Natasha immediately drove off to the country, as their dacha was not far from that of the Viardos. Speaking for myself, it was not an adventure I would care to repeat. The posters for Viardo were left at the National Hotel for me to pick up the following morning. However, when I asked for them, they had conveniently disappeared. The hotel staff knew nothing about any package having been left in my name.

Martha Hyder was usually very welcome in Moscow on her frequent visits to that city because Soviet officials knew that she would spend a good deal of money there. However, on one of her trips the United States ambassador at the time pointed out to her that pianist Viardo was not being allowed out of the USSR because of her open generosity to him. She was advised to curb her flamboyance and try to maintain a lower profile regarding the talented Soviet pianist whom she so much admired. Vladimir Viardo's absence from the stages of the Western world for so many years allowed for new and younger artists to capture the attention of concertgoing audiences. His career never reached the heights that it might otherwise have achieved.

Another product of the Moscow Conservatory, pianist Alexander Slobodyanik, had been an enormous success for us at the old Hurok Concerts, Inc. Sviatislav Richter had brought him to the attention of Sol Hurok. For some reason, Alex had not been permitted to return to the United States for many seasons following his initial successful tours here. I had hoped to make a special trip back to Moscow to request permission from Gosconcert for Alex to tour the U.S. under my management.

There was a comparatively different political climate, since Gorbachev was now premier of the USSR and perestroika was then in progress. There was talk of Gorbachev traveling to the U.S. capital at that time to confer with President Ronald Reagan in the White House. I suddenly had an idea and, in 1987, before leaving on another trip to Moscow, I telephoned Susan Tilley, who was working with Van Cliburn at that time, in Fort Worth. I suggested that it would be a wonderful bridge between the past and present to have Van Cliburn entertain for Gorbachev's tentatively planned visit to the White House. Cliburn had remained a favorite in the USSR long after his victory there in 1958 at the Tchaikovsky Competition, when Nikita Khrushchev had gone out of his way to acknowledge the American first-prize winner. Susan agreed with me, and I told her that I would try and feel out Soviet officialdom when I got to Moscow. I would call her immediately upon my return.

I was in Moscow for a stay of around three weeks. In order to get Alexander Slobodyanik onto my roster of artists, I deliberately requested the availability of four Soviet artists, knowing full well that three of the four were with other managements. In typical Gosconcert style, they said, "We will see." Then, I also casually aired my suggestion of Van Cliburn performing at the White House during Gorbachev's upcoming visit there. I was aware that the agenda of Gorbachev's visit would have to be approved by both the White House and the Kremlin. The time came for my last meeting before leaving Moscow for my return to New York. At this final meeting I was told that three of the four artists I had requested were with other managements, and that as a consolation prize, I could have Alexander Slobodyanik. I was delighted to have used their own tactics to beat them at their own game. Further, almost as a deliberately staged afterthought and adopting a casual attitude, they added, "Oh, by the way, Max, do you recall having asked about Cliburn playing for Gorbachev's visit to the White House? You must remember that it is your American White House that will be the host, and it is for them to invite Cliburn to play. As far as we are concerned, it would be okay for Gorbachev's visit."

Taking this as Gosconcert having cleared my suggestion with the Kremlin, I knew that I was expected to carry the message back to officialdom in the U.S. When I got back to New York, I telephoned Susan Tilley once again and let her know that Cliburn playing at the White House for Gorbachev's visit had a "green light" as far as the Soviets were concerned. I told Susan to go forward with informing Van and the White House. I was so enthusiastic about it that I even wrote a letter to Van.

I was very gratified to watch the televised broadcast of the performance I had orchestrated. President and Mrs. Reagan, Premier and Mrs. Gorbachev, and assorted guests were most obviously enjoying Cliburn's performance on the occasion of that state visit. The concert was an enormous success. I must also add that I had never received an acknowledgment or a thank-you from anyone, and I was later told, "It was all Nancy Reagan's idea." So much for the influence of artists' managers as opposed to the power of presidential wives.

Chapter Eleven

OVER TIME, MANY FRIENDS AND ACQUAINTANCES HAVE ENCOURAGED ME to set down my experiences in writing. I have come to the realization that I was tremendously fortunate to have worked in the performing arts during an era in which dance and music flourished in an atmosphere of thorough appreciation. As the twentieth century came to a close, that era was also coming to an end. At last I recognized a need to record some of what had occurred during that period, and my personal participation in it, lest such a history be forgotten.

During the almost thirty years that a firm bearing my name has represented artists, I have been fortunate to have associations with performers of many different nationalities: Russians, Americans, Israelis, Spaniards, Italians, Frenchmen, Portuguese, Latin Americans, Canadians, and Austrians. I have strongly favored discovering unknown and youthful talents such as the Russian émigré pianist Youri Egorov and the Israeli-Canadian cellist Ofra Harnoy.

My past associations with many artists of the Soviet Union kept me in the forefront of latter-day Russian artists' thoughts when they sought touring opportunities in North America. I also kept Russian artistry in mind, and in addition to individual artists I pondered the possibility of touring large-scale Russian attractions in the U.S. and Canada.

Moscow's Bolshoi Ballet Company had not appeared in the United States for many years. In the mid-nineties I contacted the company's management, which knew me well, to begin exploring the possibility of inviting this major attraction for a tour. It was my wish to reacquaint ballet audiences with the Bolshoi Ballet as a first-class troupe that traveled with elaborate productions worthy of any operatic stage, complemented with a full symphony orchestra. In response, I was telephoned by representatives of the Bolshoi Ballet, who seemed to be very excited about such a project and wanted to know when and in what city we could get together to discuss future plans. I suggested either New York City or somewhere in Florida. About a month and a half passed, and I received word that we should meet in Las Vegas. It came as a huge surprise to me, and I asked them why we should meet there, of all places. They totally shocked me with their reply. The

Bolshoi Ballet Company would be appearing in Las Vegas for a run of two weeks at the Aladdin Hotel's 7,000-seat theater. They would then later be traveling to Los Angeles, where they would perform for another week at the Shrine Auditorium, which seated 6,000. I was dumbfounded and asked, "Why did you do this, knowing that I have planned to offer you a tour in which you will be in proper venues and be reviewed properly?"

The Bolshoi people answered, "We needed the money."

Responding, I asked, "If you have a young daughter about whom you care and the family needs money do you put her out on the streets?"

As it turned out the Bolshoi Ballet drew a paying audience of under a hundred persons in the huge theater. Complimentary tickets were distributed throughout Las Vegas in hotels and even on buses in order that some sort of audience might fill the thousands of seats available. The company's American sponsors maintained a highly improbable hope of building an audience over the course of the two weeks. Those sponsors, however, ran out of funds by the end of the first week. They did not even have enough to pay for the rooms at the hotel housing the company. The group of investors and managers of the tour could best be described as dilettantes. Otherwise, they would never have booked the Bolshoi Ballet into such an improbable venue as the Aladdin Hotel in Las Vegas, especially after the company had not been seen in the United States for many years prior to this.

I decided to avoid Las Vegas and fly to Los Angeles, where I would also be able to see the company and its new and younger generation of dancers in the repertoire then being offered.

Upon arrival in Los Angeles and meeting the company and its administrators at the Shrine Auditorium, I was immediately informed, "Max, you were right, it is a catastrophe. But a very nice man whom we would like you to meet has saved us financially. He will tell you the rest of the story."

It was then that I met Brad Haines, a gas and oil pipeline contractor from Oklahoma who had become interested in the Bolshoi Ballet's dilemma after hearing of it from friends who had invested in the U.S. group responsible for the current tour. Brad told me that while he was not all that well versed in the arts, as an American he was embarrassed to envision the possibility of the Bolshoi Ballet's performers being evicted from their hotel in Las Vegas. To ward off such a circumstance, Brad had given half a million dollars to the American sponsors to get them through their losses during their first week in Las Vegas. As he became more and more involved, he came up with another half million to cover expenses during the Bolshoi Ballet's second week there. When the time came for their appearances in Los Angeles, Brad Haines generously proffered yet another similar sum, so that his total contribution amounted to $1.5 million. The company's

American sponsors turned over the house and one performance to Mr. Haines for the benefit of a favorite charity, so aside from aiding the company, some additional good came of his largesse because approximately $250,000 was raised for charity during that one evening.

Brad and I got along rather well and decided that we could work together to explore a proper tour of the Bolshoi Ballet in North America. The two of us flew to Moscow and stayed for several days to work out financial details and technical logistics for the potential tour. As always, the Russians were very cordial.

But still another trip to a wintry, snowbound Moscow was necessary. This second time Brad and I were accompanied by two other men, the marketing and publicity representatives who would be involved in the planned tour. We brought a final presentation and contractual proposal guaranteeing forty performances in which the full company and full symphony orchestra would be involved. The company was to be shown in the best possible light, and only in major dance venues that would include performances at the Metropolitan Opera House as part of an upcoming Lincoln Center Festival. The contract called for covering all expenses as well as a payment to the Russians of $2.5 million.

Shortly before leaving on the trip, however, we learned that a small company calling itself the "Bolshoi Ballet" and numbering around thirty dancers traveling with an "orchestra" composed of ten musicians and a synthesizer would be touring the United States in advance of the tour that Brad Haines and I were proposing. We also learned that Vladimir Vassiliev was the virtual owner of this smaller company. He was collaborating with a Russian émigré in America who was booking the lesser "Bolshoi Ballet" and sharing in the profits with Vassiliev. At that time Vassiliev was also the artistic director of the Bolshoi Theatre's entire complement of artists, which encompassed not only the ballet but an opera company and symphony orchestra as well. Boris Yeltsin, then president of the Russian Federation, had appointed Vassiliev to this position on the recommendation of Mstislav Rostropovich, whose wife, the soprano Galina Vishnevskaya, was a very important and imposing influence within the Bolshoi Opera.

We mentioned to Vassiliev that we had only just heard of the smaller company being presented in the United States in advance of the larger company. We told him that we believed this lesser company would negatively impact the image and desirability of the main company for touring in the U.S. We told him that unless he withdrew the availability of the small "Bolshoi Ballet," we could not proceed further with negotiations for the $2.5 million contract for the genuine Bolshoi Ballet Company.

Vassiliev attempted to reason that the small company would only be appearing in small cities and not in the large-scale venues proposed for our tour. We countered that such small cities had an impact on the box-office revenues in the large cities. For instance, an appearance by such a mini-Bolshoi in Evanston, Illinois, would have an effect on audience attendance in nearby Chicago or Milwaukee. People in Evanston would think that they had already seen a genuine Bolshoi Ballet troupe. Consequently, they would forgo any purchase of tickets for later appearances by the main company in Chicago.

Vassiliev refused to bend for his own personal and entirely selfish reasons, though Brad Haines had already invested $1.5 million in the Bolshoi Ballet and, by proffering the then magnanimous sum of $2.5 million as a fee over and above expenses, was ready to guarantee a genuinely profitable United States tour for the larger company. It turned out that neither party would accommodate an agreement. In actuality, Brad Haines had expended many thousands of dollars more as his funds paid for our trips to Moscow and the costs for preparation of the presentation. All efforts were made in the hope of putting a positive face on the reduced Bolshoi Ballet's appearances in America. BBC-TV filmed a documentary on the company's tour of Las Vegas and Los Angeles, which they entitled *Dancing for Dollars.* The documentary's overall impact on the reputation of the once great ballet company was an unfavorable one, especially since the program was shown on American television.

Once again, Vassiliev's behavior illustrated the self-destructive element in many artists' natures, but this time he was not just one dancer "shooting himself in the foot" but was, in effect, machine-gunning all 500 feet of his contingent of 250 Bolshoi Ballet artists. The company remained virtually unemployed the summer of our proposed tour. I later learned that a small official breakout company from the larger group did tour Scandinavia.

Our negotiations with Vassiliev were duly reported in complaints registered with the Russian ministries with authority over the Bolshoi Theatre. There were constant reports of other minor and major scandals within the artistic direction of the Bolshoi Ballet, Opera, and Symphony Orchestra over the course of the next few years. Finally, when Vladimir Putin assumed the presidency of the Russian Federation, one of his first official acts regarding the arts was to dismiss Vladimir Vassiliev as artistic director of the Bolshoi Theatre.

Brad Haines had hoped to reap a profit from our proposed tour of the Bolshoi Ballet, as well as to establish business contacts in Russia for his gas and oil pipeline construction firm. But the days of cross-country touring of the United States by huge ballet companies seem to have passed with the passing of Sol Hurok. Individual forays sponsored with funds from large foundations make possible engagements at New York City's Lincoln Center or Washington's Kennedy Center, but sustaining such major troupes for periods of a month or more is simply no longer financially feasible. American appearances for such companies as the Royal Ballet of England or the Bolshoi Ballet have become mere stopover dates on international tours encompassing engagements in Australia and Asia as well.

So, though I remain highly active in the representation of individual classical performing artists and some special attractions, I have set forth this final reporting of recent dealings with a world-class ballet company as illustrative of the end of an era in which imaginative, daring impresarios such as Sol Hurok could flourish. Symphony orchestras have floundered and disbanded across the width and length of the United States. For the first time in memory, the Chicago Symphony Orchestra, the Philadelphia Orchestra, and the New York Philharmonic are admitting to financial woes. As this is written South Florida has been without a fully professional symphony orchestra for over two years since the Florida Philharmonic Orchestra folded, and no overt signs of any pending resuscitation have been reported.

Having absorbed this memoir, perhaps the reader will now better understand why I chose as its title *It's Not All Song and Dance*. Yet I consider myself very blessed to have personally known so many artists, and especially to have witnessed so much magnificent artistry by the likes of Margot Fonteyn, Maya Plisetskaya, Leonard Bernstein, Vladimir Horowitz, Arturo Toscanini, Erik Bruhn, and Rudolf Nureyev. I have been fortunate to view such artists, who the world has known and revered as icons, as the human beings they are when not appearing on the performance stage. And to be able to report on my own good fortune here is yet another boon. I sincerely hope that I have been able to convey something of what it was like to have been a participant in those glory days.

The classics in whatever art form are classics because they have survived the centuries, and will continue to survive. I remain an optimist regarding the capacities of future generations to regenerate the traditional classics while creating new and effective works of art. Despite the problems that will present themselves along the way, including the present need for a far greater educational exposure to the arts and humanities for students in their formative years, time will prove my belief to be a valid one, as the pendulum swings back and a golden era in the performing arts takes place once again.

Afterword

PERHAPS IT IS MERELY SYMPTOMATIC OF MY ADVANCED YEARS, BUT I believe the nature of classical performing artists management has changed and not always for the better. Also, as this is being written some long-established concert artists managements are rumored to be having difficulties in meeting payrolls; still others are laying off longtime employees. It is the end of an era, and one in which I played perhaps a minor role but one which has given me enormous pleasure and pride.

The *New York Times* recently noted the passing of a leading Hollywood artists' representative by the name of Phil Gersh (born Gershowitz and no relation). The obituary remarked on this man's disappointment with his profession's "advancements." Mr. Gersh often said that he missed the golden years of Hollywood. He is reported to have said, "In the old days you dealt with producers who were creative and who were responsible financially for the picture. You take a producer like Hal Wallis or the Joe Pasternaks or the Arthur Freeds, they were creative, and they were smart businessmen. They knew about filmmaking. Not like these executives today."

Similarly, Sol Hurok was perhaps the last of the great impresarios. He defined an impresario as, in his own words, someone who "takes his risk with his own money and not other peoples.'" Such individual presenters of the finest artists in the world no longer exist today. Presentations of major ballet companies are no longer a financial risk taken by a man of sure gambling instincts but are done with little or no risk to individuals or even to the nonprofit giants doing the presenting. The John F. Kennedy Center for the Performing Arts presents the Kirov Ballet and opera companies from Russia but does so with millions of dollars from major donors available to offset the losses incurred. The Lincoln Center for the Performing Arts presents a summer festival with major performing entities from all over the world but does so only with the major financial backing of multinational corporations. Sol Hurok was the sole proprietor of Hurok Concerts, Inc., and Hurok Attractions, Inc., and, as such, personally assumed total fiscal responsibility for importing performing arts companies. These companies, such as the

Bolshoi Ballet or the Royal Ballet of England could include over two hundred people. Today, a New York City concert season that featured his artists and attractions would be considered impossible. Such a Hurok season might have included the aforementioned Bolshoi Ballet at the Metropolitan Opera House; pianists Artur Rubinstein, Emil Gilels, Ralph Votapek, Gina Bachauer, Van Cliburn, Sviatislav Richter, and Vladimir Ashkenazy; cellists Jacqueline du Pré, Mstislav Rostropovich, and Gregor Piatigorsky; violinists Nathan Milstein, David Oistrakh, Itzhak Perlman, Isaac Stern, Henryk Szeryng, and Leonid Kogan; female vocal recitalists such as Marian Anderson, Roberta Peters, Victoria de Los Angeles, Janet Baker, Grace Bumbry, and Shirley Verrett; and male operatic stars such as Jan Peerce and Jerome Hines. The Vienna Boys' Choir would be featured, as would folk-dance ensembles from Mexico, Poland, Romania, India, and Ukraine. Gilbert and Sullivan might also be performed by the D'Oyly Carte Opera Company from England along with further exotic fare such as the Bunraku Puppets of Japan.

That formidable list of artists was the sole responsibility of one man, Sol Hurok. He had a hand-picked staff to help him achieve his goals. But, all major contacts and contract negotiations were handled personally by Sol Hurok himself.

Phil Gersh lamented the passing of an era in which film producers could identify and appreciate talent and creativity. I, too, regret that while there are some exceptionally talented individuals employed by nonprofit presenting organizations, the time when a lone man could risk his own personal wealth and livelihood is now a matter of history. There were the minor-league Huroks in some of America's larger cities, such as Chicago's Harry Selzer and New Orleans's Nella Ludwig. James A. Doolittle at Los Angeles's Greek Theatre was discussed earlier in these pages. He eventually established a nonprofit corporation for his presentations in that city. There were others: the Bernardi family in Cleveland, Moe Septee in Philadelphia, Patrick Hayes in Washington, D.C., and Aaron Richmond in Boston. All of those people enriched life in their cities and all personally assumed financial responsibility.

During the final three decades of the twentieth century people began looking beyond even the west coast of the United States and across the Pacific Ocean when it came to matters of culture. Western, or "European," culture was the dominant influence on our own but is now viewed as passé and irrelevant among many academicians. Many symphony orchestras — certainly cultural beacons of European derivation — have foundered in the United States during recent times. As this country's immediate descendants of European immigrants die off, so, too, does interest in many elements of the culture into which they were born. Yet, one can maintain hope for the survival of Western art forms. Many opera and ballet companies, both traditionally European aesthetic forms, continue to flourish in the United States and offer new works by North and South Americans, Europeans, and Asians. This blending of the old and new, this genetic melting pot, is reason to be hopeful.

Maxim Gershunoff's is no longer a voice in the wilderness. He has called for "innovation, not imitation" in the presentation of the performing arts for years. His plaint is now echoed by the recently appointed president of the American Symphony Orchestra League and former president of the Chicago Symphony Orchestra, Henry Fogel. Just as the highways and byways of American cities blur together in sameness with cookie-cutter Holiday Inns, Burger Kings, MacDonald's, Denny's, Westin Hotels, and similar brand-name facilities, their concert halls present look-alike prepackaged programs offering the same brand-name artists season after season, the only hint of creative imagination being imitation.

Without venturesome individuals taking risks, unimaginative blandness will continue to characterize performing arts presentations both here and abroad. Artists are still known to be adventurous risk takers and, because of the risks they take, they often generate controversy and even derision. However, many innovative, creative artists fall prey to the powerful regressive elements of conservatism sweeping the country. The concerns of both politicians and donors turn out to be handicaps to the wider dissemination in particular of what is referred to as avant garde art. Even the vague possibility of offending any segment of the populace will have these pandering elements ready with all their armaments of suppression. The United States, where until fairly recently the arts remained largely outside the political shooting gallery, is currently embroiled in its own culture wars between political conservatives and liberals. Yet, no matter the level of recognition accorded them, artists will always continue to strive for excellence, and their representatives will faithfully continue to promote their efforts.

Leon Van Dyke
Fort Lauderdale, Florida
June 2004

Anecdotal Evidence of
a Life Enjoyed Behind the Scenes
in the Performing Arts

Royal Ballet of England Vignettes

John Lanchberry replaced Robert Irving as principal conductor of the Royal Ballet. In 1958, Irving moved to the United States and, at George Balanchine's invitation, became the principal conductor of the New York City Ballet.

Irving arrived in New York City by boat, and I met him at the pier and drove him to the Hotel Fourteen, where he established a temporary residence. I attended his first performance with the New York City Ballet. When he entered the City Center Theatre's orchestra pit as the new principal conductor, he received a standing ovation from the New York audience. Despite the initial reactions of its audiences, the New York City Ballet's administration was cautious relative to Irving's new position. They thought it best to be careful in the event that the artistic relationship between Bob and Balanchine did not work out. Time proved that the management had no need for concern. Irving and Balanchine had an exemplary working relationship. Robert Irving remained in his post for many years and became a much-admired figure with the NYCB.

Jack Lanchberry was a very exciting ballet conductor. The thrust of his rhythms, with their driving pulse, greatly contributed to the performances of the Royal Ballet. He was able to understand and accommodate the needs of the dancers without sacrificing musical values. With his keen understanding of ballet, Jack was also a very skillful arranger of many works of music. He was able to produce many interpolations, for instance, in the Tchaikovsky ballets performed by Fonteyn and Nureyev throughout the world.

Offstage, Jack was a great movie fan. He always wanted to meet movie actors and actresses that he particularly admired whenever he was in Hollywood. On one trip to the West Coast he derived great satisfaction in locating Stan Laurel of the famous movie duo of Laurel and Hardy. Surprisingly enough, he found Laurel listed in the Santa Monica telephone directory. Jack called Laurel; introducing himself on the telephone he made an appointment to visit with the legendary comedian. I accompanied Jack on the day of his meeting with Laurel. It turned out that Stan Laurel, confined to a wheelchair, lived in a modest apartment near the coast in Santa Monica. It was truly interesting to hear Laurel reminiscing and to watch his expression of delight at the fact that he still received fan mail as young audiences discovered his old films on television. Television, however, bothered him because the interruptions for commercials upset the flow of his films' humor. He said that he had spent so much time in the editing room to achieve the effects he desired, and now all of that effort was for naught if it was chopped up to advertise products. He understood the necessity of commercials, but he just did not like the effect they had on his artistic output. Although they had made a wonderful comedy team and worked in harmony, when they were finished filming on the set, Stan Laurel and Oliver Hardy shared no other interests whatsoever. Hardy would immediately leave the movie studio and could only be located at a racetrack. Stan Laurel said that he and Oliver Hardy had little or nothing in common on an intellectual basis. That afternoon, referring to his intellectual sensitivity having little comic value, he wistfully remarked, "Well, maybe Oliver was right," a line he delivered with his trademark grin while scratching the top of his head.

RETAINING A VESTIGE OF MY DIRECT INVOLVEMENT WITH ORCHESTRAL musicians, I acted as the contractor for the various ballet orchestras that Hurok Attractions, Inc., toured throughout North America. I very much enjoyed selecting the various musicians in order to assemble a good orchestra. In some instances, we kept a nucleus of principal players who were familiar with the ballet repertoire, although that could vary from company to company. I would also audition and employ young musicians, some of whom have succeeded perhaps beyond even their wildest dreams. At this juncture in my life, realizing that I played even a small role in their climb upward gives me a good deal of satisfaction. To name a few, I hired flutists Ransom Wilson, who has become a well-known soloist and conductor, and Paul Lustig Dunkel, who has achieved professional success as a conductor as well; another flutist, Paul Freed, later joined the Boston Symphony Orchestra; violinist Guy Lumia, who was a frequent concertmaster of my ballet orchestras, later became concertmaster of the Metropolitan Opera Orchestra; others, such as the violinist Emma Ricci, sister of

Ruggiero Ricci, became permanent members of the Metropolitan Opera Orchestra; and double bassist William Brohn became well known as the arranger of such Broadway musical scores as *Miss Saigon* and also rearranged Leonard Bernstein's themes from *West Side Story* for violinist Joshua Bell, who performed them on television and recorded them on compact disks (they are now popular with symphony orchestras' pops programs).

Although I selected and contracted the various musicians for our touring dance attractions at the Hurok office, I maintained a full schedule of artist managerial responsibilities as well. The New York ballet season at the Metropolitan Opera House was about ten to fifteen weeks each year, following the Metropolitan Opera's season in the spring. The Hurok ballet season at the Met was attractive as a source of employment to the musicians of the New York City Center of Music and Drama.

A proposal was brought to Hurok Attractions that involved cornering the market for the musicians who comprised the orchestra maintained by the New York City Center. That orchestra performed with both the New York City Ballet and the New York City Opera. Heading the proposed project were John Simon White (born Hans Schwartzkopf in Vienna), administrator of the New York City Opera, and Norman Singer, administrator of the New York City Center of Music and Drama. White was a member of the Austrian triumvirate that was at the helm of the New York City Opera for many years. Its other members were Julius Rudel and Felix Popper, both opera conductors. Norman Singer was a much admired arts administrator, highly regarded by his colleagues in New York City's performing arts world. White and Singer had the idea of giving their musicians more long-term employment by getting Hurok Attractions to sign them up as the orchestra for the Hurok dance attractions appearing each year at the Met. I found that they were completely disregarding the budgetary limitations of having an orchestra perform at the Met that could not then tour with the various companies following the New York engagements. Accepting this proposal would require having a completely new set of musicians go out on tour. The rehearsals required for the new musicians would cost close to $50,000. This seemed to be of no concern to White and Singer. Despite the fact that all of the musicians in the New York City Center Orchestra were members of the same union, American Federation of Musicians, Local 802, it seemed to me that White's and Singer's plan was intended to create a separate union of sorts, or a "closed shop," blocking all of the freelance members of Local 802 from employment throughout the Hurok season at the Met. I found their scheme to be highly disturbing. So, armed with the knowledge that there were exceptionally fine freelance musicians who would be happy to be employed not only at the Met but to do the touring as well, I felt it necessary to fight the City Center. I won my battle. It gave me enormous satisfaction, indeed, on behalf of the freelance musicians of Local 802, especially since I had been such a freelancer myself at one time.

ALTHOUGH CONDUCTOR JOHN LANCHBERRY AND I GOT ON QUITE WELL, and as much as I admired his talent, there was always a delicate underlying thread of unnecessary rivalry with me on his part. He could not quite absorb the fact that my position was more complex than that of just the usual orchestra personnel manager ("contractor"). I was a vice president at Hurok Concerts, Inc. and was not an instrumentalist from the orchestra doubling in the capacity of contractor, as would be the usual circumstance. My authority within the dual capacities under which I worked not only gave Jack pause, but I believe it also was a position he found difficult to accept. As an example, in Philadelphia, just at the time of race riots in that city, the orchestra was in the pit rehearsing for the first performances of a run by the Royal Ballet. There were several workers sweeping and cleaning in the empty theater, on either side of the top balcony. On occasion, the workers' whistling could be heard. Lanchberry stopped the rehearsal and, without looking in the direction of the disturbance, shouted out, "Would you please stop that infernal whistling!" The whistling stopped, but immediately some deliberate whistling started from an opposite corner of the theater. I was seated immediately behind Lanchberry in the first row of the empty auditorium, immediately adjacent to the orchestra pit. Jack, knowing that I was seated there, could have turned to me and discussed the disturbance. Instead, looking straight up at the stage with his back to me, pompously attempting to provoke and demean me, he shouted, "Mr. Gershunoff, go up to the balcony and see to it that this noise stops or I shall not rehearse." He remained frozen, looking up at the stage awaiting an action on my part. This type of posturing at my expense was a classic Lanchberry "performance."

Violence was rampant in Philadelphia in the mid-1960s. Houses were being torched, looting was taking place, and general mayhem was the order of the day. Taking into consideration the racial tensions and conflicts that were in full flower then, I had to decide very quickly whether to go up to the top balcony and risk provoking the theater's workers, which may have led to a potentially dangerous and life-threatening situation, or to simply exercise my administrative authority. I chose the latter. I rose from my seat, leaned over the rail to the musicians below, and announced, "Owing to the fact that Mr. Lanchberry does not wish to rehearse, the rehearsal is now over. You are all dismissed. See you tonight." Driving back with Lanchberry to the hotel housing the company and with the full knowledge that I had infuriated him, I said, "Jack, you know what's going on now in Philadelphia even though you are a visitor from England. I don't plan to endanger my life for you so that you can sport your ego and flaunt your authority at my expense." Fortunately, the musical performance that evening went off very well, despite the lack of a full rehearsal.

Yet another instance of his need to spark conflict with me related to a program of ballet highlights. It created possible financial problems because it included a work using extra musicians and the instruments they needed. This ballet's score required many additional percussion players, while other instrumentalists in the orchestra were not needed. After analyzing costs, I concluded that we could save $18,000 by using those other, idle instrumentalists who would, in fact, do double duty for extra pay as percussionists playing the gongs, triangles, and other instruments needed to achieve the ballet score's demands. This solution was far less costly than engaging outside musicians to achieve the same results. As performances were to take place in New York City at the Metropolitan Opera House, I naturally wanted Lanchberry's cooperation. Attempting to provoke a negative reaction on my part, Jack proposed that he would be agreeable with one proviso. He insisted that I, too, must perform along with the others on some of the percussion instruments. Either I played or there was no deal. I discovered that I had to play five instruments, ranging from a huge gong to a wood block, triangle, a gourd (with which I made a scratching sound), and a cymbal. Never having played percussion before, I found it all to be a lark. I deprived Jack Lanchberry of the satisfaction of costing Hurok Attractions, Inc., an additional $18,000 for extra outside musicians and had some fun in the process.

By the sixties, the days of overnight train rides between tour stops were long over. The Royal Ballet Company now took airplanes between engagements. A run might end in Washington, D.C., on a Sunday evening, and the company would fly on Monday to the next city, which might be Chicago. On such flights I had the opportunity to regularly observe Rudolf Nureyev, who would always be seated with Margot Fonteyn as his traveling companion. Rudy would be fine all during a flight until it came time for the plane to land. Then, acting like a scared little boy, he would bury his head in Margot's lap, and she would caress his head comfortingly. Once the plane had landed safely, Rudy would immediately perk up and upon departing the aircraft would strut forth as the star he and the world wished him to be.

Further illustrating the distance between Rudolf Nureyev in reality and the star the world recognized him as is an incident that occurred once while I was traveling with the Royal Ballet. I was having a drink with some friends in a small bar around the corner from the Masonic Temple in Detroit when Rudolf Nureyev walked in. It was following a Sunday matinee by the company. In those days, people in Michigan bars had to be seated either on stools at the bar or else be seated at a table, as there could be no standing in a barroom. Also, no alcoholic beverage other than beer could legally be sold on Sunday. This particular bar was a "Mom and Pop"–owned operation, where the very solicitous "Mom" was hostess, waitress, and, as it turned out, bouncer as well.

She hurriedly advised Rudy and his two young male friends to take a table quickly, as otherwise there would be absolutely no room in the already packed establishment. Rudy smiled as he sat down, and said, "I want Scotch."

In a pleasant manner, "Mom" explained Michigan's blue laws and said she would be happy to serve Rudy and his friends some beer. Nureyev repeated, rather arrogantly, "I want Scotch." After further back-and-forth conversation, I heard Rudy, in an angered tone, exclaim, "I not like juice." Then, and in full voice, I heard Mom say, "I don't give a damn who you are, we don't need people like you!" Whereupon she pulled him from his table and bounced him out.

His two friends, rather embarrassed, meekly made their own exit.

I must say that I was confused by her abrupt reaction and thought either it was a misunderstanding or that Rudy may have really commented about not liking "Jews." I later returned to the hotel where the entire Royal Ballet was ensconced and told conductor John Lanchberry of the incident.

Lanchberry, whom Nureyev respected enormously, always spoke to Nureyev as "Rudik" in an affectionate, almost childlike, way. Since Lanchberry adored intrigue, he said that he would call Rudy immediately and ask him what he actually had said to Mom. When that telephone conversation ended, Lanchberry looked at me and said, "Max, I have terrible news for you." The conversation went as follows: "Rudik, I understand you misbehaved this afternoon in the bar. What happened? Did you tell the lady that you didn't want 'juice' or that you 'Not like Jews'?"

Nureyev's reply, apparently, was "I not like Jews."

Lanchberry then said, "Rudik, what would Mr. Hurok think if he knew you felt that way? After all, he has been very generous to you."

Rudy's answer was "He's known worse anti-Semites than I." When I related the incident to Sol Hurok, his calm response was: "What did you expect?"

THE ROYAL BALLET HAD BEEN IN CHICAGO OVER THE NEW YEAR HOLIDAY on an earlier tour when Michael Soames was still partnering Margot Fonteyn in classical ballet repertoire. To help an intimate few welcome in the New Year, Sol Hurok hosted a New Year's Day brunch in the Pump Room of the Ambassador East Hotel. In addition to our host, the party consisted of Margot, Michael, Frederick Ashton, conductor Robert Irving, the Royal Ballet's manager Herbert Hughes, and myself. Hurok was seated in a spacious booth next to Margot. I will never forget his magnanimous gesture to Margot. As the sommelier began his ritual of opening a bottle of champagne, Hurok addressed Margot specifically, saying, "Happy New Year, and I've ordered your favorite vintage champagne for us all to enjoy." We drank a toast, and Margot said, "Oh, thank you, Sol." Then she eyed the label, leaned over to me, and whispered into my ear, "I think he has his ballerinas mixed up."

At one performance of the Royal Ballet in Boston, Margot Fonteyn and Rudolf Nureyev appeared in choreographer Kenneth MacMillan's version of *Romeo and Juliet,* set to Sergei Prokofiev's music. The performance had been going well, but at the scene where Romeo discovers the body of Juliet after she has taken the sleeping potion, the lights in the orchestra pit blacked out completely. The orchestra's musicians attempted to keep on playing whatever they could remember of the score. However, one by one each instrument gave up until it was practically like a performance of the Haydn "Farewell" Symphony. All that was missing were the candles. From the stage, Margot could be heard from Juliet's funeral bier saying, in full voice, "Rudy, either I am growing deaf or I really am dead." The curtain had to be lowered until the audience stopped laughing and the theater's electricians could restore power to the orchestra pit.

In San Francisco we had a ten-day run at the War Memorial Opera House, with poor advance box-office sales. After opening night in the hometown of the sixties "flower people," Rudy and Margot somehow ended up at a party in the much-ballyhooed Haight-Ashbury district. It was quite a shock to open the San Francisco newspapers the following morning and see a photograph of Margot Fonteyn in a crouched position, covering her head with a fur jacket, as seen atop the roof of a building that had been raided in Haight-Ashbury. The tour road manager for Hurok, Joseph Brownstone, was telephoned in the wee hours of that morning to bail Nureyev and Fonteyn out of the San Francisco jail. While they weren't participants in the drug taking going on at the party to which they had been invited, everyone at the party had been hauled into jail that night. Following the opening night, while walking to the War Memorial Opera House for the next performance, I noticed police vans and police dogs in the adjacent municipal buildings' driveways. In front of the Opera House, aside from the arriving audience, more and more flower people seemed to have gathered. At the Opera House, the press asked me if they could go backstage before the performance. They wished to interview Nureyev and Fonteyn about the circumstances surrounding their arrest and subsequent night in jail. I had to decline, knowing that Margot and Rudy were very tired, having spent a sleepless night in jail and needing all of the preperformance time now to get in shape. Perhaps naively, I asked, "Why weren't you press people here yesterday when we opened? We need all of the press coverage we can get. Your coverage might better be based on high artistry and not on silliness surrounding a bunch of hippies." The incident, however, did create a booming business for the Royal Ballet in San Francisco that season.

Before that performance, a police official wanted to speak with me. He requested that I make an announcement before the performance began requesting that the audience not leave the theater during the intermission and exit only through the side doors after the performance. He was afraid the huge crowd of hippies parading in front of the Opera House could endanger the audience. I told him I was afraid that should I make such an announcement, I would raise such fear in the audience that we would lose a great deal in ticket sales for the coming eight days. His reply was "Well then, I can't be responsible for crushed heads."

I asked him how many policemen he had on his team at the Opera House. He told me that he had fifty there. I asked, "Have you ever seen a movie premiere? Why not station twenty-five policemen on one side of the front steps of the Opera House and the other twenty-five on the opposite side. The audience will then feel protected and secure."

"Well," I was told by San Francisco's finest, "It'll be your responsibility."

Innocently, I replied, "Okay."

Having spoken with some of the local hippies and asked what brought them all to the opera that night, I learned that free buses had been chartered to bring anyone who wanted to go to the Opera House and perhaps get a glimpse of Nureyev and Fonteyn. After the previous night's scandal, the bus rides would constitute a festive activity that evening for the residents of Haight-Ashbury. A representative of one of our nation's major magazines had chartered the buses and brought the hippies to the Opera House in hopes of creating some sort of additional incident capable of making manufactured headlines. Much to the collective disappointment of the editors of that magazine, I am certain, the local hippies had a lovely evening and dispersed peacefully without incident.

ONE TOUR OF THE ROYAL BALLET FINISHED UP IN LOS ANGELES AT THE Shrine Auditorium. The final performance was to feature *Cinderella,* with Frederick Ashton and Robert Helpmann appearing as the Cinderella's ugly stepsisters. Preparing to go to the Shrine Auditorium that evening, I called up Freddy at his room at the Hollywood Roosevelt Hotel. He had a great fear of riding alone in automatic elevators, so I asked him if I should come to fetch him. He bravely said, "No, but wait for me at the lift doors in the lobby. I'll have a go at it alone." Freddy triumphantly emerged from the elevator in the lobby. He had momentarily overcome his usual fear. We drove to the Shrine Auditorium, and Freddy, in a perky mood, seemed to be choreographing some fantasy surprise in his mind. He said, "You will see when we get there."

I did see. During the performance in one scene the ugly stepsisters envision what it will be like for them to dance at the grand ball with Prince Charming. The scene calls for two violinists to be onstage in period costumes, complete with powdered wigs, and play along with the orchestra from the pit. Freddy loved to tease our concertmaster, Guy Lumia. In *Cinderella*, Guy and violinist Emma Ricci would be the costumed onstage musicians, for which they would collect extra pay. As one of the stepsisters, Freddy started to play out the choreography he had been working on while we were driving to the theater earlier. He wanted to make Guy Lumia either break up with laughter onstage or become miserably embarrassed. Freddy danced close to Guy and attempted to kiss Guy's fingertips as Guy tried to play his violin. As he tried to dodge Freddy, Guy's wig slipped off and fell to the stage. Somehow Freddy also involved Emma Ricci, the other violinist, in the horseplay, and her wig went flying as well. The audience, of course, loved it. The combination of Ashton and Helpmann as the ugly stepsisters in *Cinderella* was one that anyone who ever witnessed their performance can never forget. Their performing together was priceless. A closing night's performance always provided an opportunity for some prank onstage, and the ballet *Cinderella* offered those two talented pranksters a wonderful opportunity to treat an unsuspecting audience to their highjinks.

Mitropoulos Vignettes

THE AMERICAN SYMPHONY ORCHESTRA LEAGUE IS A STRONG ADVOCATE for the programming of new music. However, many boards of directors of America's symphony orchestras are comprised of well-meaning but musically unsophisticated donors to their organizations. They are less influenced by actual musical knowledge than by what they glean from the media. These boards, and the American Symphony Orchestra League, might be questioned as to their policy of strongly advising on the use of guest artists for the purpose of selling tickets. This policy serves only as a self-defeating and temporary Band-Aid. Overexposure on the concert stage has seen many well-known "names" deteriorate in their level of performance as the fees those performances command escalate. Audiences, consequently desensitized by such overexposure, drop their subscriptions. They have not found any exhilaration from "stars" cranking out less-than-exciting performances. Meanwhile, there are exceptionally talented, superb young unknown artists available and anxious to perform. Hiding behind their buzzword, "marketing," administrators, for the most part, do not have the "nose" needed for self-confidence in such artistic matters. They are leading themselves down a dead-end street where they will not find any new stars to replace the fading ones in whom they have placed so much faith.

The groups usually in charge of selecting conductors to be music directors of symphony orchestras in today's world are known as "music director search committees." Hearing of outrageous temperamental outbursts, like those of the late, great Arturo Toscanini, by a prospective candidate for their orchestra, would immediately mark such an individual as "psychologically unstable," and financially too risky to serve their needs. Such search committees will gladly accept a conductor more limited than a Toscanini, sacrificing a more exciting musical product in the interests of peace. Unfortunately, along the way audiences have been lost through such priorities.

When I was still freelancing with the NBC Symphony, I remember one rehearsal when Toscanini seemed to be disturbed by the constant tearing of his eyes. He went through the first half of the rehearsal dabbing away at his eyes. During intermission, some of the violinists placed neatly folded, clean handkerchiefs on the maestro's music stand. When Toscanini returned to continue the rehearsal he looked down and noticed the handkerchiefs. A normal reaction might have been "Thank you, gentlemen." Instead, he grabbed at the buttons of his black rehearsal jacket, seeming to want to tear it off, and blasted the company of musicians by saying, "This is not a laundry. This is not a laundry." The rehearsal ended there, and we were all dismissed. Over one hundred musicians were being paid that afternoon to do nothing.

During a performance in Carnegie Hall, once again perhaps reflecting Toscanini's battles with failing eyesight as he aged, it became very important to him that the elevation of his podium not be too high. It had to be constructed to be an exact height. He had made his entrance onto the stage for the concert on this particular day, and the podium seemed not to be what he had expected. He conducted magnificently for the entire first half of the program, restraining his frustration with the podium until he stomped off the stage for the intermission. He then darted up to his dressing room, taking the stairway two steps at a time, screaming all the way at the top of his lungs, "I am not a ballerina," along with a constant stream of assorted vulgarities in English and Italian. Though Toscanini had seemingly unlimited compassion for others' shortcomings or physical limitations, he could not accept anyone viewing his own capacities as being limited. Toscanini commanded and won the respect of his musicians, but in today's world his behavior would be considered unacceptable, and he could not get away with it.

It was an unenviable position for any conductor to follow Arturo Toscanini as a guest conductor of the NBC Symphony Orchestra. It was a hard act to follow with his national radio audience of fans and an international reputation. For the guest conductor, it was more like walking into a minefield peopled with enemies gunning for his every vulnerability. His talents, the most publicized assets of a guest conductor in his first confrontation with the instrumentalists of the NBC ensemble, were most susceptible to attack by those musicians. Individually, musicians are very different in their behavior than when met as an often challenging group. On the part of the guest conductor, this first time out required a very careful balance of diplomacy, maintenance of discipline and the earning of respect needed to achieve artistic goals.

I can recall the very first time that Dimitri Mitropoulos conducted the NBC Symphony Orchestra. All of the musicians in the orchestra were talking about the sensational Greek whom Serge Koussevitzky had earlier invited to conduct the Boston Symphony Orchestra. Their colleagues in Boston had been telling them of their experiences with Mitropoulos. He was said to have a photographic memory, and once he had studied an orchestra's seating chart, he could address each member by name from the first rehearsal, which was also conducted from memory. Referring to Mitropoulos's not-so-secret homosexuality, the NBC Symphony Orchestra members jokingly cautioned one another not to "bend over" in the Greek's presence.

The NBC Symphony's French horn section consisted of four horn players, three of whom were brothers. They were Arthur, Jack, and Harry Berv. That first rehearsal began with a very cordial, businesslike, authoritative work session led by Mitropoulos without the aid of a printed score. As is usual during rehearsals, there were various exchanges between orchestral musicians and the conductor. At one point, when Mitropoulos was explaining his desires to the orchestra, Harry Berv shouted from his seat, "Oh, Maestro, at Letter 83, is the third horn marked 'muted' or 'open?'" Dimitri asked, "Why are you asking me this now, we passed it a long time ago?" Harry Berv remarked, "I didn't want to interrupt the rehearsal, but now that you've stopped, I need to know." Dimitri immediately replied to Berv's deliberate testing by saying, "It's marked 'mute' in red pencil. I put it in your part myself." We in the orchestra shuffled our feet in unison in our own form of approval of Dimitri's unusual talent. In that moment he had won our respect and admiration.

Dimitri did not recognize the concept of "photographic memory" as such, but believed his ability was simply a form of mental discipline. As to his homosexuality, I remember his commenting to me at one time, "What a pity it is that I am being condemned for a luxury that I don't even have time for."

I had introduced myself to Mitropoulos following that first rehearsal and expressed my admiration. We came to know one another over the course of the next few years, and he was aware that I had moved back to California.

As mentioned previously, Mitropoulos stayed with me in California during his recuperation from a heart attack. During that period in 1951, as Dimitri became stronger, he felt obliged to make some social visits, as well as to receive visitors on occasion. There was one very persistent man who telephoned many times. He mentioned that he was of Greek extraction and that his name was Kourisis. Dimitri would joke, "If it's a Greek, it's undoubtedly to ask a favor of some sort." The persistence of Mr. Kourisis won over Dimitri's good nature, and he finally acquiesced and requested that Mr. Kourisis drop by at 2:30 of an afternoon. During the meeting, it turned out that Kourisis was in the early stages of his career as a booking agent, placing conductors as guest artists with smaller orchestras. For his visit with Dimitri, he was acting on behalf of the Portland Symphony Orchestra (now the Oregon Symphony Orchestra). The orchestra was experiencing financial difficulties and any fee for a guest conductor would be negligible. Kourisis had already been able to enlist the services of such conductors as Otto Klemperer and Igor Stravinsky to help the orchestra out of its financial doldrums. Dimitri also agreed to conduct the Portland Symphony Orchestra with the proviso that his protégé, Paul Strauss, also be engaged. Dimitri would not only conduct one concert but would remain and appear as piano soloist when Strauss conducted. Paul Strauss at the time was the conductor of the Ballet Russe de Monte Carlo. Inquiring into the Greek heritage of his guest, Dimitri learned that he had been manipulated to some degree. His guest disclosed the fact that he had merely used his family's Greek name so that the maestro would meet with him. He had actually changed his name, and told Dimitri that it was now Ronald Wilford. He felt it necessary to have altered his name in order to avoid the prejudices surrounding Greeks at that time. As the Anglicized Ronald Wilford, today he is the well-known chairman of Columbia Artists Management, Inc., who arranged for me to leave CAMI after completing only two years of my three-year contract.

ON A SOCIAL OUTING, I ACCOMPANIED DIMITRI TO THE HOME OF JOSEPH Szygeti and his wife in Palos Verdes, an exclusive suburb south of Los Angeles. Their home, overlooking the Pacific Ocean, was a beautiful villa with a swimming pool on spacious grounds on which they maintained beehives. Szygeti had appeared as a guest artist with the Pittsburgh Symphony Orchestra in 1942, with Fritz Reiner conducting, when I had been a member of that orchestra at the age of nineteen. It had never occurred to me then that one day I would be welcomed into the home of this famous artist as a privileged guest along with an even more privileged guest, Dimitiri Mitropoulos. Our host was a highly intellectual man who maintained an extensive library in his home. He also had a very valuable collection of string instruments, all of which he proudly showed us as he conducted us through his house. We went upstairs, where he wanted Dimitri to see the guest room which was to have been set aside for him had he chosen to stay with the Szygetis. With his playful sense of humor, Dimitri excused himself and said that "like a doggie" he would use the bathroom to "mark his territory." We were then led into the Szygetis' bedroom with large Romanesque windows with a view of the Pacific Ocean. Dimitri said he was overwhelmed by the beauty of both the room and its view. Szygeti concurred and commented that on the many nights he was unable to sleep, he enjoyed looking out at the view. He then added, "Maybe if I didn't have all of this, I would be able to sleep." I found the contrasts between these two highly successful musicians and their quite different attitudes about finances to be a source of both wonder and amusement. Dimitri Mitropoulos valued money only as a tool and lived exceptionally modestly, whereas Joseph Szigeti chose to live very luxuriously.

After a long prologue of arrangements, we visited Arnold Schoenberg's widow, Gertrud. Dimitri had invited Madame Schoenberg to New York City as his guest for two weeks on an occasion when he had performed one of her late husband's compositions with the New York Philharmonic, and he had even raised funds for her personal needs at a time when these needs had come to his attention.

Dimitri gave me the address of the Schoenbergs' Westwood Village residence off Sunset Boulevard and the Westwood Circle of the time. He felt that the visit was incumbent upon him, but that it needn't be too long. We arrived around 5:30 in the afternoon, and as we approached the address, Dimitri said, "Oh, it cannot be here." The impressive two-story house was behind a gated circular driveway and in no way matched the pathos of the story he had in his mind regarding the Widow Schoenberg. He insisted that the house I had driven to was the wrong one. I insisted that it was the one at the address he had given me and that we ring the doorbell and see who answered. It turned out to be the correct address for Madame Schoenberg. We had some sherry and Gertrud Schoenberg brought out some of her husband's scores about which Dimitri had expressed some curiosity. It was a short but sweet visit until we got back into the car. Dimitri then, in attempting to sort out the conflict in his mind, questioned the idea of the widows of great men who so often could not adjust to living on in a more modest lifestyle than the one they had enjoyed during their husbands' lifetimes of relative fame. He said, "I cannot afford to live that well. How could she have given me the idea that her circumstances were limited when she is able to live as well as she does now?" I commented by conjecturing that the University of California at Los Angeles, where her husband had taught, could possibly own the property on which Madame Schoenberg was living. However, the whole experience was more than he wanted to cope with at the time and, as if to ease his mind, he said, "You know what? Let's have dinner and go see a bad movie." The worse the movie was, the better Dimitri's estimation of it. He loved inconsequential films. "It's like a can of soup, you drink it and it's over," was his summation of his filmgoing.

DIMITRI MITROPOULOS WAS AN ARDENT SUPPORTER OF "NEW" MUSIC AND championed living composers in whichever artistic positions of authority he held. He also championed the works of Gustav Mahler and was a principal influence on those who came after him and also promoted the Austrian genius's symphonies, including Leonard Bernstein. Mitropoulos's interpretations of Mahler served as role models for Bernstein, who eventually recorded the entire Mahler symphonic repertoire, a feat that would have been unheard of two decades previously. Once again, Leonard Bernstein was in the right place at the right time. With the advent of worldwide communications capability in television, Lenny had greater exposure as a conductor than any who had preceded him. His ability to promote Mahler was partially due to the prominence he had gained through the medium of television.

One day during his recuperation at my home in California, Mitropoulos received a letter from the New York Philharmonic's music adviser, Bruno Walter. According to Walter's letter, the board of directors of the Philharmonic had requested that he convey to Maestro Mitropoulos a directive that Mitropoulos confine his programming to a menu "more consistent with a formula of Beethoven, Brahms and Tchaikovsky." In other words, "no more of that 'new' music" that Mitropoulos felt so obliged to foster or "steps might have to be taken for your dismissal" from the Philharmonic. It is my understanding that the New York Philharmonic has denied knowledge of any such letter. Be that as it may, Dimitri was very deeply disturbed with this intrusion on his mission to expose his audiences to new music. After 1950, most symphony orchestra audiences in the United States became less and less accepting of new compositions.

Earlier, Dimitri had asked me to drive him to the Los Angeles airport. Composer Leon Kirschner, on his way to New York from the Northwest, had arranged a brief stopover at Los Angeles. He could say hello to Dimitri and give him a Kirschner score that Dimitri had hoped to study for future use. Instead, after receiving Bruno Walter's letter, he called Kirschner and explained that he would not be able to consider Kirschner's new composition for programming purposes, at least not in the then foreseeable future. Kirschner should fly directly to New York without stopping in Los Angeles. The prospect of what that letter meant for his future so depressed him that Dimitri spoke of leaving the New York Philharmonic. Dimitri, my father, and I discussed the dangers of overreacting and defeating one's mission entirely. Perhaps it would be best to minimize his fervor for new music for the present. A few weeks passed, and one morning, as he paced the kitchen floor sipping the strong coffee he loved, Dimitri thoughtfully announced, "I have made my decision. I shall no longer be a missionary of music but remain as a mere entertainer."

A COUPLE OF YEARS AFTER HIS STAY IN CALIFORNIA, MY FATHER AND I RAN into Dimitri just after my father had arrived in New York City from Los Angeles for a short visit. We had just left the Carnegie Tavern on West 56th Street around midnight when Dimitri rounded the corner from Sixth Avenue on his way home to the Great Northern Hotel. We crossed the street to say hello, only to find that Dimitri had been walking down the street with tears in his eyes. His sad expression could not be hidden. My father asked, "Dimitri, what's wrong?" Hoping to make him feel a little better, my dad said that he had brought Dimitri a box of my mother's homemade cookies that he loved. Dad also suggested that Dimitri return to us in California for a rest. Dimitri acknowledged the gift and invitation and quietly said, "Aaron, you know, my days of fun are over." I believe that following that episode with the New York Philharmonic, Dimitri Mitropoulos suffered from a deep depression for the rest of his life that lasted until death.

Bernstein Vignettes

IN 1951, LENNY WAS MAKING HIS FIRST TOUR OF THE UNITED STATES WITH the then newly formed Israel Philharmonic Orchestra. Following a concert scheduled earlier in the week in Pasadena, California, there was one on Friday evening in Los Angeles. A very dear friend of Lenny's, originally from Philadelphia and then living in Los Angeles because he was connected with the movie industry, was hosting a postconcert reception in Lenny's honor. The party was to be held at the host's beautiful home in the Hollywood Hills. He asked Lenny to give him a written list of personal friends whom Lenny wished to have at the reception. Among the names that Lenny provided to his host was the name "Chaplin." Lenny, still new to the Hollywood scene, was looking forward to meeting glamorous movie folk. I drove Lenny from the concert in Pasadena to the party. When we arrived I noted that, indeed, Lenny's host had assembled an illustrious grouping of Hollywood's notables. As we both mixed and mingled, his host said to Lenny, "Why don't you say hello to your friend Chaplin, who's sitting on the stairway in the entry hall talking to a bunch of people there?" Lenny, glancing in that direction, said, "Oh my! That's Charlie Chaplin — but I don't know him." His host remarked, "But you asked me to invite him." Lenny said, "No, I didn't mean Charlie Chaplin, I meant the other Chaplin, Sidney Chaplin"

I learned there, as well as at other parties, that Charlie Chaplin never completely entered into a party scene when he first arrived. He would only feel secure after he had engaged a group in conversation in an entry area. Then, once safely surrounded by a newly formed admiring entourage, Charlie would make his entrance. The effect was that of a pied piper being dutifully followed. No one at a party would fail to notice the well-executed arrival of this shy artistic genius. Oona O'Neill, his wife, would already have made her own way into a party room and be comfortably seated somewhere. Once the party was well under way, Charlie took center stage and delighted everyone with pantomime renditions, reciting Shakespeare while picking his nose, and doing a satirical take on a couple on safari being filmed by a bad movie director. Charlie was absolutely free of inhibition and gave a no-holds-barred demonstration of how bad direction can lead an audience's imagination into sexual areas never intended by a movie script.

The mood of the party was very warm and outgoing, and I was standing with Lenny when he asked Charlie Chaplin how he had enjoyed his concert. Charlie replied that he had not been to the concert. However, he had heard that it was very wonderful. Lenny then said, "Well, you must come to my Friday concert in Los Angeles." Charlie said that it might be difficult for him to get there, and perhaps if I took him, he would go. He asked me for my telephone number, and we planned to coordinate our meeting on Friday. On that day, Chaplin called with apologies and said he hoped that Lenny would understand. He explained that in view of the political climate (it was the heyday of Senator Joseph McCarthy and the House Un-American Activities Committee) he would be unable to attend. *Life* magazine had recently published several pages of postage-sized photos of people in the arts, including actors, writers, composers, and directors, who were listed as either Communist dupes or actual Communists. Those photos included both Bernstein and Chaplin. Chaplin said since then he had not gone to any public events and, as much as he would have liked to hear Lenny's concert, he felt that he might possibly do Lenny more harm than good by attending. Should the press write about Charlie Chaplin surfacing in public to attend a concert by Leonard Bernstein, they would have a field day by intimating that "fellow travelers" were getting together. Some sort of political camaraderie could be implied by Charlie's attendance at the concert. I explained it all to Lenny later that night at the concert and he understood only too well. Charlie Chaplin and Leonard Bernstein subsequently partied together in New York City, getting to know one another better at a later time.

During that 1951 tour of the U.S. by the Israel Philharmonic, Lenny discussed the makeup of the orchestra with me. He felt that it could be improved with a new principal horn and new principal trumpet. He asked if I might be interested and also whether Joseph Eger, then the principal horn of the Los Angeles Philharmonic, could also be persuaded to join the Israel Philharmonic. The three of us had known one another from our days as students at the Curtis Institute of Music. As added incentive, Lenny noted that the Israel Philharmonic would not only find me a very hard-to-get apartment in Tel Aviv but would have my auto transported from Los Angeles to Israel as well. My cars were important to me at the time, and I was the proud owner of a brand-new Nash Rambler. Our employment as musicians being of major concern to us at all times, we felt that we should have a serious talk with Lenny regarding his suggestion of our joining him and the orchestra in Israel. We wanted Lenny to provide us with a more detailed description of what our lives might be like living in Israel.

Lenny first pointed out that while it was not an absolute requirement, whomever he hired would ultimately be expected to live in Israel permanently. Knowing us both personally as Lenny did, he felt that Joe Eger would love it, since Joe was always interested in complex social issues and Israel, as a new nation, had plenty. When it came to me, on the other hand, Lenny said, "Max, you will probably find it a very interesting academic exercise for about six weeks. You'll find the landscape to be somewhat like Los Angeles, Santa Barbara, and Palm Springs ... and that's it. But knowing you personally, as a way of life living there would not be your style." Joe expressed some misgivings, saying, "Why is it so good for me and not for Max?" We enjoyed a laugh, and, ultimately, Joe accepted Lenny's offer and left the Los Angeles Philharmonic. He remained in Tel Aviv for only several seasons. I, however, respectfully declined this offer, with many thanks to Lenny for knowing me so well.

In 1987 a retirement party was given for Ralph Gomberg, principal oboist of the Boston Symphony Orchestra and a fellow Curtis alumnus. The festivities were held at the former home of Serge Koussevitzky at Tanglewood in Massachusetts. Lenny had chartered a plane in order to avoid missing the event. He arrived complete with entourage, of course. At one point a small circle surrounded him, and someone dared to ask if he had read Joan Peyser's recently published biography of him. Looking down, he gruffly responded, "No. I'm told it would be a waste of my time to open the cover." I kind of smiled, and, looking at me, Lenny asked, "Did you?" I replied in the affirmative. He then said, questioningly, "Nu?" Knowing that there were scandalous stories in the book, my reply was "Lenny, if ever you do open the book, I hope you will notice the absence of my name in the index." He smiled in appreciation.

I HAD MOVED TO FLORIDA IN 1990 AND THEN LAST SAW LENNY IN DECEMBER of that year when he was honored as *Musical America*'s Musician of the Year at a party that took place at the Tavern on the Green restaurant in New York City's Central Park. Lenny told me about how much he liked Florida, particularly the Keys. I mentioned seeing a photograph of him in a pool frolicking with a dolphin. He was surprised that I had seen that picture. He said he was so fascinated by that dolphin that he fell in love with it. He then looked at me and laughing, proudly said, "And it was a girl!" He then reached into his pocket and took out his wallet. He said, "Don't laugh. I carry a picture of her with me." Maintaining that same level of humor, I commented on how pleased I was, since I knew he had frolicked with just about everything else. Lenny asked, "Max, why don't I see more of you?"

I replied quite honestly, "Lenny, I don't feel very comfortable with the so-called friends that hover around you."

He had no response for that, but getting even more serious with me, he said, "I envy you so, living in Florida. Where else can you have such a climate, still be close to New York and breathe clean air, unless you live in Tibet, which is too damn far away — and who the hell would want to live there anyway?" This all said while his usual cloud of cigarette smoke surrounded us. I said, "Lenny, put your cigarettes away and simply come on down."

He then leaned over to me and the last thing he ever said to me was said in a sad and pensive voice: "Max, I can't get off the merry-go-round."

With that, Lenny seemed to be finally acknowledging the Faustian debt owed for his phenomenal success. The ruthlessly ambitious and outrageously multitalented youth and fellow student in Philadelphia I had first known fifty years previously was finally admitting there had been a price to pay for constantly maintaining his fame and success.

Index